Mammon's Ecology

Mammon's Ecology

Metaphysic of the Empty Sign

Stan Goff

FOREWORD BY
Ched Myers

CASCADE *Books* · Eugene, Oregon

MAMMON'S ECOLOGY
Metaphysic of the Empty Sign

Cascade Books
An Imprint of Wipf and Stock Publishers
199 W. 8th Ave., Suite 3
Eugene, OR 97401

www.wipfandstock.com

PAPERBACK ISBN: 978-1-5326-1768-3
HARDCOVER ISBN: 978-1-4982-4255-4
EBOOK ISBN: 978-1-4982-4254-7

Cataloguing-in-Publication data:

Names: Goff, Stan, author. | Myers, Ched, foreword.

Title: Mammon's ecology : metaphysic of the empty sign / Stan Goff ; foreword by Ched Myers.

Description: Eugene, OR : Cascade Books, 2018 | Includes bibliographical references and index.

Identifiers: ISBN 978-1-5326-1768-3 (paperback) | ISBN 978-1-4982-4255-4 (hardcover) | ISBN 978-1-4982-4254-7 (ebook)

Subjects: LCSH: Economics—Religious aspects—Christianity. | Money—Religious aspects—Christianity.

Classification: BR115.E3 G64 2018 (print) | BR115.E3 G64 (ebook)

Manufactured in the U.S.A.   04/17/18

For Daddy, Mimi, and Glen, who beat me to the barn.

No servant can serve two masters: for either he will hate the one, and love the other; or else he will hold to one, and despise the other. You cannot serve God and mammon.

—LUKE 16:13

Contents

Foreword

STAN GOFF, FOR THOSE unfamiliar with his growing body of work, is an extraordinary and conscientious organic intellectual. He has traversed a fascinating life-journey, from Vietnam to West Point, from Special Forces operations in Haiti (where he began his radical transformation) to peace activist, and post-Marxist social analyst to Christian disciple. In his quest to get to the roots of both public and personal pathologies, he has increasingly "followed the money." This has led him to tackle, in this his sixth book, the unorthodox but compelling thesis that "general-purpose money" is the *central ecological issue of our time.*

Goff's important study is a demanding read. This is because he is, on one hand, trying to make a complicated thing simple enough to be intelligible to laypeople, thus summarizing and distilling a vast body of economic and philosophical thought; and on the other hand, trying to make that simple thing complicated again by challenging us to move beyond rhetorical sound bites to greater precision in our analysis and vocabulary of political economics. This is a *work*book, which invites us to become fellow "detectives" in discovering what we might call "the secret life of money." I commend it to all who want to go deeper in their diagnosis of the dysfunction of our historical inheritance—*especially* if you chafe, as I do, at the popular current maxim that "it is easier to imagine the end of the world than the end of capitalism" (the provenance of which Goff correctly identifies).

Goff chooses to frame this complicated terrain "simply" in terms of the ancient trope of *Mammon.* We find this term in a key, if routinely mishandled, parable (and commentary) of Jesus as recorded in Luke 16:1–15. This teaching represents the heart of Luke's theology of economic justice—and mirrors much of the argument of this book. So it is worth exploring here as a portal into Goff's project.

Jesus' story begins: "There was a rich man who . . ." (16:1). Luke's chapter will close with a second parable that repeats this phrase (16:19), revealing this narrative sequence as a carefully composed chiasm, in which the two parables bracket Jesus' teaching concerning Mammon and the "love of money" (16:9–15). Both parables are poignant fables that illustrate, in different ways, a world caught between what Wendell Berry calls the "Two Economies"—one in which money is used to repair social and ecological relations, and one in which both are sacrificed to accumulate capital.[1] Here I want to focus on the first parable which, as a tale about subverting a money system, both illumines and is illumined by Goff's study.

To subtitle this as the "Parable of the Dishonest Steward" (as so many versions of the New Testament do) already biases how it is read. Indeed, churches usually approach this text with an unconscious hermeneutic of capitalist moralism, implicitly taking the "side" of the boss while vilifying the worker—despite the fact that in the narrative, both the Master and Jesus *commend* the steward's insubordinate initiatives![2]

I prefer to think of the main character as a "defective manager," using the modern analogy of a mid-level bureaucrat in a large corporation. Just as he is about to be sacked because of below-expected sales numbers, he improvises a desperate but ingenuous "fire sale" on credit that ingratiates him to his clients, in hopes they will reciprocate when he's out on his ear. In so doing he turns his allegiances toward an alternative, local, *relational* economy of mutual aid, one that ever persists just below the surface of the dominant market system. In this reading, the manager is not the villain but the hero of the story. He represents a sort of archetype for all of us who: (1) are captive to a toxic and oppressive economic system; (2) realize that we too are becoming disenfranchised; and (3) consequently try to "monkeywrench" whatever leverage we have to effect a modicum of redistributive justice. The story gives dignity to such partial but meaningful efforts to "build a new world within the shell of the old," as Dorothy Day famously put it.

Like so many of Jesus' parables about the rich, this one acknowledges that the world is ruled by the "rentier" class (an important term that Goff defines in chapter 7). Luke's Jesus has already made his attitude to the "1

---

1. Berry, "Two Economies."

2. Myers, "Capital to Community." A more detailed treatment of this text, and how it correlates to critiques of capitalism, can be found in Wendell Berry, Ferdinand Tonnies, Hazel Henderson, and Karl Polanyi.

percent" painfully clear in an earlier folktale about a wealthy farmer who knew only how to accumulate (12:16–21), and does so again in the parable that closes our sequence . . . in which a self-indulgent Dives must face the cruel truth of the gulf between the opulent and the destitute from Lazarus' vantage point (12:19–31). Interestingly, in both tales the elite come to terms with their contradictions *only in death*; the Bible is so much less equivocal in its judgment on wealth disparity than we are!

The "steward" of 16:1 (Greek *oikonomos*, whence our word economics) belonged to what sociologist Gerhard Lenski called a dependent "retainer" class, literate bureaucrats whose job was to secure exorbitant profits for the master through merciless resource-extraction and labor exploitation, while at the same time maintaining working relations with peasant producers, competitive merchants, and customers. Here the analogy with modern, middle-class, educated white-collar workers is fitting: we too are people who are privileged within, yet subservient to, an economic system that both benefits and victimizes us. So whereas most of Jesus' parables feature peasants as protagonists, this story uniquely calls *us* to discipleship.

"Charges were brought to the Master that this manager was wasting his goods" (16:1c).[3] The resulting dismissal of the latter is summary, confirming the absolute authority of the former (16:2). The accused neither argues nor defends himself, knowing there is no due process in this system. Instead, in a poignant internal dialogue, he focuses on the stark alternatives facing him (16:3). This soft-handed bureaucrat realizes he cannot physically endure the brutal lot of day-laborers, while resorting to alms would obliterate what remained of his "class" honor. The story turns on the fired manager's conclusion (16:4).

Though his plan is not yet revealed, the hoped-for result is: he is going to do whatever it takes to "cross-over" from the economy engineered by (and for) the rich to the remnant village economy of mutual aid. By redistributing some of his Master's wealth at his (temporary) disposal, he seeks

---

3. The two verbs here tell an interesting story. The first connotes accusations made "with hostile intent, either falsely or slanderously." This manager is likely being undermined by fellow stewards, who are ever competing for increased prestige and influence in the system. The second (Gk *diaskorpizōn*) normally refers to a physical or geographic "scattering" of people or seed; only here and in the immediately preceding parable of the Prodigal Son is it translated "squandering" (Luke 15:13)—again, thanks to capitalist hermeneutics. However, in the context of this story one could argue that it implies the manager is *already* "skimming" and redistributing some of the assets under his control, a practice he will shortly intensify. Indeed, earlier in Luke, *diaskorpizō* appears in a key phrase of Mary's "Magnificat": Jesus' mother sings about the "proud" being "scattered" (Luke 1:51f.), a reference to the demise of precisely the sort of rich landowners portrayed in this parable!

to re-enter the traditional ethos of "generalized reciprocity," by which the communities exploited by his Master manage to survive. A key value of that older economy is *hospitality*, and the hope is that in return for his facilitation of debt-relief, "they will receive me into their homes." Having been kicked out of the Great Household, he must now rely on what feminist economist Hazel Henderson calls the "love economy" for survival.[4] It is precisely this older tradition of economic culture, Goff argues in his conclusion, that we must rehabilitate if we are to restore ecological and social equilibrium to a world plundered by our toxic and terminal money-system.

The rest of Luke's story unfolds quickly (16:5–7). The defecting manager hurries to his place of business and—still acting as the Master's agent before news of his termination is broadcast—summons his clients. "Tell me how much you owe," he barks, indicating that he no longer has the books; he does, however, ask for their signature on the revised bill to make the transaction official. This represents a sort of "Jubilee" strategy, re-enacting the old biblical vision (Lev 25:36; Deut 15:1) that forever stands in tension with ruling economies, as Goff notes.

The next verse brings the "punchline" (after all, parables mean to turn the world upside down to crack open our political imaginations). Strangely, the Master *commends* his feral manager (Luke 16:8a). As in the more well-known (and equally misunderstood) parable of the Talents (Matt 25:26–29; Luke 19:22b), the Master here concedes that his system is corrupt, acknowledging the one he fired as a "manager of injustice." Yet he "gives him credit for being shrewd." In fact, the plutocrat has been outsmarted: since recipients of the debt amnesty would praise the *patrón* for presumably authorizing it, to save face he must begrudgingly honor the write-off, so as not to jeopardize the system with a "credibility" crisis. Meanwhile, "Robin Hood's" fate is in the hands of the villagers.

Luke now switches abruptly to Jesus' "decoding" of the parable: "For the children of this age are shrewder than the children of light in dealing with their own generation" (16:8b). This aphorism has an apocalyptic tone, the traditional rhetoric of resistance in Jewish antiquity. It conveys an indictment of the "filthy rotten system" (again, Dorothy Day) that must "pass away." Yet also implied is an acknowledgment that as long as it persists, "shrewdness" (repeating the Master's approbation) will be required to survive it.[5] In this case, a manager has defected from his upwardly mobile track and linked his fate instead to the debtor class below him, helping them

4. Henderson, "The Love Economy."

5. Matthew 10:16: "Behold, I send you out as sheep in the midst of wolves; so be *shrewd as serpents* and innocent as doves" (italics added).

in order to help himself. His Jubilary gesture gives hard-pressed peasants a measure of relief and secures "refuge" among them.

This brings us to the moral of the story, the crucial lesson for the "children of light." It is here that Luke introduces the infamous trope Goff has invoked: "Make friends for yourselves, therefore, by means of the '*Mammon* of injustice'" (16:9a). *Mamōnās*, which only appears here in the New Testament (and its parallel in Matt 6:24), is an Aramaic word that probably stems from the Hebrew for "that in which one trusts." Though not in the Hebrew Bible, the term does appear in later Jewish writings. In the Mishnah it connotes property, often as contrasted with life; in the Targum it is an epithet for profit made through exploitation: "He destroys his house who *gathers* the mammon of injustice" (*Targ Prov* 15:27, italics added). A possible etymology could be from the Babylonian *manman*, connoting "filth of hell." *Mammon* thus seems to be, for Jesus, a dark metaphor for the economic system of domination—or as Goff puts it (following Ellul and Stringfellow), money as deadly principality and power.

In the second part of his lesson we see clear resonance between Jesus' exhortation and the manager's strategy at the center of the parable: "in order that when I am put out of the economy they may receive me into their homes" (16:4); "in order that when it fails [Gk. *eklipē*] they may receive you into the eternal tents" (16:9b). From Jesus' perspective, the question is not *whether* the unsustainable Mammon system will be "eclipsed"; only *when*.

Significantly, the radical alternative for those displaced by the Mammon system is the hospitality of "eternal tents." This suggests that healing lies in a return to Israel's primal wilderness traditions, specifically regarding what I call "Sabbath Economics," summarized in four principles narrated in Exodus 16: (1) creation is understood as a divine gift (symbolized by the mysterious *Manna*); (2) people are to gather that gift equitably (no one taking too much, everyone having enough); (3) the gift must not be turned into a possession to be accumulated privately; and (4) Sabbath practices of communal self-limitation must be observed.[6]

The only antidote to *Mammon* culture, in other words, is *Manna* culture.

But ideals are only made flesh in practices. Jesus seems to acknowledge in this parable that in the real world, improvisational attempts to re-deploy Capital on behalf of Community will be necessarily partial and inevitably ambiguous—especially when initiated by those with privilege. Still, all of us who are caught and complicit in the *Mammon* system must figure out ways to defect from it, while trying to rehabilitate traditional ways of *Manna*

6. Myers, *Sabbath Economics*.

sharing. If we so dare, we will be dismissed by our Masters as "defective," and perhaps even punished—a prospect made explicit in Luke's very last parable "of the ten pounds" (19:11–27) about a whistleblowing manager who is criminalized and executed (as the Teacher himself will be in this story). But according to Jesus, this "risky business" is the *only way the managerial class can become "trustworthy,"* as the following verses argue (16:10–12). It is an unsettling challenge Goff reiterates in this book.

So as not to be misunderstood as advocating incremental reformism or merely symbolic gestures, however, Jesus concludes with an unequivocal reiteration of the incompatibility of the Two Economies: "You cannot serve God and Mammon" (16:13). Such apocalyptic dualism provides rhetorical heat and is Jesus' way of "politicizing" the issue. As Wendell Berry paraphrases: "If we do not serve what coheres and endures, we serve what disintegrates and destroys."[7]

Jesus has spun a tale about the rapacious, predatory world of ancient commodity managing, presided over by the "children of this age." Stan Goff has done the same concerning our own world in this book, tutoring us on how to unveil the awful truth about *Mammon.* Luke's parable and Goff's study both articulate a difficult "trialectic" for persons of privilege: (1) We must realize that the money system which *appears* to benefit us is in fact an end-game, and thus figure out how to act creatively and concretely to use whatever economic means are at our disposal to stop ecological plunder and to rebuild social relations with those oppressed by this system. (2) Our best efforts will only ever bring *partial* relief or justice in a world ruled by Capital; but we must nevertheless persist, knowing that the system is ultimately unstable and unsustainable. (3) The ambiguity of our position (complicit) and our conflicted efforts to resist (fractional) should not delude us (as it has mainstream economic theologians) into believing that the Two Economies are perhaps *not* after all absolutely incompatible. They are, and the struggle to defect from one to the other is the essence of Jesus' call to discipleship.[8]

Yet we are deeply entwined in capitalist culture, and for the foreseeable future are "stuck" with the money system (at least until the kind of systemic transformation imagined by Goff in his conclusion). No amount of

7. Berry, *Home Economics,* 74.

8. This requirement of redistributive justice is illustrated in Luke's last two (contrasting) stories about rich men: one rejects Jesus' invitation to follow the Way because he cannot "sell all he has and give it to the poor" (18:18–30), the other makes extraordinary restitution (19:1–9).

dissociative rhetoric or oppositional activism exonerates us, therefore, from our practical responsibility to handle the money we *do* have subversively and constructively, even as we labor for radical structural change.

As this book argues repeatedly, we must be clear that money is neither a rational exchange mechanism nor a morally neutral tool, but a Lie—what elsewhere scripture calls "the root of all evil" (1 Tim 6:10). How we work with it will either help destroy or help nurture social and ecological relationships. We middle-class Christians have far more choice about this than we are socialized to imagine, as growing movements such as fair trade, community supported agriculture, sustainable building and social investing suggest. Only conscious, critical and creative practices will begin to change the economic narrative that is killing us, and animate our political imaginations to embody ever more radical alternatives to the *Mammon* system. This book's analysis is an important contribution to that animation.

Ched Myers
Bartimaeus Cooperative Ministries

Preface

IN THE MID-1990S, NOT long out of the army and suddenly possessed of a restless curiosity about the political and economic world that had swallowed up half of my life, I joined a listserv called *Crashlist*. Remember listservs?

Crashlist was a discussion list that promoted rigorous and sometimes tense discussions about two related kinds of probable-future collapse: economic and ecological. It was there that I was exposed to economic critics Henry C. K. Liu and Michael Hudson, both of whom eventually predicted with uncanny accuracy what we would see in the 2001 dotcom bubble collapse and the 2007 housing bubble crash, the very phenomena that mainstream economists later claimed to have been extraordinary and unpredictable anomalies. The late Andre Gunder Frank participated in the list, lending his considerable influence with "world system" and "dependency" theory. My late friend Mark Jones, a Welsh historian who had spent many years in both Soviet and post-Soviet Russia, participated, holding everyone's feet to the fire with his broad learning, provocations, and straight-razor critique.

In 2001, Andre and Mark were debating the role of oil in world system theory. Mark had written, "In any case the idea that the laws of thermodynamics have social effects is not new and goes back to at least Justus von Liebig if not to Aristotle . . . Alf Hornborg has recently written good stuff on this, as has Stan Goff on this list."

That was the first time I'd heard of Alf Hornborg, and it was after I'd been dismissed by several listserv members for saying that Ilya Prigogine's concept of "dissipative structures" in physics had direct material consequences on social organization. I might as well have said that I could make rain by dancing. The "culture-nature division" was for some a mental electrocution fence. I wasn't totally prepared to defend this idea in any depth at the time (I was only five years out of the army), but I was alerted by Mark's comments to the man with the Scandinavian name, a Swedish anthropologist who taught something called "human ecology."

It was Alf Hornborg's work, then, that introduced me for the first time to a systematic treatment of my fuzzy intuition that physical entropy materially affects social order. But more than that, Hornborg helped me understand that to comprehend today's world, we need an ecological, and even a *thermodynamic*,[1] account of money.

That account was expanded substantially for me in Jason Moore's ecological history of capitalism that incorporated Hornborg's suspicion of Descartes' dualizing influence on modern thought, a geographer's attention to historical development, and the integration of feminist insights into his project—the latter something I appreciated, having tried to do the same thing for more than twenty years.

In subsequent discussions and debates over the last sixteen years, especially as they stumbled up against the thorny hedgerows where questions of justice and governance meet, I found myself repeatedly returning to this question of money and ecology because so much of our thinking— even among those who engage these issues out of selfless compassion—is rooted in a *way of knowing* that conceals the deeply ecological nature of money. The superficial account that most of us have of money leads us to default again and again to several popular misconceptions into which we are all indoctrinated, misconceptions that are mutually reinforced by habit, by our formal education, and by mass media. This is true throughout our ideological landscape, and so demands an approach radical enough to dig down into the subsoil.

The best literature on the ecological nature of money, unfortunately, is still restricted largely to an academic sphere and written in a language that restricts itself to that sphere. Given the terrifying political, economic, and ecological crises in which we find ourselves now, if people like Alf Hornborg and Jason Moore are right—which I believe they are—the task of clarifying and deepening our understanding of this combined crisis has become urgent. Deficient interpretation is an obstacle to appropriate practical action; and our popular understandings are, frankly, abysmally oblivious to politics, economics, and ecology *as a single and inseparable phenomenon.* And so this book is a first attempt to translate the crucial work of these academics and economic critics out past the campus and into bedrooms, libraries, reading circles, and churches.

---

1. Science dealing with energy.

This is a book about money, and only coincidentally about "economics." Reading about economics is the world's most effective antidote to insomnia. This is a book about nature, knowledge, and power. As a Christian, I have to be interested in power. In our founding story, Jesus has been seen for the first time as the Christ by the wild man John, and upon being baptized, Jesus hikes deep into a mountainous wilderness, where he encounters The Tempter. The Tempter asks for Jesus' loyalty, and in exchange offers Jesus three things: the ability to turn stones into bread, the ability to be thrown from the temple wall and land as safely as a bird, and the ability to command every kingdom on earth. These were the temptations of *power*. The Roman emperors of the time distributed bread to Roman citizens to keep them docile. Being thrown from the temple wall was a punishment for crime, and Caesar had impunity. And kings had the authority to govern by decree. Domesticate the population with loaves of bread as numerous as the stones. Be immune from punishment. Have the authority to issue commands and decrees that affect the known world.

During a lunch at Duke University in February 2017 with Amy Laura Hall, Kara Slade, and Stanley Hauerwas, Stanley asked if I was working on anything. A book about money, I said, whereupon—as he is known to do—he immediately said there was a book I needed to read on the subject. I needed to read *Christ, Power, and Mammon*, by one of his former students, Scott Thomas Prather. As is frequently the case, Stanley was right. Scott Prather is also studying money as a species of power, and as a coequal partner with the state. Mammon and Leviathan, Prather calls that partnership, improbably combining a term from Jesus with one from Thomas Hobbes. Prather's study of the principalities and powers is likewise a synthesis, one including the Reformed theologian Karl Barth and the Mennonite theologian John Howard Yoder,[2] and by extension Yoder's study of another Reformed theologian, Hendrik Berkhof. These theologians, writes Prather, "name the great opponent of God who the Gospel of Matthew calls 'Mammon' as both a commodifying spirit and as a world-ordering form

2. Yoder's concept of the powers-as-*structures* figures significantly into the synthesis in this book between thinkers like Alf Hornborg and Jason Moore and Christian thought. It is not in the way of self-righteous ritual denunciation of John Howard Yoder that I take note here of Yoder's infamous exposure as a serial sexual predator, the pain of his victims casting a terrible dark shadow over his theological work. If Yoder had attended to the structures of gendered power as closely as he did those of state power, perhaps he would not have so cavalierly abused the women with whom he worked over the years. In the same way, many of us who are Christians need to become aware of how the way we use money implicates us, albeit less directly and often unknowingly, in the perpetuation of structural injustices.

of power."[3] This book agrees emphatically with that dual-characterization; and while this book will continue to unpack the relation between state and money, my strokes will not be nearly as broad. *General-purpose money* will be differentiated from earlier forms in order to describe fairly specifically how it works hand in hand with the modern nation-state, while aiming to place particular emphasis on money as an ecological phenomenon that defies the culture-nature dichotomy.

We will study how money relates to domination—the will to dominate others and the mad desire to dominate nature itself—as if we are ourselves an aspect of nature. Perhaps more importantly, we want to show how modern, general-purpose money has secured our complicity in domination, our complicity in apathy, our complicity in injustice, and our complicity in the progressive disassembly of the very natural systems of which we are ourselves a part and upon which we absolutely depend. Only with a fuller understanding of these things can we hope to begin the long, complex, and difficult path out of that complicity and away from that power.

A good part of the foundation for this book involved the work of ecofeminists, in particular Carolyn Merchant and Maria Mies. Whereas this is not a book about feminism, as my last book was, the debt this book owes to feminism, and the importance of its deconstruction of ideas that originated as male ideas in a male-normative society, and were therefore taken to be simply generic *ideas*, is incalculable. There is a direct connection between the unfortunate presidency of Donald Trump, the money-centric American cult of success, and the dangerously reactive and pugnacious locker room stupidity expressed or cosigned by his supporters, which I have called "conquest masculinity."[4]

There is perhaps no issue more morally challenging for the church than money. Money as an accelerator that compels us to "get things done," even when it may be time to "stop doing something, and just sit there." Money as a quick and easy substitute for face-to-face friendship with the

---

3. Prather, *Christ, Power, and Mammon*, 1.

4. Mies, *Patriarchy and Accumulation*, 75. The reason feminists have been more sensitive to the gendered character of this notion of the conquest of nature is that women have long experienced the imperial patriarchal trope of having been "defined into nature," along with colonies. Mies notes that the three forms of archetypal (imperial) male conquest have been conquest-of-women, conquest-of-nature, and conquest-of-colonies. Man equals subject. Nature (with colonies and women "defined into nature") equals object.

marginalized. Money as the strange attractor that pressures pastors to attend more closely to the most lavish monetary supporters in a congregation, determining whose priorities get done with the finite time and energy of a congregation. Money misunderstood in ways that may make us complicit in distant injustices, or misguided in how we tackle problems. Money that fastens us to the world in ways contrary to our aspiration to be witnesses *to* and resident aliens with primary citizenship *in* the Realm of God. My hope is that this book, if nothing else, will help us think more deeply and clearly about that.

Any Christian discussion of principalities and powers, in addition to beginning with a Christian idiom that strikes nonbelievers as strangely archaic, is fraught with controversy, because the writ-large church's relationship to politico-economic power has staggered from Amish-like withdrawal to grotesque church-state alliances like the rule of the Borgias to jackleg pseudo-theology like the televangelists who now provide cover for jackleg leaders like Donald Trump. Proof-texting Scripture in support of a preexisting commitment is an irksome and apparently interminable practice that muddies the waters for Christians and gives those who speciously claim that "religion" is the source of all our woes a stout stick with which to beat us—and no one is quicker to proof-text in support of conformity and obedience than those who profit by our conformity and require our obedience to sustain that profit.

Like Kathryn Tanner and Scott Prather, who echo Barth and Yoder before them, we see money as one of those powers, and we cannot explicate that claim without attending to the political regimes, ideologies, and human ecologies through which money asserts this power. Everyone knows that "money equals power." It is a truism, and merely stating it in these terms leaves us resting comfortably on a host of assumptions and beliefs that, frankly, are part of the ideology that gives money its peculiar kind of power *without* implicating political regimes or acknowledging how money-politics reshapes our *ecology*.

As a Christian pacifist, I frequently encounter the conundrum that Christian "realists" attend closely to political economy, as do many fellow pacifists, though many pacifists and the pacifist-curious, in their close attention to eschatological matters, edge toward a position of withdrawal that tempts us with another distinctly Christian truism: the world is fallen. Not that the world is not fallen. This is an article of faith. But the subtext can be: "And that's the end of it. Nothing to be done." I have to insist first of all that we cannot withdraw, even as we stand apart in our political loyalty to the Realm of God; and I feel compelled to further insist that we go beyond a declaration of fallenness to the discernment of the particular ways that we are fallen *now*. This is only decipherable, in my opinion, through attention to history. Not history as a collection of dead facts but history as a process among us creatures that situates each of us in a specific time and place, among specific kinds of power structures. As Prather says,

> Theologically speaking, [the] sociopolitical dimension is simply an issue of whether the works of historical forces that structure social life are, in any given instance, to be construed as a service to God's bringing about a new humanity in Christ, or as moments of the great creaturely rebellion against the divine-human reality, and so as claimants to the feigned dominion and authority of an idol . . . The structural dimension of creaturely rebellion is then a necessary complement—not a replacement or exclusion—of traditional bibilical language of "the heart," and of traditional (Western) theological emphasis upon human will.[5]

Political economy is such a structure; but this book will expand on that—just as *Borderline*[6] did by incorporating the structures of gender as a system dividing power—by showing that what is structured is not merely *society*—or relations between people—but a whole *ecology* that includes the complex and interconnected relations that constitute all of earthly creation, human and nonhuman together.

The general deficiency of understanding with regard to this larger relation is not specifically Christian. In fact, Christian scholars are, at least, frequently more well-grounded in philosophy, especially moral philosophy, than scholars from other fields; and so in this respect, those scholars have a leg up already. But this book is written for the layperson; and it aims to give us a little more clarity about how to be faithful Christians, lay or clerical.

Our modest ambition in this book is to add to our own general awareness that the structures of exchange, technology, and governance, facilitated by general-purpose money, are together an *ecology*, their own form of order in the world. In turn, how the world is ordered influences the formation of the people in it.

5. Prather, *Christ, Power and Mammon*, 70–71.
6. Goff, *Borderline* (2015)—the author's last book, on gender, militarism, and church.

Acknowledgments

THIS BOOK COMES ON the heels of a hell of a year in which I lost my mother and brother just days apart. And so before giving credit where it is due—and it is due to many—I have to acknowledge family—siblings, kids, grandkids, cousins, nieces, nephews, in-laws, and close family friends—all of us who sat at bedsides, tended, ate, cooked, cleaned, reminisced, and cried together; and those who pulled us close when we met on the road. All of you still here, and those who went ahead. I'll single Sherry out by name, at my side almost every minute, and remaining tirelessly there even when health issues of my own intervened as I began work on this book. Without you, this little tome would never have seen the light of day. All my love, for all you are and all you do.

To Vandana Shiva, whom I only met once, and Maria Mies as well as Carolyn Merchant, neither of whom I've ever laid eyes on, your integrations of feminist insight with ecological concerns are at the absolute center of anything I pretend to understand here.

Charlie Collier, I owe you my gratitude again, for opening the door to this one.

Jason Moore and Alf Hornborg, for your groundbreaking work, and your willingness to correspond: this is y'all, being dragged into church by a crazy old vet. Wherever I have come up short in representing you, I take full responsibility.

Thanks to Ched Myers, who spent a week teaching me the Gospel of Mark. Your efforts to move the church toward an ecologically informed discipleship are recommended at the close of this book. Your presentation in Durham one day many years ago, when I stood by as one of the resident "secular" lefties, was one of the things that inaugurated the process that led eventually to my conversion. And your editorial suggestions for this book have made it eminently more readable.

To the holy women of the Adrian Dominican Sisters, my exemplars, combining compassion, intelligence, and a good deal of earthy resilience: this is your book, too.

Introduction

Behold, I send you out as sheep in the midst of wolves; so be shrewd as serpents and innocent as doves.

—MATTHEW 10:16

"LONG, LONG AGO IN a galaxy far, far away," I was in the infantry. There I learned a form of dismounted military patrol called a "cloverleaf reconnaissance." Reconnaissance patrols are not combat patrols; they are performed for the sole purpose of gathering information. The cloverleaf recon was a method for surveilling a fixed installation of some kind, in which the patrol moves up to a surveillance point within view of the reconnaissance target, where the patrol takes photographs, makes sketches, and writes copious notes on activities, then backs away. The recon circles around to another surveillance point—again doing the same things—then another, and another, all the way around. Plotted from above, the pattern of approach looks like joined semicircles, or a cloverleaf. During a cloverleaf recon, one comes to appreciate how a single place appears very differently as one changes points of view. At the end of the reconnaissance, when the patrol returns to debrief and collate its information, these multiple points of view are merged into more than a snapshot of the installation—that is, into actual knowledge of the installation based on how each aspect of that target *relates* to the others. Other questions are then posed by the reconnaissance. How does that installation function in relation to what we know about the surrounding area? How critical is it? How accessible is it? How recognizable is it? How vulnerable is it? How recuperable is it if it is damaged? What are its effects on the local population?

This book is a cloverleaf recon of the phenomenon of modern, general-purpose money, not to eventually attack it, but to more fully understand how it fits into and redesigns nature, of which we are a part. We are going to find the target on a map, so to speak, before we go in close enough to put eyes on it. Then we are going to study it from the point of view of natural laws, of particular ways of knowing, of technology, and of its relation to the power of civil society[1] and the state. The binoculars we are going to use, or the lens, is going to be *exchange*: exchange in nature, exchange in human metabolism, exchange in economics, exchange in technology, and so forth. Once we have a handle on money from these different points of view, we are going to see how the different aspects of money relate to each other. After relating its aspects, we will begin asking more complex questions about the actual ways we see money used in different situations and at greater and greater scales, and the actual consequences of those uses in our world.

The first few chapters, which, apart from an outline in chapter 1, will not zero in much on money, may lead the reader to ask, "What about money? I thought this was a book about money." Returning to our cloverleaf recon analogy, however, before we can fully characterize our target, we need these various perspectives. Be patient, because what makes this investigation of money different are analytical methods and interpretive frameworks that are unfamiliar to some of us and so at first may seem strange. The first few chapters are to familiarize readers with those alternative frameworks and to de-familiarize the conventional ones.

Mammon's Ecology is designed to constantly circle back on itself. We will lay out a concept, then another, then another; but every so often, we will go back and grab a concept we covered earlier to stack that concept into the others. Think of it as making bricks, then using the bricks to build a patio or a wall. Sometimes we have to handle the same brick more than once.

Because of the potential unfamiliarity of some of these ideas, we will take our time with each idea until we become accustomed to it. You may never have heard of an *Umwelt* or *semiosphere* before, I don't know. But be not afraid. We will sneak up on these things, circle around them, get hold of them, stroke them, touch them with the tip of the tongue, knock them against a tree, hold them up to the light, sniff them, bounce them like a ball, tie them onto a roller skate and pull them with a string, until you can walk them out your front door and introduce them to your neighbors like a new pet.

We don't want you to go into the front door of this book and come out the back door the same as you went in. We want you (figuratively) armed

---

1. Nonstate persons and organizations that heavily influence culture and politics; mostly from the professional classes, and employing trained spokespersons through the various media to shape public thinking and gain acquiescence to the agendas of that class, the class that manages and patronizes them, and the state—which today is the political expression of the monied/business class.

and dangerous at the exit, more ready than when you went in to play intellectual hardball on a topic we all only thought we understood. We want you lit up, questioning, subversive, primed.

We are saving the action parts for the last. This will be like a Charles Dickens novel in that respect. By the final chapter, there will be reasons to be happy or at least hopeful-in-action; but all the chapters before that will be a little scary and sad. We are the people of the cross, and there is nothing that will throw us off the path to that cross quicker than the counterfeit optimisms of privilege and denial. For most of the people in the world now, life is already quite scary and sad. Forty percent of the world lives on less than two dollars a day. Fifty percent lives on less than $3.50 a day. Eighty percent lives on less than ten dollars a day. Thirteen percent do not eat enough to properly maintain their body metabolism. And the fact that we measure their well-being with money is precisely the problem.

Money, we will learn, is as dangerous as dynamite; and yet we allow children to use it. Money is as corrosive as muriatic acid, and yet we adults are promiscuous and uncritical in its use. Money is useful, just as knives are useful, but do we always understand (1) if that usefulness is a good and (2) if that usefulness before us conceals something more malignant beyond its immediate convenience? We will learn how money has become the mindless and merciless umpire of world governance and how money makes us all involuntarily complicit in a host of sins.

One of the paths taken in this book will inevitably lead through the subject of *energy*. In studying money's ecological impacts, the corresponding study of energy is a necessary bridge between money and ecology. As it turns out, just as we need to grasp the simple and stable laws of thermodynamics—of energy and heat—to understand how they discipline the universe, we will need a review of them to apprehend the ecological nature of money, too.

I am a hopeless fan of crime fiction. Numbered among my closest and never-seen friends are Denise Mina, Walter Moseley, John le Carré, P. D. James, Laura Lippman, Gillian Flynn, Graham Greene, Tana French, Stuart Kaminsky, Ian Rankin . . . I could go on. At its best, crime fiction is social criticism, the exposure of mortal sins writhing beneath a veil of respectability. Good crime fiction, in addition to being good literature (there's the gauntlet thrown before the snobs) uses conditions of extremity to confront protagonists and readers with tough moral questions. Good crime fiction attends to the ways we are undone by disordered desire; and the detective—official or private, the injured party looking for answers, the curious questioner who gets in over her head, or the investigative journalist, whichever the protagonist is—systematically peels back the mask to reveal that disordered desire through the revelation of something that happened and was hidden. In the best examples, crime fiction reveals that disorder in ourselves, too. So readers must forgive me for making the reader a "detective" in this book, a detective on the trail of money along the streets and alleys of exchange. It was an irresistible conceit.

Apart from our detective metaphor, the language in this book will strike many people as strange. The language will reflect a scientific sensibility that is modern and an interdisciplinary sensibility that defies modernity's categories and sets limitations upon them. History, science, philosophy, and geography will all be whizzed together like a ten-berry smoothie. The language is intended to be *accessible*, but not *popular* in the sense of our postmodern affinity for being ever-so-ironic or the unfortunate tendency of some "Christian literature" to aim at being as dreamily, optimistically vague as possible, presumably to achieve an aura of disembodied spirituality. This book's language is intended as a bridge—whether it succeeds at this or not—between professional intellectuals and non-professionals who are called to become more organically aware. Our present-day intellectual division of labor is part of the problem this book describes.

Money is an *ecological phenomenon*. That's what the first part of this book is about; then we'll see how that branches out into socio-ecological structures and consequences. But this book is also an invitation. I invite every reader, every parishioner, every academic, every deacon, every teacher, every pastor, and every student to add his or her own thinking to this. The implications are what matter, after all, and for that I am inadequate to the task.

Because there are numerous unfamiliar (for many) terms and concepts in the book, I am using same-page footnotes throughout, which will include citations, editorial asides, and excursive outtakes with more detailed discussion of certain aspects of the subject that would otherwise interrupt the narrative flow. Meanwhile, "stay awake." And pray.

1

Detectives

Don't take advantage of the poor just because you can; don't take
advantage of those who stand helpless in court.

—Proverbs 22:22

Nodes and Flows

A *node* is a point of interchange.

Every hour a healthy adult casts off in the range of 30–40,000 dead
skins cells from the *stratum corneum*, our outer layer of skin. The stuff is
raining off of us all the time, drifting around us in little clouds, depositing
itself in our clothes, making maps of itself on our beds. We breathe these in
from ourselves and others, ingest it from our food, and massively exchange
it during intimacy.

All day long, we exchange atmospheric oxygen for metabolically produced carbon dioxide and gaseous water, with an average tidal volume of
500 milliliters per breath. If you brightly backlight two people having a conversation, you will see whole sprays of breath, material otherwise invisible.
The subjects, like all of us who have face-to-face discussions, are actually
steaming and spitting—storming steam and spit—onto each other.

We drink around 2 liters of water each day, which is exchanged everywhere throughout our bodies for metabolic wastes. The water is then run
through a couple of complicated filters called kidneys just underneath our
inferior-posterior ribs, whereupon it is mixed with other filtrates, like urea,
and passed back out of the body again at a rate generally corresponding to
the fluid intake.

We take in fuel (energy) from the sun every day, which has been
stored in plants, and from plants eaten by animals. We eat the fuel, or food,

1

which is then converted into biological maintenance materials and useable energy. The parts unused for maintenance or energy are consolidated into feces, which is then passed out of the body and into the surround again, where it breaks down and is reincorporated into other materials. To aid in the digestion of that food, there is a megacity along the walls of your gut of around 100 trillion various bacteria, about three pounds worth of living things that are not you, making trillions of little exchanges per second, without which you would die.

The stuff coming off of you all the time is so uniquely mixed that for a good tracking dog it might as well be a fingerprint or a DNA sample. You leave behind molecular clues about your past whereabouts in such profusion that large hounds, the kind with three million scent receptors, can find you ten miles away and three days later if you are moving on foot.

A human being observed as a *location* is the hub, or *node*, of multiple *exchanges*; flows of materials in, and flows of changed materials out. We are mixed into our environment, a part of it and not apart from it. If we could simply see the invisible gases moving through a person, respiratory and otherwise, a crowd of people would appear to boil in front of us, each person another bubble rising from the bottom of the pan.

A family domicile is such an *exchange node*, too. Things flow in. Things flow out. Think of what happens when flows are disrupted. What an emergency when the electricity fails! When the sewer pipe becomes obstructed, or the water shuts off, or the trash haulers go on strike! Disrupted flows, many of those flows that we take for granted, are crises—times of difficulty, disorientation, and even danger. This is true of a cell, a body, a home, a community, a biome,[1] a watershed,[2] an ecosystem,[3] or a nation.

This is also true of technologies. The car that supports the family and the family's dwelling can also be seen as an *exchange node*. Gasoline fuel, other fluids, and lubricants go in; heat and work (movement of mass) come out. New parts replace old ones that flow into a trash bin, and from there into a landfill. New paint and epoxies are needed to fix damaged spots that have disappeared with rust. The machine is not a thing-in-itself any more than we are. In its own way, on its own timetable, it eats and excretes, or it will slowly dissolve.

The car gets you to a grocery store, where that most common of *exchanges* takes place, money for food, carried back to the car, and by car

1. Communities of living species within a habitat.

2. A region within which all rainfall and water drains into a particular river, lake, or sea.

3. An interdependent combination of geography, climate, soil, water, and biomes seen as a self-organized dynamic.

back into the input stream for the household, where the *metabolic* flows are maintained for all those warm bodies.

In this book, we are going to become detectives. *Exchange* detectives. Let's open that grocery bag.

Exchange Detection

What do we have here? Bread. Frozen fish. Cheese slices. Pasta noodles. Pasta sauce. Fresh cherries. Bell peppers. Olive oil. Canned soup. Breakfast cereal. Salad greens. Eggs. Milk. This will be a short list, or we'd have a whole book, an encyclopedia, on the *nodes* and *flows* of foods. What is the first question the exchange detective asks? Where did each item originate? Okay, the bread was made one state over, the frozen fish was packed in California, the cheese slices came from a factory in Illinois, the pasta noodles from a factory in Atlanta, the cherries from an orchard in Chile, the peppers from a farm in Texas, the olive oil (which is mixed with other oils to make it cheaper) was harvested in Spain and Iowa then mixed in Mexico, the breakfast cereal hails from a factory in Michigan, the soup was made in a factory in China, the salad greens were brought in from Mississippi, the eggs from a distributor 150 miles away (God knows where the actual egg factory is with the captive chickens), the milk from the same distributor (and the actual cows?). The frozen fish is being kept frozen in a machine made of X number of materials, and kept running with energy scraped out of a coal seam uncovered by removing a mountaintop in West Virginia or Wyoming, using more big machines that run on diesel fuel, etc.

What does the exchange detective ask next? Where were the exchanges that preceded the last exchange? Those cherries from Chile, how much land, water, labor, chemicals, and money had to flow into an orchard somewhere in Chile to make cherries come out the other end? How were the cherries transported from Chile to your grocery store? In this way, the exchange detective begins to draw mental maps, *flow-maps*.

The next step in exchange detection, after gathering information about flows, is to begin to focus on the points of exchange, or nodes, to ascertain the actual *form* of the exchange. When a bully steals a smaller child's lunch money that *is* an exchange. Likewise, when I trade my blue marble for your yellow one, this is an exchange. If my daughter gives me a watch for Christmas, this is an exchange. All exchanges are not equal. Exchanges between people have *moral* content. My daughter's gift is different from the bully's extortion.

What are the working conditions of the Chilean who picks the cherries? How was the land acquired? What kinds of inputs go into the tractors on the farm? During an exchange, do all parties benefit? Equally? Is the threat of poverty or violence an element of the exchange? What is the moral substance of the exchange? What moral questions are raised by the actual form of the exchange? How is the exchange facilitated? What cultural doors open and close during an exchange? Do we sign a paper or not? Do we use money or not? Are we having a conversation or merely transacting at a fixed place for a fixed price with someone who might as well be a robot? Self-checkout at the grocery store *is* a robot. Are there protocols, rules, languages, symbols, signs that are necessary for the exchange? When present-day exchange detectives begin this final phase of detection, they will inevitably confront a simple question that raises a host of new questions: *What is money?*

2

The Heat

He changes rivers into a wilderness
And springs of water into a thirsty ground;
A fruitful land into a salt waste,
Because of the wickedness of those who dwell in it.

—Psalm 107:33–34

A Southern preacher once told me, "When the Bible says 'you,' that translates into 'y'all.'" "You" in the Bible most often means the second person plural. We are in this together. This brings to mind a conversation with friend of mine, a geologist who I've known since he was a graduate student in the nineties. He said, "The three scariest words in the English language are 'Pine Island Glacier.'"

Warming

Think of a world map, Detective. A huge topographical map with contour lines indicating elevations above mean sea level. Think of contour lines indexed at one meter, then two, then three, then four. What you are imagining are future coastlines. And as they rise, people will move further inland. Where will they go? What will they do? How will the *nodes and flows of exchange* change when they do?

In 2015, a 225-square-mile island of ice broke free from West Antarctica. The boundary shelf of West Antarctica includes a mass called the Pine Island Glacier where the ice sheared off. The particulars of this breakaway ice may be too much information for most readers, but the up and the down of it is that earth scientists are now quite sure that the West Antarctic ice is melting from below. This is not a good thing. More alarmingly, they are now confident that the question of whether West Antarctica will melt is not a matter of *if*, but *when*, and the timetable for *when* has been moved up.[1]

Conservatively, this means that my grandchildren in thirty-five years may be able to walk along the shore of Myrtle Beach—well, it won't be a beach any more—around Highway 31. "Family Kingdom Amusement Park" and "Broadway at the Beach" will be fish habitat, depending on which species survive further ocean acidification[2] and the massive injections of fresh water from melting ice around the world.

Half of the fresh water in the world is locked up as ice in Antarctica. West Antarctica alone, if melted, could raise sea levels ten feet . . . bye-bye Miami, bye-bye Manhattan, bye-bye New Orleans. Shanghai, look out! The United States would have more than 3 million people directly affected. Myanmar, 4 million plus. Philippines, more than 6 million. Netherlands and Thailand, 8 million each. Indonesia and Bangladesh, 10 million each. India and Japan, nearly 13 million each. Vietnam, more than 23 million. China, 50 million.[3]

This does not take into account sea-level rise caused by other melts which are already in progress and accelerating in the Northern hemisphere. Greenland alone now loses 269 billion tons a year, and that rate is increasing every year.[4]

Two percent of earth's 7 billion humans live within one vertical meter of the coast. Six percent live within five meters. Ten percent live within ten meters.[5]

Waters cool, changing currents. Changed currents change weather. Desalination and cooler temperatures kill coral and plankton, disrupting whole food chains. Coastal waters become petri dishes for algae blooms that decay and de-oxygenate water, killing aquatic life. Inundation by rising water means whole islands will sink. Whole habitats will disappear. Estuaries will reach back into mainlands, salting the surrounding soils. Drinking water will be contaminated. Homes will be abandoned. Fortunes will be lost. Those who are driven away will move inland creating new stressors

1. Waldman, "Antarctic Ice Shelf," para. 6.

2. Ocean water, like any other fluid, has a pH, the measure of where it falls along a line from the most alkaline (high pH) to the most acid (low pH). Atmospheric carbon increases are causing ocean water to move closer to the acidic pole of that line, which is changing the environment of everything that lives in the ocean, many species of which will not survive a dramatic pH drop.

3. Strauss, "20 Countries Most at Risk."

4. Harvey, "Climate Change," para. 7.

5. Bollman et al., *World Ocean Review 1*, 68–72.

on infrastructure there. Farms will be ruined. More species will die out. Storms will damage more and damage further inland. Communication and transportation lines will be destroyed and rerouted. Fisheries will collapse. And these are only the effects of sea level rise.

As Dahr Jamail writes, "Everything in the planet's climate system is linked, and when one part of it changes, all the other parts will respond."[6] We have only glimpsed the changes ahead in the form of superstorms or the wildfires that consume Appalachia and California.

These inevitable scenarios, bad as they are, however, are not the worst. The most terrifying scenario of all is something called *runaway warming*. Runaway warming is when a "tipping point" is reached wherein warming quits being the effect of a cause (greenhouse gases introduced by industrial and agricultural activity) and becomes a self-reinforcing feedback loop. Warming begets warming.

Locked into the world's permafrosts are unknown quantities of carbon (estimates are around 1.4 trillion tons for just the Siberian Shelf[7]) that can be converted into methane, a gas that is 84 times as powerful a greenhouse vector as carbon dioxide per molecule over a period of twenty years.[8] When the permafrost melts, as *it is now melting*, this carbon-methane cocktail will be released. Though some methane is routinely released even from frozen mass in the arctic, no one currently knows how much greater the releases of methane will be as permafrost melts.[9]

Here is what we do know. Carbonaceous material—dead plants and other organic matter—that are thawed will rot. Microbial activity with oxygen (aerobic) will convert that organic material into atmospheric carbon. Microbial activity underground, without oxygen (anaerobic), will produce methane. Methane forms bubbles that then migrate to the surface. Because we cannot be sure how far or fast this process will go, we simply cannot know if or when such a tipping point might arrive. Climate scientists have consistently said this is unlikely; but in recent years, more and more climate scientists have walked back their own certainties about this. One researcher published a 2015 article in *Scientific American* that estimated we could reach a "point of no return" as early as 2042.[10] Twenty-four years. Within most readers' lifetimes. Additionally, the ice that is melting reflects heat from the

6. Jamail, "Melting Arctic," para. 41.
7. Simpson, "Arctic Thaw," para. 25.
8. Hamburg, "Methane," para. 3.
9. Shaefer, "Tipping Point."
10. Johnston, "Point of No Return," para. 2.

sun back into space, so there's that, too. Less reflection, more absorption, greater acceleration of warming. Happy days.

Paradoxically, generalized warming could lead to unseasonably cold weather in some places. What we do know to nearly an absolute certainty is that some of our grandchildren will live to see, conservatively, a rise of eight degrees Fahrenheit in global average temperature. That may not sound like much, but it is, in combination with the consequences of sea level rise and ocean acidification, downright apocalyptic. I hope churches and church people are thinking about this and resisting the temptations of ostrich optimism.

Crop failures, migrating diseases, deadly heat waves, killer storms, extreme drought, uncontrollable wildfires, lowered air quality, losses of potable water, and population migrations will have not only their direct effects, but will inevitably result in economic catastrophes compounded by political destabilization—the latter almost certainly characterized by a drift toward increasing authoritarianism and ever more draconian population control measures, which will likely in turn lead to civil strife, even civil wars. Few people today recognize, for example, the key role that *water*—not ideology or even "religion"—played in the Syrian Civil War,[11] and continues to play in the brutal Israeli occupation and dispossession[12] of the Palestinians.[13]

Hornborg's Coca-Cola

Without general-purpose money, there would be no climate crisis. We'll prove that as we go along; but we will warn you now that this does not automatically lead to the conclusion that the solution is as easy as abolishing money (likely impossible). For now, we will simply assert that money has every bit as much of an impact on our environment as acids, bases, solvents, atmospheric carbon, or atomic bombs. Thinking seriously about the implications of *thermodynamics* (the branch of physics that deals with *energy and heat*) for political economy, we have to ask how this aspect of nature—thermodynamics—determines the cultural practice some call "political economy," that arena of power that regulates and enforces various social *exchange* relations.

In Hornborg's *Power of the Machine* he wrote, "Viewed from outer space, money is an ecosemiotic[14] phenomenon that has very tangible effects

11. Hammer, "Lack of Water."

12. Arnaud, "Occupied Palestine."

13. Corradin, "Water as a Tool."

14. Having both material and cultural/communicative features, analogous to

on ecosystems and the biosphere as a whole. If it were not for general-purpose money, we could not trade tracts of rainforest for Coca-Cola."[15] Soon enough, you will understand exactly what "ecosemiotic" means.

Onward.

---

wave-particle duality in subatomic physics.

15. Hornborg, *Power of the Machine*, 170.

3

Nature

"But now ask the beasts, and let them teach you;
And the birds of the heavens, and let them tell you.
"Or speak to the earth, and let it teach you;
And let the fish of the sea declare to you.
"Who among all these does not know
That the hand of the Creator has done this,
In whose hand is the life of every living thing,
And the breath of all humankind?"

—Job 12:7–10

As exchange detectives, before we can understand money as an ecological phenomenon, we need to have a shared understanding of *nature*. By that, we do not mean something apart from humans, because we are part of nature. We mean the forms, functions, and relationships that play by certain changeless physical rules. The sugar maple behind my house obeys those rules, but so does this computer, the lamp next to it, and the train I hear in the distance. By *nature*, I do not mean sentimentalized things that seem untouched or less-touched by humans. We are, as we said, part of nature's equation. I mean what some call "the material world," or those phenomena that consistently *obey* those changeless rules by which nature plays. My fantasies may not obey those rules, but my brain as an organ certainly does. I can imagine I am not part of nature, but that does not make it so.

The Second Law

This chapter will require a quick remedial science lesson.

> Life on Earth is driven by energy. Autotrophs take it from solar radiation and heterotrophs take it from autotrophs. Energy captured slowly by photosynthesis is stored up. As denser reservoirs of energy have come into being over the course of Earth's history, heterotrophs that could use more energy evolved to exploit them. Homo sapiens is such a heterotroph; indeed, the ability to use energy exosomatically (outside the body) enables human beings to use far more energy than any other heterotroph that has ever evolved. The control of fire and the exploitation of fossil fuels have made it possible for Homo sapiens to release, in a short time, vast amounts of energy that accumulated long before the species appeared.[1]

One of the rules to which we'll pay particularly close attention is the *Second Law of Thermodynamics*. Don't close the book. It's not that scary. The shorthand for the law is "entropy." If you put ice into a glass of water, the ice melts instead of the water freezing around the ice. Heat seeks the cool, moving outward (and seemingly inward as it penetrates our ice cube) as microscopically agitated material seeking its ultimate rest. Orderly things, unless interfered with, become more disorderly over time (and very quickly during combustion).[2] The arrow of time points only one way. There are no do-overs. Entropy is a great and universal unwinding. Stuff that is in a state "far from equilibrium" (fire, for example) seeks a state closer to equilibrium (the ashes and smoke passively dissipated by the breeze). These are ways to describe entropy, which is the basis of that mysterious thing we call *time*.

Entropy is important in the study of heat and energy. As exchange detectives, we map flows, so we need to map the flows of energy, but also what happens at the point of exchange, or the exchange *node*, how inputs are

---

1. Price, "Energy and Evolution."

2. We will use the terms "order" and "disorder" throughout the book as shorthand. These sound like evaluations rather than physical properties, as if we are judging nature's "order" as good and "disorder" as bad. There is a grain of truth in that, because we are looking at human beings and nature as part of the same reality, so what benefits humans is certainly a factor. But what the shorthand "order" stands for, which is "observable" in the scientific sense, is compact, serviceable, and energy-dense; whereas "disorder" stands for diffused, no-longer-serviceable, and energy-uncompressed.

The author's second book's title, *Full Spectrum Disorder*, was an ironic mash-up of Prigogine's concept of entropic *disorder* and then-Secretary of Defense Donald Rumsfeld's war doctrine of "full spectrum dominance."

converted into more *entropic* outputs.[3] Energy for our discussion is something that can *move* things, or does *work*. And once energy moves things,
entropy being what it is, the energy itself is *dissipated*.

That drop of gasoline that explodes[4] in the combustion chamber of
your car's motor begins with .35 calories of super-concentrated energy. That
intense heat and shock from combustion is channeled by technology (applied knowledge) into a drive train that hauls nearly a ton of metal, plastic,
rubber, ceramics, fibers, and people. All of that energy, once the drop of
gasoline explodes and pushes the piston against friction, is lost for any practical purpose as heat. The heat rapidly *dissipates* apart from the operation of
the machine, and no longer has the concentration necessary to push a ton
of metal around on inflatable tires.

Let's categorize the energy as it goes through this exchange. Nature
does not make more energy or destroy it,[5] *and neither can we*, but nature
commands it to *diffuse*[6] (the *Second Law*) except during special interventions, like tension, gravity, or photosynthesis.[7]

The energy that was stored in the gasoline had all this volatile potential stored inside itself. The gasoline energy was *concentrated* and *portable*.
The unused gasoline energy was *against-entropy* or entropy-resistant; it had
been through a multi-million-year process of concentration, the opposite of
dissipation.[8] Its volatile concentration is pushing back against the door of
nature's tendency to seek equilibrium, or dissipation, or rest.[9]

Some scientists call this kind of concentrated energy *negentropy*,
shortened from "negative entropy," even though it is more like stubborn but
ultimately futile opposition to entropy. The point is, *negentropy*, or "against-
entropy-energy," is highly *ordered* with regard to its capacity for work. The
embodied energy is available to push a piston with the force generated inside a combustion chamber. The moment after combustion, however, that
energy begins dissipating (moving toward disorder) into media (like air)
that do not concentrate energy or through the friction-heat along the piston

3. At some level, it is indistinguishable from matter, but that's not the court we are
playing on today.

4. Explosions are simply combustion (fire) at very high velocity.

5. The First Law of Thermodynamics.

6. Spread out; the verb *diffuse* is the opposite of the verb *concentrate*. When sugar
dissolves into hot coffee, the sugar is diffusing.

7. When life forms, mostly plants, use sunlight ("photo") and carbon dioxide to
make, or "synthesize" their own food.

8. In reality, that concentration process over time dissipated a great deal more
energy over time than it stored. Entropy always wins.

9. Perfect equilibrium is nothingness, everything completely at rest, "heat death."

shaft, that itself then dissipates. We can think of this used-up energy then as diffuse, disordered, no longer concentrated, portable, or directable.

Overwhelmingly, that energy originates from the sun. At any given moment, 1.74×10^{17} watts of power slams into the earth's atmosphere at 186,000 miles per second from the sun. Some bounces back into space. Some warms the oceans. Some moves the air to make the wind.

Some solar energy is captured and transformed into biotic (life-based) energy storage. For our analysis, the main counter-entropic process, or process that concentrates *negentropy*, is photosynthesis. If you are munching on a piece of bacon right now, you are still eating solar energy. The corn captured it, and the pig ate the sun-to-corn energy. Then we slaughtered the pig, whereupon you, with that bacon in your greasy fingers, consume a piece of the pig to get a portion of the energy that passed from the sun through the corn and to the pig.[10] Now you can use some of that energy to read this book.

Energy is the force that drives all change. Combined with matter, energy provides the motion that is necessary for change. The solar energy used by life on earth is chemically bound up and concentrated by organic matter. The biosphere—the sum of all ecosystems across the planet—emerged as an ever more complex architecture of consolidated energy, first as simple life forms that gained energy directly from the sun, then as *autotrophs*[11] that converted sunlight into metabolic fuel, and later as *heterotrophs*[12] that consume autotrophs for the energy stored within them.

The net energy available for "work" within the biosphere was increased over billions of years. Even though heterotrophs receive nourishment from other organic matter, most heterotrophs still exploit[13] energy inside their own bodies. This energy-transfer inside the body is called *endosomatic*. *Endo* means "inside." *Somatic* means "body." Inside-the-body. Eating is an *endosomatic* process. Only with the appearance of humans was the biosphere introduced to intentional, systematic, *exosomatic*, or outside-the-body, *exploitation* of biologically-concentrated energy, first through the use of fire to burn plants, dung, and other readily available organic materials,

10. And at each step along the way, some of that energy was dissipated, though during photosynthesis—a unique process—that loss is nearly immeasurable. This makes photosynthesis one of the most remarkable things in nature.

11. Organisms that synthesize their own food, using light or chemical energy to convert inorganic substances. Most plants are autotrophs.

12. Organisms that cannot synthesize their own food and must obtain it by consuming other organisms. All animals are heterotrophs, as well as all fungi and protozoa. Most bacteria are heterotrophs.

13. Take advantage of; use for itself.

then through the domestication of animals, and finally through the burning of organic material that was hundreds of millions of years in the making—fossil hydrocarbons, or fossil fuels.

Energy is a material basis of *all* development[14] without exception. Any real account of our circumstance must be based significantly on an account of where energy originated, how it is changed into useful forms, and how society is organized to use that energy. As exchange detectives, we already know that this means *identifying exchange nodes and seeing what happens there.* This chapter is a necessary reality check before we get to general-purpose money.

Energy impacts *all* social relationships. Bureaucratic and profit-motivated organizations, however, are driven by the dual compulsion that defines them—*self-preservation* and *expansion,* nowadays through the accumulation of money. This disqualifies these institutions as "experts" on energy ecology and its relation to money, because they have privileged *money* prior to providing an account of energy. We are going to correct that by providing an account of energy first, then money.

> Energy has always been the basis of cultural complexity and it always will be. The past clarifies potential paths to the future. One often-discussed path is cultural and economic simplicity and lower energy costs. This could come about through the "crash" that many fear—a genuine collapse over a period of one or two generations, with much violence, starvation, and loss of population. The alternative is the "soft landing" that many people hope for—a voluntary change to solar energy and green fuels, energy-conserving technologies, and less overall consumption. This is a utopian alternative that, as suggested above, will come about only if severe, prolonged hardship in industrial nations makes it attractive, and if economic growth and consumerism can be removed from the realm of ideology.[15]

14. Social change, usually with increasing complexity.
15. Tainter, "Complexity."

Energy Primer

Proponents of alternative energy speak of achieving "sustainability," or avoiding using things up for good when we use them. To be *sustainable*, however, an energy source would have to be perpetual by its very nature (wind, solar, wave), replaceable through re-concentration (e.g., photosynthetic biological mass, growing more trees for fuel), or rely on some nearly inexhaustible resource not only for the energy, but in some schemes like "hydrogen energy," for the technological base.[16]

Advocates of "green energy" love data. How many kilocalories (thousand calories)[17] a day of solar energy hit the earth, etc.? As if that means all those kilocalories are available to us. Sometimes they simply present alternatives that can transform energy into useful energy, with no reference to ultimate capacity, density, portability, stability, safety, ease of extraction, etc. Most of the chatter about alternative energy and "sustainable" energy emits more heat than light, forgive the pun, because it *conceals* more than it *reveals*. We will show you how.

Before reviewing so-called alternatives, it is important to review some energy basics.[18]

In physics, *force* pushes against resistance. Press your foot into the floor, and you exert *force*. If resistance is overcome to any degree, that is, if something is moved—you lift yourself up from the chair—that is *work*.

Work, in the physics sense, is measured by an arbitrary but consistent standard. For example, if a force can lift a one pound weight one foot straight up (directly away from the center of the earth) at mean sea level, we refer to the quantity of that *force* as *one foot-pound*. The work is performed *on* the weight. The energy that holds a spring closed is a *force*, but not yet work. Work has to move something. The spring in that old wind-up clock

16. Wise, "The Truth about Hydrogen." Hydrogen is touted as the coming miracle in energy, but it is far more useful at producing research grants than it is at producing energy. In fact, not only does hydrogen not fit the bill with regard to production, storage, distribution, and use, as a carrier and not a source it consumes more energy in feedstocks than it makes available for work. The actual potential for hydrogen fuel cells is extremely limited. Some critics of the hydrogen hype compare it to "snake oil" and "alchemy." The author agrees.

17. A calorie is enough energy to raise the temperature of one gram of water one degree Celsius at one atmosphere of pressure.

18. Lancaster, "Some Energy Fundamentals."

is actually performing *work*, moving the hands around the clock. When the spring is uncoiled and loses its *force*, it quits working.

Energy means *capacity to perform work*, not work. It can be *latent* (available, but not currently moving anything, like the coiled spring in that old clock before you release the winder) or *actual* (moving something now). Energy comes in *forms*: thermal, chemical, electrical, etc. Using heating as one example, think of heat directly from sunlight, heat from combustion, heat from animal metabolism, heat from friction. Of course, heat is a by-product of energy *use*, and as soon as that heat is produced, it begins its entropic dissipation.[19]

Power is a combination of *intensity* and *time*. That is, power is the quantity of energy delivered for work over a specific time. One horsepower, for example is defined as 550 foot-pounds *per second*, which someone apparently determined was about the pulling capacity of an average adult draft horse.

Different energy sources are measured in different ways. British Thermal Units (BTU) measure heat. One BTU is sufficient heat-energy to raise the temperature of one pound of uncontaminated water by one degree Fahrenheit at mean sea level. One *volt* of electrical flow-force successfully overcoming one *Ohm* of resistance is a current of one *Ampere*. The heat generated and lost to the environment by that resistance is one *Watt*. The power of one Watt (quantity) for one second (time) is called a *joule*. The power of a Watt over one hour is one Watt-hour. So it goes.

An energy *source* embodies energy, or holds the energy as a structure like a molecule. Oil and sugar are energy sources. An energy *carrier* only transfers energy sources from one place to another. A battery is an energy *carrier*. Hydrogen is an energy *carrier*. All energy carriers, with no exceptions in the physical universe, are energy *sinks*, places where more energy is consumed to produce it than is ultimately available for work. The measure of invested versus returned energy is Energy Return on Energy Invested (EROEI). The formula is Energy Yield ÷ Energy Expended. If 500 calories of fossil energy is used to generate 400 calories in a hydrogen fuel cell, the EROEI is 8/10, which is less than one. Any energy production process that is less than one ERORI is an energy sink.

Energy sinks are more than just energy production processes. An *energy sink* is also any situation where more useful energy is dissipated than gained in work. *Energy sinks* are where net *negentropy* is lost. Your car is an

---

19. Take special note of the concept of *dissipation*—spreading thin until something appears to vanish. We will place special emphasis on the contrast between *dissipation*—using up—and its opposite *generation*, like the process of photosynthesis. Likewise, we will discuss *dissipative structures*—structures that "use up energy."

energy sink. A city is an energy sink. Your body is an energy sink. A battery is an energy sink. More negative entropy (concentrated energy) goes in than comes out through the work performed. Understood as time—also a function of the Second Law—an energy *sink* is any process that uses up more "past" energy than it returns as "present and future" energy. The universe as a whole, as far as we can tell, is a vast energy sink.

Energy *density* refers to how much energy is stored by *volume* and *weight*. These are not the same, and they are important for us. *Volumetric energy* density is X number of *watt-hours per liter* (a size). *Gravimetric energy* density is X number of *watt-hours per kilogram* (a weight). Gasoline has a volumetric value of 9,000 watt-hours per liter. 150 Bar gaseous hydrogen, on the other hand, contains 405 watt-hours per liter.[20] A 15-gallon gas tank would have to be replaced by a 334-gallon-capacity high-pressure tank, fitted with a host of new safety devices, beginning with high-pressure regulators. *Portability*[21] is a big issue related to energy, and one related to volumetric energy. Gasoline is relatively easy to contain and transport. Natural gas is far more difficult. Natural gas, then, cannot replace gasoline in most cases, because it has less *volumetric energy* than gasoline. This is why when someone says we can mine X kilocalories of natural gas to substitute for X kilocalories of oil, that person is either misinformed or deceptive, because they are ignoring *volumetric* and *gravimetric* differences.

Taking all these factors into account, we can now get the rest of our energy reality-check.

The simple fact is that the world economic system as it is now constituted, in every facet, including technological development and population, has been fueled predominantly by fossil hydrocarbons (oil, gas, and coal), exclusively and irreplaceably in many sectors by oil (because it is highly-concentrated, liquid, and portable). Any analysis that fails to confront this fact squarely is neglecting physics, specifically the Second Law of Thermodynamics. The reason this physical law—related to energy—is so important is that it is a law that cannot be broken. We cannot "make" energy, and when we use up highly concentrated energy in work, it is—practically speaking—"gone baby gone." You cannot re-use your burnt gasoline.

---

20. Ibid., 71.1–71.3.

21. Easily carried. The more portable a thing is, the easier it is to carry. A briefcase is more portable than a suitcase, a suitcase more portable than a mattress.

The Second Law states that heat can never pass spontaneously from a colder to a hotter body. Refrigerators and air conditioners warm more air than they cool, generally by burning coal for electricity, in addition to producing powerful greenhouse gases at the point of use.[22] The cool air you enjoy from that AC is *exchanged*, Detective, for more heated air elsewhere. We import X degrees into the air conditioned building and export X degrees plus Y back to the outside (somewhere). As a result of this fact, natural processes that involve *energy transfer* always have one ultimate "direction," toward dissipation, and that dissipation is absolutely irreversible.

This law also predicts that the entropy, the disorder in an isolated system, *always* increases with time. "You can't win. You can't break even. You can't get out of the game."[23] If time is conceived as "linear," the line—or arrow—of time aims in only one direction, and that direction is toward disorder. This is what we know right now about energy, entropy, and time. This is what makes death inevitable and travel "back" in time a Hollywood fantasy.

The central question regarding "alternative" energy is whether and how it can *replace* fossil fuel—and I will concentrate here on two sectors, transportation and electricity, beginning with oil. The first premise we have to face is that neither wood, hydropower, solar, wind, wave, tides, fission, geothermal, batteries, nor gas hydrates are interchangeable with oil. These can produce electricity, but electric batteries that store it cannot replace oil. Walter Youngquist explains:

> How to use electricity to efficiently replace oil (gasoline, diesel, kerosene) in the more than 700 million vehicles worldwide has not yet been satisfactorily solved. There are severe limitations of the storage batteries involved. For example, a gallon of gasoline weighing about 8 pounds has the same energy as one ton of conventional lead-acid storage batteries. Fifteen gallons of gasoline in a car's tank are the energy equal of 15 tons of storage batteries. Even if much improved storage batteries were devised, they cannot compete with gasoline or diesel fuel in energy density. Also, storage batteries become almost useless in very cold weather, storage capacity is limited, and batteries need to be replaced after a few years use at large cost. There is no battery pack which can effectively move heavy farm machinery over miles of farm fields, and no electric battery system seems even remotely able to propel a Boeing 747 14 hours nonstop at 600 miles an hour from New York to Cape Town (now the longest scheduled plane flight). Also, the considerable additional weight to any vehicle

22. Rosenthal and Lehren, "Relief in Every Window."
23. Quoted from a friend, D. A. Clarke.

using batteries is a severe handicap in itself. In transport machines, electricity is not a good replacement for oil. This is a
limitation in the use of alternative sources where electricity is
the end product.[24]

Batteries cannot become a wholesale replacement for gasoline in vehicles. To think otherwise is not merely technological optimism; it is technological delusion—the belief that somewhere, somehow, *technology* can
solve any problem.[25] But technology is bound by the Second Law just as
everything else is. It may seem controversial for us to say that science fiction involving the colonization of space is an unrealizable fantasy—this is
an idea that is tied up with "progress" narratives. But we can make a pretty
solid case, based on the Second Law, that aside from a few minor forays into
space, human beings will never get off this rock. We have neither the energy
nor the resources to do so. We are contained not by lack of imagination, but
by an unbreakable physical law.

All units of energy are not equal in form. We not only will never use
batteries to fly airplanes or run eighteen wheelers, we will never use coal,
wind, solar, geothermal, hydroelectric, or wave power to run these vehicles
except to make the electricity to fill the batteries of electric cars. The average
electric car ultimately uses as many or more calories of fossil energy than a
gasoline-powered car.[26] You just don't see it, because the coal mine is on a
ruined mountain in rural West Virginia somewhere, and you plug your car
into an outlet in a suburban garage in Atlanta or San Jose.[27]

24. Youngquist, "Alternative Energy Sources."

25. Yes, there are some electric cars; but that does not mean it is ecologically or
economically feasible to replace the gasoline-powered world fleet with them. It is not.
And if attempted, it would ultimately generate more greenhouse gases than we currently emit from gasoline transport. The Second Law says "There's no such thing as
free lunch."

26. Bielo, "Electric cars." "[S]mokestacks, many attached to coal-fired power plants,
are the single-largest source of greenhouse gas pollution in the US, at two billion metric
tons of CO_2 per year. *That source would grow as electric cars demand more and more
electricity,* unless tighter pollution controls are placed on power plants." (Italics added.)

27. Sovacool, "Valuing the Greenhouse Emissions from Nuclear Power." Many
people advocate for nuclear energy to produce the electricity to power automobiles.
There are three significant problems with this. First, when you take into account the
energy and environmental costs of mining, milling, and refining uranium for nuclear
fuel, building and operating plants, processing and disposing of waste, etc., nuclear is
only marginally better from an emissions standpoint than a combined fuel plant. Second, nuclear is so potentially dangerous that no private insurance company will cover
them (their insurance is subsidized heavily through tax revenues). Third, remembering
flows as inputs and outputs, spent nuclear fuel has to be expensively contained and
guarded for thousands of years before it is safe to return to the environment. Given that

Volumetric and gravimetric (portability) considerations are inescapable for specific energy applications. There are a handful of highly expensive, science-project electrical cars, but in the world there are now more than a billion automobiles (75 percent of them are private cars),[28] a massive increase since Walter Youngquist wrote the previously mentioned quote in 1999.[29] They consume approximately half of the world's gasoline. They continue to be produced along with replacement parts, and will continue to be produced—barring some massive social cataclysm or transformation—until the petroleum is no longer *economically* available.[30]

Water, Water Everywhere, or Not

Food is the way nature exchanges energy in plants and animals. Food is where actual persons get the energy they require to support their basic metabolism—that is, those bodily *exchanges* necessary to survive. The other things these biotic energy transfers require is *water*, that universal solvent. And humans, as well as other *animals*, need access to *oxygen* to "burn" the fuel in the body. The most basic connection between the person and nature, each coextensive with the other, is through exchanges of air, water, and food.

All of these exchanges are conducted in certain ways for certain cultures and in certain ways for certain natural conditions.[31] Food and water are on land. There are spaces on or near the surface of the earth where the water is concentrated, and likewise spaces where water and soil come together to support terrestrial life. Land and water are aspects of *nature* that have to be taken into account when we look at money, the *cultural* product, as an *ecological* (natural, material) phenomenon.

no human civilization has yet lasted as long as the half-life of plutonium-239, which is 24,000 years.

28. Tencer, "Number of Cars Worldwide."

29. LeBeau, "Whoa!" The United States accounts for far more than its share. Worldwide, in 2000, there were four automobiles for every thousand people. By 2010, there were forty per thousand. In the United States, in 2012, we had 600 per thousand people.

30. By this we do not mean the oil "runs out." At some point, it will take more energy to pull the oil out of the ground than what the oil itself yields. This may still be economically feasible because of gasoline's criticality, if for example coal-generated electricity is used to get the oil. While the EROEI (energy return on energy investment) may be negative from coal to oil, the energy loss in the transaction is "paid" by gasoline's portability and volumetric power. The other factor, apart from EROEI is what Jason Moore calls EROCI (energy returned on capital invested).

31. There is no actual boundary between "culture" and "nature," between subject and object, between "material conditions" and "cultural construction." These can only be sufficiently understood in relation to one another.

"Water is life," say the indigenous water protectors. Every human society is situated near water. Water, in conjunction with culture, places limits on societies. Wars are fought over water. Water forces people to reach agreements on what happens upstream and downstream. Water runs over, under, around, and through our boundaries. Perhaps a sounder basis for political mapping would be watersheds—regions where water drains into common rivers, lakes, and seas—instead of the artificial lines we often use now. My current state of residence, Michigan, has eighty-seven watersheds and sub-watersheds that may make more sense than the current eighty-three counties that look mostly like boxes drawn on the map.

In late 1999 and early 2000, Bolivians—mostly indigenous—in the city of Cochabamba took to the streets in what would come to be known as the Cochabamba Water War.[32] A huge American company, *Bechtel*, the one-time employer of former Secretary of State George Schultz, fronted by the local corporation, *Aguas del Tunari*, and backed by the World Bank, made a deal with the municipal government to privatize the water system. That is, the company would claim *ownership of water*, which it would then sell to everyone who needed it.

That went over like the proverbial fart in choir practice. The police then reacted badly to the resulting mass demonstrations—surprise, surprise—and things spun nearly out of control. This continued for weeks and ended badly all around. But when Evo Morales, an indigenous agrarian organizer, became the public spokesperson against the "privatization" of water, he ran for President as an agrarian socialist and was elected—to the chagrin of the Bolivian elite as well as Washington—in 2006. Messing with peoples' water can have consequences.

In 2016, we saw the rise of the "water protectors" among indigenous North Americans standing fast in front of an oil pipeline at the Standing Rock Reservation in North Dakota. By February 2017, they were removed by militarized police in actions that shocked the world with its echoes of past genocidal land grabs by European settlers against the same people. The greatest conflicts and crimes coming out of the Israeli occupation of Palestine, seldom mentioned by the press, have to do with water.[33] The land grabs, not dissimilar from those made by European settlers in North America a century and a half earlier, are all made at water points. The Syrian Civil War began with a drought that drove a million farmers into

32. Strother, "On Water Scarcity."
33. Arnaud, "Occupied Palestine."

the cities where social services were already being dismantled, and that extra million in urban centers overloaded the infrastructure and threw the country into crisis.[34]

The United States as a whole uses water at staggering rates, most of it on bad practices, wasting an enormous fraction of it. Industrial agriculture and now hydraulic fracturing oil and gas wells are pumping out major US aquifers faster than they can recharge, poisoning more water every day, lowering the tables until wells go dry, drawing off rivers and streams, and destabilizing soils, all by pump-pumping away with eyes fixed on the next business cycle and not on the threatening horizon of inescapable consequence. The problem with this is that businesspeople cannot make water. What they are doing instead is abusing water, abusing others by misusing the water, and making water ever scarcer. Scarcity strengthens the potential for conflict. Water is a natural phenomenon, essential to all life, and not reducible to a mere "resource."

Land and Mr. Malthus

We hesitate to even use the word *population*, because it has so many Malthusian and even eugenic echoes.[35] We need to say in advance that we do not see the world's conditions as first a "population problem"; nonetheless how many of us there are, in conjunction with how much we use, what we make, where we live, how we relate to each other, *is* part of our "material reality," our human/non-human ecology.[36] So we are seven billion more or

34. Hammer, "Lack of Water."

35. Malthus was a social theorist in the later eighteenth century who said that population increases faster than land can support them. Malthusianism has come to mean those who see the world's problems are primarily a problem of "overpopulation." Many Malthusians have advocated policies like mandatory sterilization and birth control, or eugenics—the attempt to selectively breed "better" humans. Malthusianism does not always entail racist ideas, though it often has. In the Chinese case, mandatory population control measures have targeted women, and have resulted in far fewer female births (because traditional ideas favor male children and females are aborted). Anti-Malthusians (like the author) point out that population does not increase *in advance* of land use, but *in response* to it. When more food is available (due to changes in land use and agriculture), then the population increases in response. The problem we face now is that we have increased food production and thereby increased population based on a model of agriculture that is not sustainable. This still does not mean that the prime directive is population decrease, but that land use must again be redesigned. In fact, intensive hand-tended polyculture can produce far more and far more variable food per hectare than extractive industrial agriculture and actually restore soils to biotic health. See Li Ching, "Is Ecological Agriculture Productive?"

36. Moore, "Transcending the Metabolic Rift." Moore shows that ecology is

less, spread all over the place, clustered around water, depending on land to produce food, shelter, fuel, fiber, minerals, livestock, etc.

Exchange detectives makes maps. They map patterns. What is the per capita energy consumption of energy (in gigajoules) in the following nations?[37]

Afghanistan	3.78
Benin	17.34
China	75.88
Dominican Republic	35.28
Honduras	25.24
Greece	102.5
Kenya	20.28
Mexico	65.95
Nicaragua	22.76
Russia	207.61
United States	300.91

When we call this era of climate change the "Anthropocene" era (literally, "made-by-humans"), we conceal the fact that *industrial capitalism*[38] is the specific social organization that has led to both the over-carbonization of the atmosphere and to the abrupt outgrowth of general human population, beginning in the sixteenth century, taking off with industrial expansion in the early nineteenth century, then at a far steeper rate after World

---

something of which we are a part, inflecting the ecology and being inflected by it. This includes the ways in which the existing ecological reality is determined by political economy. He therefore calls our current ecology the "capitalist world-ecology."

37. Global Energy Statistical Yearbook 2016, https://yearbook.enerdata.net/.

38. My use of the term "capitalism" throughout the book is in every case qualified. Any number of historians and theorists have established a sound historical case for the claim that "capitalism" is an overgeneralization, that the term did not come into use until the eighteenth century, that by any of its various definitions it is difficult to fix its "origins," and that it is—except as a familiar linguistic marker as it is used here—an essentially ideological category, whether used by "pro-capitalists" or "anti-capitalists." Capitalism, for our purposes, as will be described, is an economic regime based on monetary accumulation through ceaseless "expansion," or what is often called "growth." We will explain as we go what is problematic about this; and this is not an endorsement of the repressive state socialisms of the twentieth century, which were not the only alternative to industrial capitalism—in fact, they adopted many of the ideas and practices of industrial capitalism.

War II.[39] When we say we have a "population problem," we are excusing the consumption of the rich person in the United States and making the Afghani peasant equally responsible. Some have suggested this be called the Capitalocene era instead.[40] Calling it a "human-made problem" (Anthropocene) or a "population problem" is a way of "naturalizing" the issue, spreading the blame to all and pretending it is just part of a "natural" process as a way of immunizing powerful people and their politico-economic structures from criticism. A good detective will do well to remember: "This-is-how-it-works" does not mean "This-is-how-it-*has-to*-work."

Even with Russia's colder climate (which is a factor in gas consumption for heat, for example), the US as a whole still consumes more per capita. A hundred times more than the average Afghani. And yet, we can support an Afghani on an average of $421 a year, whereas it costs $30,240 a year to keep up the Average American who is hoovering up a hundred times the energy.[41]

Our system, based on general-purpose money, pays *more* for the person who uses up the *most* negentropic resources than the other person who does far less damage. How do we come to a place where we reward the *worst* with the *most*? Because natural ecosystems work in the opposite direction of general-purpose money with regard to the Second Law![42] This is one key reason that profit-seeking is an *inherently* wasteful practice. We will learn more about this in chapter 7, on money.

When we name the crises in air, land, and water as "population" problems, we are concealing the obviously unequal social relationships that show how the birth of a rich child is far more damaging to the biosphere than the birth of a poor child.

Where culture meets land, we call it a *landscape*. How many landscapes do we see, and how many do we not? Which landscapes do we see that conceal

39. Rademacher, "Three Agricultural Revolutions."

40. Moore, "Anthropocene or Capitalocene?"

41. Phelps and Crabtree, "Worldwide, Median Household Income."

42. Hornborg, *Power of the Machine*, 14. "Most fundamental is the fact that, by and large, prices must be inversely related to the productive potential of the traded products. This becomes apparent once we realize that production is dissipative rather than generative. It is simply a logical consequence of what the idea of money implies in a universe complying with the Second Law of Thermodynamics. Any stage in the productive process aiming to enhance the utility of substances thus transformed will reduce the sum of their productive potential (e.g., the availability of energy)."

other landscapes? Exchange detectives make maps. One kind of map back-traces land *use*. How many hectares[43] of land do you require? Ecological "footprints" are maps that imply flows. Ecological footprints are not synonymous with land, but land is part of the formula for ecological footprints, and the footprint itself is measured in landesque units, i.e., hectares. The ecological footprint of the average US citizen is eight hectares; whereas the average Honduran uses 1.91. For a poor city dweller in the United States, however, that might be 4 hectares; and for Donald Trump 50,000 hectares. Averages never tell the whole story; but they can at least help us see beyond categories like "population."[44]

Recapping, then, nature is energy and matter. Matter is air, land, and water, as well as the things that come from them. These phenomena *obey* the laws of nature. But they also *respond* to *knowledge*, the subject of the next chapter, which does not obey laws of nature and seldom corresponds to natural laws. Therein is the rub.

43. 10,000 square meters.

44. In chapter 10, we will criticize our own use of the "ecological footprint" metaphor, but for now it is an analytical tool in the early part of a process of de-familiarization. When we use this metaphor, we have *culture* making a footprint on *nature*—two separate entities. Our basic argument in this book is that this is a false division.

4

Knowledge

For the wisdom of this world is foolishness with God. For it is written, He that takes the wise in their craftiness: and again, The Lord knows the reasonings of the wise that they are vain.

—1 CORINTHIANS 3:19–20

IVAN ILLICH CONFRONTS US with a question.

> Look at the change in the meaning of nature between classical and modern times, as the historian Carolyn Merchant[1] has done . . . One thing was certain in antiquity: nature was alive. There were different and conflicting philosophical interpretations of what nature was; but to all of them was common the certainty that . . . nature is a concept, an idea, an experience derived from birth-giving . . . If, therefore, we look at the rise of natural science, and science altogether, in the seventeenth and eighteenth centuries, we are faced with research on a nature which not only lies outside the hands of God, but has lost its basic character of aliveness . . . You can call it mechanical, you can call it necessary or give it any name you want—an issue comes up which is characteristically modern: How do you explain, how do you speak about life in a nature and among natural things which are not born but are, so to speak, mathematically programmed?[2]

Let's answer that question in bite-sized pieces.

---

1. Merchant, *The Death of Nature*.
2. Illich, *Rivers North of the Future*, 69–70.

One, Not Two

Sometime just before that period broadly and somewhat pridefully called the Enlightenment, we changed *the way we know*. Philosophers have a fancy word for "the way we know," called *epistemology*,[3] but what we mean is that knowledge is not a simple mental mirror of what is. Knowledge is not fixed and permanent. We no longer "know" our bodies through humors, or "know" the stars through celestial spheres. Half of all scientific knowledge today will likely be considered somehow wrong in forty-five years.[4] We *know* things in different times and places in a particular *way*.

By the arrival of the Enlightenment,[5] we began to see the universe as a giant clock, many parts moving unconsciously in response to one another to create a synchronized whole. Some call this "clockwork determinism," because this way of knowing leads us to believe that things are predictable, or *determined*, as a series of precise physical causes and effects like the parts of an old-fashioned spring-powered watch.

Around the same time we were going through this shift in ways of knowing, we began to understand the person—ourselves—as isolated, like a soldier in the foxhole of his or her body, looking out onto a world apart from him.[6] We divided the world into the *subject* (the person, you or me) and the *object* (everything outside the person, outside you or me, including other people! "I am a subject. You are an object.").

With this idea, we came to "know" that the *subject* was unreliable because of illusions, desires, and emotions, whereas the *object* could yield the truth to the subject using various forms of mathematics. This gave us the idea of *object*ivity as a superior way of knowing. The key notion here is that the two—subject and object—are completely separate. This way of knowing came to be called *subject-object duality*.[7]

3. The study of knowledge.

4. Arbesman, *Half-Life of Knowledge*. This concept is used by quantitative analysts. Fifty years ago we *knew* dinosaurs were reptiles. We now *know* they were more closely related to birds. When the author was a child, doctors recommended smoking to their adult patients as an "aid to digestion."

5. *Merriam-Webster Dictionary*: The Enlightenment—a philosophical movement of the seventeenth through nineteenth centuries marked by a rejection of traditional social, religious, and political ideas and an emphasis on rationalism.

6. The normative *person* then was a male.

7. This way of knowing was very useful in certain kinds of scientific discovery; and its practical applications were so effective in many instances (in "dominating" nature) that it led people to conclude something that *did not follow* from the premise of being effective: that science, as practiced through measuring discrete things mathematically, is the singular source of truth.

Between these two ideas—clockwork determinism and subject-object *duality* (two-ness)—we came to understand the (objective) universe as essentially passive and unaware, and we created an imaginary but powerful borderline of "knowing" between persons (one thing) and the environment (something outside persons). These ideas are still extremely influential, making it difficult to imagine anything apart from them.

The reason we began the first chapter with the Rain of the Skin Flakes is that we need an image, from reality, that helps us to think past those imaginary borders. We need an image of something real that demonstrates what might be unreal about this subject-object split. Ivan Illich said that there is "a structural kinship between subject and object; the indwelling of one in the other."[8]

As to "dead" nature, we are going to start with a radical claim. We are, each of us—and in that "us" we include every *thing*, down to every atom, photon, and quark—in some way *aware*. If I aggressively till the sod on a sunny lawn here in Southern Michigan in June, and it rains heavily for a day or two, that patch of earth will burst forth with a plant called purslane.[9] The purslane seeds that have lain dormant are *aware* of temperature and moisture in the soil, and they respond to it. If we watch this on time-lapse photography, that living awareness will be very apparent. This is not animism, where a tree has *thoughts* like a human. It is to say that we are not merely joined to our environments, but that our environments themselves are joined with us through many, many forms of *awareness*. The environment does not play a merely "passive" role, first because it is not *apart* from us, and second because every aspect of "it," in "its" many forms, responds to other aspects of "it." We may see the passage of energy from one billiard ball to the next and assume that these objects, being unalive, have no awareness. But the fact that they respond to one another is indicative of *some form of awareness*, or perception, even if it is not awareness like our "consciousness." Non-human nature does not respond *passively* to human interventions, even if is not responding *consciously* in the sense we experience, with a capacity for conscious *choice*.[10]

A corresponding dualism is the separation of *culture* from *nature*. The culture-nature split is a *way of knowing* that makes culture (and humans, as *subjects*) one thing and nature (an imaginary Nature without humans, as

8. Illich, *Energy and Equity*, xviii.

9. Many people spray purslane, calling it "pigweed." In fact, it is one of the most nutritious and delicious green vegetables around, and the highest in Omega-3 fatty acids. In Latin America it is routinely eaten, and called *verdolagas*. Nature communicates with us all the time. We have proven sometimes, however, to be bad listeners.

10. A power we frequently overstate in ourselves.

object) another.[11] Overcoming this *dualism* opens a path along which we can observe *money* as a natural, or ecological, phenomenon; even though money cannot be reduced to nature as something that itself obeys the most immutable laws of nature. The main boundary we want to erase in this exchange detection exercise is between money (a cultural creation—something we have *made*) and the environment ("material reality," or those things we can understand using observation and physical laws—some made and some created). We will show how this thing—*money*—this sign, this code, this institution, has direct and discernable effects on the material world, effects that are *unique to money*, and that make general-purpose money in many ways extremely dangerous.

Things Not Seen

Remember earlier when we spoke of electric cars? We said that this was not "green" technology, because the actual energy drawn from the California garage wall socket is being made elsewhere by burning coal that was mined by mountaintop removal in West Virginia. We are fooled by what we don't see.

In the 1970s, anthropologists Michael Taussig and June Nash studied peasants in Colombia and Bolivia who had been taken off their land in the countryside to force them into dependence on wage labor, cutting sugar cane and mining.[12] The peasants developed the belief that a person could make a pact with the devil, whereupon they would make a lot more money. But there was a catch, two catches actually. First, the money made on the deal with the devil could only be spent on foolish impractical goods, and second, the person who made the deal with the devil would die early and painfully. Talk about living dangerously!

There was also a corresponding practice. The peasant-laborers would baptize the money they received in wages, which "brought the money to life," and ensured that the money spent would eventually return to its baptizing recipient.[13]

11. Moore, "The Capitalocene, Part II," para. 2: "The problem of dualism is an onion problem; we are dealing with layers within layers. To critique Nature/Society dualism is to implicate not one but many binaries: the repertoire of 'interrelated and mutually reinforcing dualisms' immanent to modernist though. The terrain of this critique is vast and I will not reprise it here. What I should like to highlight is the especially tight connection between three sets of dualisms that cannot be ignored: nature/society, base/ superstructure, local/global."

12. Taussig, *The Devil and Commodity Fetishism*.

13. Ibid., 126-42.

Taussig was confronted by the opinion of some anthropologists that these beliefs and practices were mere holdovers from their more "primitive" days before being turned into wage laborers "as a response to anxiety and thwarted desire."[14] On the contrary, said Taussig, "Magical beliefs are revelatory and fascinating not because they are ill-conceived instruments of *utility*,[15] but because they are poetic echoes of the cadences that guide the innermost course of the world. Magic takes language, symbols, and intelligibility to their outermost limits, to explore life and thereby change its destination."[16] These peasants were adapting with a form of resistance to the new waged-economy into which they'd been conscripted by stripping them of their land. In particular, they were resisting their oppressors' characterization of *money*, the thing that tied them to those oppressors. The devil *described and validated* their alienation from the work of the plantations and mines. They weren't going to allow the oppressors *account* of money to colonize their thoughts.

Taussig takes this examination of indigenous peasant-laborer belief and holds it up it as a mirror to our own "superstitions" about money, for example, that money "grows." Money, of course, does not *grow*. It is printed in response to bank credit,[17] just as it once was minted out of precious metals; but it never "grows" in the way a baby grows or a plum forms on a tree. The appearance of "growth" is an aspect of money *accumulation*.[18] But our imagination of money "growing" is every bit as magical a form of thinking as that of the "primitive" peasant-laborers; only in this case, we *are* accepting the dominator's *account*.

The bank loans you $100 and you pay back the $100 with six percent interest. From the standpoint of the bank, they began with $100 and ended up with $106, so the appearance of growth is sustained by the disappearance of every other aspect of that transaction by what is kept "off the books," so to speak. Like the magical *appearance* of electricity in a California suburban garage outlet to power the trendy "green" electric car. The extra work you did to get the extra six dollars for your loan, like the Appalachian coal field that produces power to the electrical grid, are *out of sight and out of mind*.[19] It is only our own familiarity with this "money grows" notion that allows us

14. Ibid., 14.

15. *Utility* is an idea that industrialized Western culture projects onto other cultures.

16. Ibid., 15.

17. A system called "fractional reserve banking."

18. The gathering of more and more money by one person, family, enterprise, or social class.

19. "*Out of sight and out of mind*" is a recurring point throughout the book. That is why we will continue to italicize it.

to substitute this magical belief about the money for what is real, yet *out of sight and out of mind*.

This is why, as exchange detectives, we look past the immediate and into the nodes and flows. We are revealing the truth that is cloaked by the deceptive power of *what-we-see* and, as we have been trained to do, ignoring what is *out of sight*. This deeper look is not the dominant *way of knowing* for us. It is *epistemologically* strange to us. The exchanges at the bank and in the garage and with the electric company are mystified by what is *out of sight and out of mind*; and detectives reveal what is behind the veil. Consider this European folk tale that Hornborg relates:

> The tramp is reluctantly admitted into a kitchen, but the housewife has no intention of serving him any food. He pulls a stone out of his pocket, asking merely for a pot of water to boil some soup on it. The housewife is too intrigued to deny his request. After a while, stirring and carefully tasting the water, the tramp observes that it could do with some flour, as if this was the one missing ingredient. The housewife consents to offer him some. Then, one by one, he similarly manages to lure her to add the various other ingredients, until, finally, she is amazed to find a delicious soup cooked on a stone.[20]

Just as the interest appears to the banker and the electricity magically appears to fill the batteries for the electric car, this folk story shows how our attention is focused on the thing in front of us, distracting us from the whole truth. As Hornborg says, "It transfers our attention from the wider *context*[21] to the imaginary center"[22] (italics added).

What is the *context* of money as our imaginary center? Let's move along, Detective.

Abstraction

> Money has become abstract because the individual can no longer hold in his hands something that is valuable in itself; he can no longer attach a fixed meaning to the money he uses. Coins as well as paper money have become abstract symbols. The individual is attached not to his ten-dollar bill or ten-franc piece, but

---

20. Hornborg, *Power of the Machine*, 151. European folk tale as related by Hornborg.

21. Latin: *Con* means "together," *texere* means "weave." Con-Text is "woven-together." *Merriam-Webster* defines "context" as "the interrelated conditions in which something exists or occurs," how things are woven together.

22. Hornborg, *Power of the Machine*, 151.

only to its buying power. The symbol itself, like the economic
reality for which it stands, has become more abstract.[23]

—JACQUES ELLUL

Our *way of knowing* is still more than the apprehension of facts and signs, of
dualism (two-ness) versus monism.[24] Our *way of knowing* is also more than
the tendency to see what is there while failing to understand what is *out of
sight and out of mind*. We also often perform *abstractions* that can conceal
more than they reveal.

Abstraction can be understood as folding something into something
bigger, or *encompassing*.[25] You, the individually unique person named Janie
in Oakland with her two kids and a job at the dentist's office, might also be
an American—but there are many Americans who are not Janie, a female—
and there are many females who are not Janie, an African American—and
there are many African Americans who are not Janie. Any of those latter
categories wraps around the personhood of Janie and submerges it into a
more abstract category. As a human, Janie is a member of a species, yet
more abstraction—more encompassment. As a Homo sapiens, Janie is of
the Family Hominoidea, the Order of Primates, the Class of Mammals, the
Phylum of Chordata, the Kingdom Animalia, and then within the overall
category Life. Each stage in this taxonomy further *abstracts* Janie or *encompasses* Janie. The "biosphere" to which we have referred and of which we are
a part is an abstraction that encompasses unimaginable local complexity in
every continent and ocean, every region, every watershed, every field and
pond and town, even every unique inch of soil.

Abstraction is a trade-off. We get more clarity about what differentiates a category from everything apart from it,[26] or conversely we demon-
strate what joins more than one thing into a greater whole. Janie's American
citizenship qualifies her to vote, for example; and Janie's status as an African
American in a racialized culture creates a kind of solidarity—a political
identity—with other African Americans that may influence if and for whom
she votes. But we also conceal/erase the differences between everything
captured *inside* the abstraction. Janie can interpret her status as a mammal
in ways that are helpful, for example, in determining certain valid medical

23. Ellul, *Money and Power*, 10.

24. The idea that Being is one, inclusive of *subject-object*.

25. Surround and hold within.

26. An orca and a bottlenose dolphin can be differentiated from non-whales within
the category "whale," even though we are ignoring much about an individual orca or
bottlenose dolphin.

generalizations.[27] On the other hand, her status as a mammal does little to resolve her conflict with an insurance company, or help her figure out what to do with her visiting grandmother, or which movie she and her husband want to watch with the kids on Friday night. The real danger of abstraction is that it can lead to lazy thinking in the guise of serious thinking, or worse, self-deception. Janie herself cannot be boiled down to any of those encompassing categories, nor is it advisable to *uncritically* project group characteristics on her. Janie is one generation from a Louisiana Creole family that lived near the coast, for example, and so she can catch and clean fish unlike many other females, she speaks a second language unlike many Americans, and she is Catholic unlike most African Americans.

Every social theory trades in abstractions, because these theories are concerned with humans as organized aggregates, not simply as singular persons. This is helpful as long as we don't begin to impose the abstractions back onto the specific persons; and the way we do that is by shifting focus back and forth between the abstract and the concrete—called a dialectical (two-sided) approach—to make sure these two domains continue to agree, that the abstract and concrete constantly correspond to each other. We say something about women, then something about Janie, then we see if these two statements agree. When they don't agree, this contradiction is telling us there is something faulty about our assumptions or methods, or that we need to further specify our claims. There are sometimes exceptions that do not totally disprove the rule; but they do preclude us claiming the rule is absolute. If I say, "All generalizations are false, including this one," then I need to revise my statement to, "Most generalizations are false." This book deals in several abstractions, but we also want to constantly check in with the concrete, the local, the specific.

Divide and Conquer

In 1811 England, a group of textile workers began destroying the machinery of the newly developed and "Satanic" textile mills. This group of labor activists were called the Luddites.[28] They did not believe the machines to be demons, *per se*, but they did clearly recognize that those machines would replace workers and create terrible conditions for the workers who remained employed. They are now the butt of jokes about people who are averse to

27. There is actually something in medicine called the *mammalian* reflex, which is important to scuba divers and hypothermia victims. Janie may—as a mammal—nurse a child, and what we know about nursing children generally can be helpful to Janie.

28. Conniff, "What the Luddites Really Fought Against."

certain technologies, but they actually had the insight that machines were not morally neutral just because they were not alive.

Technology is not generally thought of as anything except *dead*, "a material, intrinsically meaningless, but essentially knowable reality."[29] Technology in itself is considered morally neutral. We will challenge that idea in chapter 5, but for now we need to show how we arrive at this *way of knowing*. This is a dualistic stance, one that is upheld by the related ideas of clean separations between *subjects* and *objects*, as well as between *culture* and *nature*.

We measure nature in the natural sciences with mathematics, and economics reduces everything to (money) numbers in order to pretend it is a science.[30] Philosopher Alasdair MacIntyre can help us see through this trick:

> We might begin by noticing that 'exists' as used by modern quantification theorists can be said equally of numbers and oak trees. "There is a prime number greater than seventeen and less than twenty-three" and "There is an oak tree in Sherwood Forest" make use of the same "There is." But the oak tree, if it exists, has a kind of actuality that the prime number lacks.[31]

Without an example like this, it is difficult to grasp how terms can differ even when they use the same language. The number *exists* as does the tree, but "exists" has two different realms to which it refers that radically differentiate the meaning of "exists." One is an idea and the other is a material thing. Both things are true, but their truth has to be established in different ways. This is a fairly easy mental exercise as far as it goes; and most of us easily recognize that these two realms, ideas and material things, co-exist within the same reality. A person, in the day-to-day conduct of her or his life, does not and cannot separate ideas and material things. We need both; and we know intuitively that ideas penetrate the material and the material penetrates our ideas in our lives. Whether one is reading a map or building a bird house or measuring out a dose of medicine, our understanding is incomplete if we fail to integrate these supposedly separate realms that we can only mentally separate. And yet, higher education now strives to represent knowledge itself as separable by realm to such an

---

29. Hornborg, *Global Ecology*, 31.

30. Natural sciences, under rigorous conditions, can at least establish certain patterns that lead to predictable outcomes. Economics has never displayed any such consistent predictive power, and is therefore not a science in the same sense, but a pseudo-science.

31. MacIntyre, *God, Philosophy, and Universities*, 40.

extent that integration of various realms of knowledge is made increasingly difficult by endless specialization.

> Disaggregation, the separation of reality into dissociated tax-onomies, the pretense that reality can be separated into various parts which can then be studied and evaluated independent of one another, begins with Descartes's "thing in-itself." It can be seen most clearly today in the organization of the modern uni-versity. MacIntyre outlined three developments in the modern research university that could be traced to the displacement of Aristotle's universalism by Cartesian atomism. First, the univer-sity made extraordinary discoveries in various fields, especially the sciences. These discoveries, however, required funding, and so the direction of research efforts was determined in large part by who funded the research and to what purpose. Second, the new universities provided an increasing pool of specialized ex-perts to support the expansion of an industrial capitalist society. Undergraduate studies are now largely an initiation into gradu-ate specialties that are determined by professional job markets. Increasing specialization is an aspect of de-skilling. In the acad-emy, this has led to a proliferation of disciplines, subdisciplines, and sub-subdisciplines, in which the graduate student and eventual professional or expert neither comprehends nor needs to know the larger social, moral, political, or economic context of the work that he or she does. Third, as research dedicated to both economic expansion and greater specialization goes deeper into ever more specialized fields of inquiry, universities become increasingly expensive and come to resemble for-profit corporations producing commodities.[32]

This division of "knowledge" contributes from the top down to the culturally dominant idea that a cultural product like *money* can be under-stood apart from natural phenomena like *ecosystems*, and vice versa. This division serves a purpose with regard to our politico-economic thinking, in that it allows us to embrace the illusion that money—as a "mere" sign—is not an ecological phenomenon, or that machines are "mere" objects with no ethical implications. It excuses us from using both without discomfiting ethical considerations.

When we said above that economics pretends to be a science by using mathematics apart from other considerations, we meant two things: first,

---

32. Goff, *Borderline*, 145–46. Jason W. Moore describes this as dividing the world into pieces and giving each piece the status of ontology—an actually existing and sepa-rate *being* prior to our perception of it.

this trick allows us to maintain the illusion that ideas and material things can actually be separated, and the second thing is that whereas actual sciences using mathematical methods prove themselves with the ability to predict outcomes and to establish what MacIntyre calls "law-like generalizations," economics has never been capable of either. We will show, in the course of the rest of this book, how economics functions more as a belief-system or an ideology[33] than a science—almost, at times, as a form of propaganda.

Let's move our detective's inquiry forward again, now, to *exchange* itself.

---

33. A set of ideas that serve a political or economic program. Dominant ideologies can simultaneously conceal and reproduce the nature of power.

5

Exchange

He has filled the hungry with good things,
And sent away the rich empty-handed.

—LUKE 1:53

THE LIVING CELLS THAT comprise your body *exchange* ions internally to stay alive. They *exchange* nutrients taken in from outside themselves for waste products that are excreted. They process nutrients internally through a set of molecular *exchanges*. I am composing this in a house in Michigan. It is now January and quite cold outside. My house is pulling in gas to burn in order to heat the house, and the heat is diffusing through the attic; the house is drawing water from the water grid and sending used water into the sewage grid. *Exchange* is a term that encompasses processes that apply to almost every aspect of existence. When we *separate* subjects or disciplines, as MacIntyre pointed out happens in universities, we *conceal* many exchanges and many relationships. When things are concealed, they are thought of less, if at all; and this is the essence of *out of sight and out of mind*.

When we talk about *exchange* here, however, we are being somewhat more specific. We are talking about intentional exchanges between people within that field of activity we call economy. This book, this exercise in detection, is aimed at a revised *way of knowing*, a revised form of discernment, about *exchange* that unveils those things concealed and therefore *out of sight and out of mind*.

Velocity

A place designated for money-facilitated exchange is called *a* market. I've shopped in open air markets in Haiti, Venezuela, Peru and Somalia. I've

37

shopped in strip malls and box stores and grocery outlets (indoor markets) in the United States. These were specific *places*. The abstract sphere across place and culture within which money-facilitated exchange takes place is called *the* market, an abstraction and not a place.

Market economy is fast! That's why we like markets. I need sealant to fix a leak, a puzzle for our grandson's birthday, the latest copy of *Mother Earth News*, a new umbrella to replace my raggedy old one, and a gallon of milk. I don't need to make birdhouses, or bone knives, or down pillows at home, then dicker trades with an epoxy factory, a puzzle company, a publisher, an umbrella-maker, and a dairy farm. They use money, and I use money, and I can pick everything up within an hour or so. That *velocity* is generally experienced as a good thing. We call it *convenience*. It becomes a problem when whatever is being done to get these goods to market is harmful, because we are not merely causing harm, we are causing harm faster and faster.[1] One pound of kitchen waste in a trash can bound for the landfill (instead of a compost heap), where it will be buried and converted into methane—a powerful greenhouse gas—is negligible in the larger scheme of things. A hundred million households doing the same thing is not.

In our detection exercise earlier, we learned that a good detective follows exchanges through nodes to look for those things that are *out of sight and out of mind*. Behind those *goods* are some *bads*. The epoxy, the puzzle, the magazine, the umbrella, and the milk, for example, are all produced and delivered using energy (since we've talked about this), as does the car I drive to pick up all those things. Behind that energy, there are trash and toxic waste, pipeline spills, water and soil contamination, shipping pollution, carbon emissions, ocean acidification, worker exploitation, land exhaustion, and wars. We don't see any of this when we scan the umbrella at the self-checkout.

There is a direct relation between the speed of exchange and the increasing speed of travel. "No, wait a minute," you may be saying. "You are confusing apples and oranges! The speed of buying and selling are different than the speed of an automobile or an airplane." I think I can convince you otherwise.

1. Turgeon, "The Great Pacific Garbage Patch." Two enormous islands of plastic trash are now floating on the Pacific Ocean along a current called the North Pacific Subtropical Gyre. Nearly all plastic ever produced is still with us. These "islands" swap trash back and forth near Hawaii. It is estimated that it would take sixty-seven ships working full time to clean up one percent of this trash. It kills fish and other aquatic mammals and leeches toxins into the water. Estimates are that eighty percent of plastic discarded in the ocean sinks, so these islands are just a snapshot. Plastic is an item of convenience. We might name these toxic plastic islands the Isles of Convenience.

Ivan Illich, writing in 1974, drew a distinction between *traffic, transit,* and *transport*. Though somewhat arbitrary, he meant that *traffic* (as he used the word) meant the movement of people anywhere outside the home; by *transit*, he meant movement of people and goods using animal metabolic energy (e.g., walking, draft animals, or bicycles); *transport* meant the movement of people and goods using outside energy sources.[2] He was writing about energy, and we learned earlier how central energy is to everything.

A person on foot can cover three to four miles an hour. A bicycle, which is an engineering wonder of user-friendly technology, using human metabolic power, can cover ten to fifteen miles an hour. A person can walk around freely without much infrastructure, though she may avoid thickets and swamps and have difficulty with deep rivers. A bicycle requires at least a path, but not a big one. These forms of *traffic*, however, are systematically overtaken by fueled *transport*, and human-energized *transit* is constrained and even blocked by the infrastructure for fueled transport.

In looking at physical speed, Illich showed how beyond certain velocities, an increase in speed by one person or group is "purchased" at the cost of slowing someone else down. This is a physical analysis of a social inequality; but it is not—just like those other *out of sight and out of mind* examples we saw earlier—immediately visible. When I, a privileged first world person in my expensive automobile, am blazing down the expensive and material-heavy interstate at seventy miles per hour, I do not see the person on foot or on a bicycle who is blocked and rerouted by that Interstate. The only clue I have, which I ignore as best I can because it makes me a little sad, is the string of dead animals I encounter that did not understand this linear danger zone that had been constructed in their paths. They follow smells, in accordance with their natures, and encounter fatal ambush by machine.

The velocity of money represents an *entitlement* that also allows time to be appropriated by one person from another; and the modern speed of transport is not possible without the velocity of money . . . and vice-versa. Two aspects of the same process. Money allows forests to be traded for soda pop.

Carlton Reid wrote in April 2012 about what the actual average net velocity is for an automobile. Looking into every conceivable way to back-trace the energy as speed (power), checking how much was used in the production,

2. Illich, *Energy and Equity*, 15.

transportation, and maintenance, and further into pre-production-produc-
tion, and factoring in social as well as economic costs, he determined that
the average speed of the average car worldwide in 2012 was 3.7 miles per
hour.[3] About the rate at which the average healthy adult can walk. This sym-
metry is not accidental. We are pushing around X amount of weight against
Y amount of resistance, which requires Y amount of energy. It would be difficult to backtrack a lot further, because the other energy is human (which
means you'd have to measure caloric intake and output). Whether we can
measure it or not, we can at least be aware that there is some actually existing amount for how much X, Y, and Z are, whether we know that number or
not. The energy expended *here* in excess of the average everywhere comes at
the expense of energy appropriated *elsewhere*. Second Law.

When Monsignor Illich wrote *Energy and Equity* in 1974, his title
was direct and to the point. Illich observed how energy-use, especially fossil energy, since it is still the predominant energy commodity, crosses a
threshold, whereupon the use of *energy* itself creates, sustains, and expands
social *inequalities*. Above, we said, "There is a direct relation between the
speed of exchange and the increasing speed of travel." There is a threshold at
which the increased velocity of our activities, powered by "energy-slaves,"
begins to materially produce greater social inequality. We'll quickly review
Illich's thesis now, and from there try to relate this to see how money is in
the other half of an energy-money connection, a material-communication
connection, a natural-cultural connection. Culture and nature, to again
crib Illich, mirror "a structural kinship between subject and object; the
indwelling of one in the other."

Illich also spoke about velocity in terms of our earlier discussion of
price as the abstraction that makes unlike things alike in their exchangeabili-
ty for money. Going back to his distinction between transit (non-motorized)
and transport (motorized), and their relation to traffic (the movement of
people and things), Illich made special note that "Transit is not the product

3. Reid, "Speed of Cars." This number, ascertained in 1974 admittedly, was calculated by dividing the average number of miles driven by 1600 (hours), a number that
included driving, making and pumping the fuel, work hours paying for the car, emergency room hours lost from motor vehicle accidents, etc. A blogger named "CelloMom"
updated the figures in 2012 for just the United States (which skews the velocity upward,
because it doesn't account for the horrific traffic jams in many large cities abroad), and
kicked the net velocity up to a blazing 13 miles per hour, slightly faster than the average
bicycle at about 10 miles per hour. This does not account for space, wherein a line of
sixty pedestrians can easily walk along a four-feet-wide foot path going both directions,
without delays, compared to sixty car passengers, at the national average of 1.55 passengers per car, using 39 cars, that take 72 square feet of ground space, requiring 24 feet
of road width for two-way traffic, which can be jammed by one mishap. (http://www.
cellomomcars.com/2013/01/the-average-speed-of-average-car.html)

of an industry, but the independent enterprise of transients." Take note now of the term *independent* and its opposite *dependent* (or *dependency*), because this is the crux of the problem we will encounter further along about the money-energy nexus, which is that *we depend absolutely on both money and fossil energy* . . . and they come to us in our age as a package deal. Continuing with Illich: "It [transit] has use-value [the value of a thing apart from price, a teapot has value for making tea] by definition, but it need not have exchange-value [price]. The ability to engage in transit is native to man [*sic*] and more or less equally distributed among healthy people of the same age."[4]

Illich goes on to compare transit and transport. So both have use-value, but only one is a collection of things for sale. *Transit* is available if you can walk and have space. *Transport* means you have to build and buy cars, invoke immanent domain and pay for materials to make roads, pump oil out of the ground and refine it, and train emergency room doctors and nurses for motor vehicle trauma. As Illich said, "*Transport* stands for the capital-intensive mode of *traffic*, and *transit* indicates the labor-intensive mode."[5]

Thermodynamically, as we see with Reid, greater speed is achieved only with the input of greater useable energy (negentropy). Socially, as suggested by Illich, there is no gain in speed as a total quantity, but the stratification of society between those who must continue to walk—albeit with restrictions imposed by the new transport landscape—and those who have the wherewithal to ride. With regard to money, then, we will see that the greater speed that is afforded the privileged by social power and fossil energy is underpinned by the speed of commerce. The reason we can trade tropical forests for Coke, in Hornborg's example, is because the transaction is based not on use, but on *price*. Everything for sale is exchangeable for everything else for sale. Without that interchangeability based on price, we could not gather the materials from several continents, or refine and ship the fuels, or gather the building materials from hither and yon, to make the cars, the highways, the gas stations, and the emergency rooms. The velocity of our society is based absolutely on this *property* of money. Unlike some earlier cultures, who would say that two currencies—one for subsistence and one for luxury—must be used to prevent commensurability between forests (a necessity) and Coca-Cola (a frivolous and unhealthy luxury),[6]

4. Illich, *Energy and Equity*, 44.

5. Ibid., 43.

6. Further along in the book, we will look more closely at one such group, the Tiv people of Nigeria.

our use of general-purpose money tells us that the forest and the soft drink are equally valuable.

General-purpose money removes things from their context using price and speeds their exchange; and fossil energy moves them into new contexts at breakneck speed to effect more exchanges. One cannot work without the other in today's economy.

Inequality

In 1997, Nike Corporation employed around 100,000 Indonesian factory workers to make some of their shoes. The workers there made around $3.50 a day, working six days a week, totaling $21 a week, with zero insurance or benefits. Forty-four percent of their sales were in the United States and Canada, the largest fraction by far of its sales market. A US factory line worker, on average, costed a company around $12.45 an hour plus around five additional dollars an hour for mandatory insurances, totaling around $17.45 an hour in labor costs. The American worker was producing on average about $67 in monetary value per hour, meaning the company got a net boost of $49.55 an hour. Assuming then, that Indonesian factory workers were approximately as efficient as Americans using the same machinery, the net benefit per worker per hour to the same company in Indonesia was (with a 44 cents per hour wage rate) $66.56. The difference, then, between the American and Indonesian profit before transport, was $17.01 per hour per 100,000 workers, coming to $1.7 million an hour, eight hours a day, six days a week: more than $81.6 million a week. A pair of these $70 shoes, then, costed around nine dollars in materials and energy, six dollars in rentals and duties, and fifty cents to ship.[7]

The shoes sold to the American consumer, who may or may not be a factory worker, represented an exchange between that consumer and the producer, an Indonesian line worker—probably a young woman. It is fairly easy to see the differences in pay between the two, which would seem to make the high cost of the shoes (unreachably high for an Indonesian making forty-four cents an hour) appropriate for the American who makes $12–15 an hour or more. Since the report from the University of Michigan's "Just Don't Do It" campaign reported these numbers in 1997, we might assume that this has all changed. But another analysis in 2015, after Indonesia as a nation had an 800 percent jump in GDP between 1998 and 2013, shows that an American factory laborer still earns seventy-six times as much per

7. "Just Don't Do It," *University of Michigan*, 1997.

capita as an Indonesian. So who got the benefit of that 800 percent increase in GDP? It wasn't the average Indonesian.[8]

The difference between production costs and profit do not serve to narrow the distance between the Indonesian worker and the American consumer. It is absorbed by the third-party company. Class economics 101. The real question is, however, "How are we able to pay the Indonesian less than a dollar an hour, when the American could not even hope to live on that?" The reason is ecological and *gendered*, when we include the built environment in the ecology—or the sum of relationships in the overall environment.

The cost of day-to-day survival for the Indonesian is far lower than for the American.[9] The former does not have electricity, running water, or plumbing. She cooks on a small brazier using charcoal (which deforests an already denuded landscape), and washes by hand in a sewage-polluted river. The vast majority of this unpaid day-to-day survival work is being done by women, many of whom have also been impressed into wage labor, and who now—between paid and unpaid labor—work a hundred hours a week.[10]

Understood thermodynamically and seen statistically, we can compare the average energy consumed per person each year in Indonesia and the United States, which is 850 gigajoules and 6,916 gigajoules respectively. The amount of land, measured in hectares, required to support the average citizen of Indonesia is 1.6. For the United States, that number is 8.2 hectares.[11] The American is not even *allowed* to live without electricity, running water, or indoor plumbing, and not allowed to wash clothes in the river. Even if the American tried, she would not be able to find work without an automobile or be prepared to show up for work in accordance with even the

8. Ghogomu, "US Factory Workers."

9. Hartsock, *Money, Sex, and Power*. Sometimes called the cost of "social reproduction." Feminist Nancy C. M. Hartsock corrected Marxist economists who concentrated their analysis of profit at the "point of production," showing how the "cost of social reproduction," *i.e.*, unpaid labor by women. Illich called this "shadow work." World system theory, which takes into account differences in "technological development," incorporates the differences in social reproduction costs based on the money necessary to support industrialized social reproduction, *e.g.*, washing clothes in a machine versus in a river.

10. Peck, "Women Work More Hours." This is, to some extent the case in more metropolitan countries as well, where women who have joined paid-work forces are still coming home to do "women's work." In the US, the average woman with full-time work puts in an additional 16 hours of work at home each week, whereas men's "unpaid" work averages around seven hours. While at work, doing similar tasks, women earn 80 cents for every dollar earned by a male.

11. Global Footprint Network, http://www.footprintnetwork.org/content/documents/ecological_footprint_nations/.

job's basic dress and appearance standards without the American technological infrastructure.[12]

We do not see unequal exchange, in any guise, because it is *out of sight
and out of mind*. But the more difficult thing still is to see the *relationship*
between unequal exchange stated as *wage difference* (money) and unequal
exchange stated as *ecological difference* (energy/land, time/space). An important thesis for this book, and the case we intend to make by the time we
reach the end, is that understanding the nature of money as an ecological
phenomenon will reveal the ways in which economic inequality and environmental destruction are not two separate problems, but two faces of the
same coin. If there is a solution for this, it will require that both be addressed
simultaneously.

Illich, in speaking of *Energy* (material) *and Equity* (cultural), said that
the velocity achieved by one group using *transport* comes at the expense of
those with less, who still rely on (transport-restricted) *transit*. Hornborg,
likewise, suggests that in terms of land, energy (including labor), and social
organization, we are playing a "zero-sum game"; that is, the gains of some
are always at the expense of others, and the Second Law of Thermodynamics
is an equally harsh master in terms of how we extract material and energy
from the biosphere. Many people, however, believe that we can cut corners
and that we can cheat the Second Law and escape from the social inequality
our violations of it (facilitated by money) create, using new technologies.

> The habitual passenger must adopt a new set of beliefs and ex-
> pectations if he is to feel secure in the strange world where both
> liaisons and loneliness are products of conveyance. To "gather"
> for him means to be brought together by vehicles. He comes
> to believe that political power grows out of the capacity of a
> transportation system, and in its absence is the result of access
> to the television screen. He takes freedom of movement to be
> the same as one's claim on propulsion. He believes that the level
> of democratic process correlates to the power of transportation
> and communications systems. He has lost faith in the political
> power of the feet and of the tongue. As a result, what he wants
> is not more liberty as a citizen but better service as a client. He
> does not insist on his freedom to move and to speak to people
> but on his claim to be shipped and to be informed by media. He
> wants a better product rather than freedom from servitude to it.
> It is vital that he come to see that the acceleration he demands
> is self-defeating, and that it must result in a further decline of
> equity, leisure, and autonomy.[13]

12. Built and maintained by the same unequal exchange from abroad.
13. Illich, "Speed Stunned Imagination," *Energy and Equity*, chapter 3.

6

Technology

I looked on the earth, and behold, it was formless and void;
And to the heavens, and they had no light.
I looked on the mountains, and behold, they were quaking,
And all the hills moved to and fro.
I looked, and behold, there was no man,
And all the birds of the heavens had fled.
I looked, and behold, the fruitful land was a wilderness,
And all its cities were pulled down
Before the Lord, before His fierce anger.

—JEREMIAH 4:23–26

Our society resembles the ultimate machine which I once saw in a New York toy shop. It was a metal casket which, when you touched a switch, snapped open to reveal a mechanical hand. Chromed fingers reached out for the lid, pulled it down, and locked it from the inside. It was a box; you expected to be able to take something out of it; yet all it contained was a mechanism for closing the cover. This contraption is the opposite of Pandora's "box."

The original Pandora, the All-Giver, was an Earth goddess in prehistoric matriarchal Greece. She let all ills escape from her amphora *(pythos)*. But she closed the lid before Hope could escape. The history of modern man begins with the degradation of Pandora's myth and comes to an end in the self-sealing casket. It is the history of the Promethean endeavor to forge institutions in order to corral each of the rampant ills. It is the history of fading hope and rising expectations.

> To understand what this means we must rediscover the
> distinction between hope and expectation. Hope, in its strong
> sense, means trusting faith in the goodness of nature, while
> expectation, as I will use it here, means reliance on results
> which are planned and controlled . . . Hope centers desire on a
> person from whom we await a gift. Expectation looks forward
> to satisfaction from a predictable process which will produce
> what we have the right to claim. The Promethean ethos has
> now eclipsed hope.[1]

IN 1964, THE FRENCH Christian philosopher and social critic Jacques Ellul published *The Technological Society* (the original French title translates literally: *Technique: The Stake of the Century*).[2] The English edition's title is confusing, because Ellul wasn't talking about technology apart from it being one manifestation of *technique*, which also translates badly. What Ellul was describing was a *practice*, not a series of designs, even though the practices of *technique* gave rise to designs to achieve the goal of *technique*—efficiency.

This was not like, "She has a nice technique with that hook shot." *Technique* (italicized in Ellul) means the self-propelling, connected, and strictly fixed relations between the parts of a whole thing (like a machine or factory, including the workers), a collection of directives and mechanisms to support them, and the spread of this practice until it becomes universal, all in the interest of improved "production." The worker in the factory, for example, is *fitted to* the demands of the machine, in a system designed by an efficiency expert. The suburban commuter moves along pre-laid corridors of Illich's transport systems.[3] We move from the life-support system of a highly technological house to the life-support system of an ever more technologically sophisticated car to the technological life-support system at work, then back again.

Ellul said that *technique* has displaced our former relation to nature, where our practices were "the uncertain and incomplete intermediary between humanity and the natural milieu,"[4] and into a time and place where nature is completely dominated by *technique*.[5] In a sense, Ellul called

---

1. Illich, *Deschooling Society*, 105.

2. Ellul, *The Technological Society*.

3. How many times have you been trapped in a traffic jam to get to your job? And when will cars be equipped with something to discreetly relieve your bladder during a traffic jam?

4. Ellul is still trapped here by *the way we know* into that split between humanity and nature.

5. We will insist that the "domination of nature," while it is a powerful ideological construct that is also gendered male, serves to reinforce the culture-nature split and conceal the fact that technology becomes part of nature and nature part of technology.

modernity a kind of obsessive-compulsive disorder about "productivity," in which we are all imprisoned and yet convinced that by *technique* we have been liberated.

Technique is driven by the desire for increased velocity of both transit and exchange.

Sometimes, we have to begin with experience and work our way deeper. Who of us has not experienced the sense of separation, remoteness, and even hostility toward our work, our built environment, our culture? Psychologists and philosophers call this sense of separation *alienation*.[6] Ellul said that the ever more complete mechanization of society led us into a general sense of alienation; and this is our entry point into *technology*, or if you prefer, machines.

This chapter is related to *technique* but will explore the actual hardware as opposed to the practice. The reason this hardware—or technology, or machines—is shoved into the middle of a book allegedly about "money as an ecological phenomenon" is that the technologies, or machines, are what *mediate*, or direct traffic if you will, between money, knowledge, and nature in our cultures. Even when we say that solar power or wind power is "free," for example, we are ignoring, as if the sunlight or wind magically transmutes into electricity, the massive and expensive *mediation* of solar panels[7] and wind turbines[8] that convert that energy into something we can use.

The last time human beings were exploiting nature's useful energy (negentropy) *without* tools was when they snatched fire from along the edge of burning grasslands. Not long afterward, they figured out how to make fire-bows, as well as axes, knives, hammers, probes, baskets, pots, fish traps, etc., and tools have ever since been the *mediators* that change humans by changing nature and change nature by changing humans—because we cannot be separated.

Technology is composed of three essential things: nature, knowledge, and exchange.[9] When we get our heads around that, we will see that, just

6. A feeling of isolation, boredom, indifference, and even hostility. One's own circumstances begin to feel *alien*.

7. Hill, "Solar Panels." After forty years of solar panel use, it was not until late 2016 that the world collective of solar panels quit being an energy sink.

8. Hall, Lambert, and Balogh, "EROI of Different Fuels," 141–52. Wind power has an EROI (Energy return on [energy] investment) of only around 17 (17 percent above energy invested over time), which is favorable compared to coal at 12 or nuclear at 14, and without the carbon output of coal or the dangers of nuclear. Nonetheless, as we will show, the actual materials for the wind turbines, like steel, carbon filament, copper, aluminum, epoxies, plastics, and concrete each represent exchanges that are potentially unequal. It may not be possible to wind power a nation like Germany or France without exporting environmental damage to the countries where these materials are extracted.

9. Hornborg, *Power of the Machine*, 10.

as cars hardly increase our overall miles per hour per calorie, technology is not as self-propelled, or *autonomous*, as Ellul and others suggest. And that *exchange* cannot achieve "technical velocity" without the mediation of general-purpose money.

Energy Slaves

> The advocates of an energy crisis believe in and continue to propagate a peculiar vision of man. According to this notion, man is born into perpetual dependence on slaves which he must painfully learn to master. If he does not employ prisoners, then he needs machines to do most of his work. According to this doctrine, the well-being of a society can be measured by the number of years its members have gone to school and by the number of energy slaves they have thereby learned to command. This belief is common to the conflicting economic ideologies now in vogue. It is threatened by the obvious inequity, harried-ness, and impotence that appear everywhere once the voracious hordes of energy slaves outnumber people by a certain propor-tion. The energy crisis focuses concern on the scarcity of fodder for these slaves. I prefer to ask whether free men need them.[10]

So here we are, back with energy . . . again. Unavoidable. Forgiving Illich his archaic reference to humanity as *man*, this way of thinking about oil, coal, and gas, as *slaves*, puts our theme into perspective. People managed to get animals to do work for them many thousands of years ago, and as they became more settled and some learned to profit by violence, they founded whole societies on the institution of slavery. The point, apart from the sin-ful satisfaction of counting oneself superior somehow, has generally been to get more work done with less of our own effort, something any child understands perfectly well, which meant objectifying some people as draft animals.[11] At the beginning of the scientific era, people even spoke explicitly about making Nature (who was seen as female, of course) our slave.[12]

---

10. Illich, *Energy and Equity*, 3–4.

11. Hughes, "Environmental Impacts of the Roman Economy," 31. Slaves in the Roman Empire were called *instrumentum vocale*, "talking tools."

12. Merchant, "Women and Nature," 2. "The experimental method evolved from a vision of extracting Nature's secrets to the process of devising experiments on liv-ing nature depicted in the female gender. Francis Bacon urged his contemporaries to hound Nature in her wanderings, to extract her secrets, to vex her, and to transform and fundamentally alter her. Bacon's vision, which he meant as a method for improving the lot of humankind, eventually led to seventeenth-century experiments on animals. Scientists experimented with transfusions, such as exchanging the blood of dogs with

Many thought they had figured this out with fire-powered machinery, and they ignored the destructive costs. Even in ancient Rome, the fuel demands of metallurgy, weapons production, concrete production, expanded grain production, and heating for a large city, led to massive deforestation. By 200 BCE, the resulting soil erosion had ruined the land for cultivation and sent so much silt downstream that the Port of Pasteum became a shrinking, poverty-stricken, inland shanty town.[13] Few people have been conditioned to think of ecology with regard to the eventual fall of Rome, but it was a decisive factor. Historians do not generally, however, write history from an ecological perspective, choosing instead to focus on kings and generals.

What fundamentally connects velocity-of-exchange to social inequality and environmental degradation is the velocity of exchange outrunning the velocity of non-economic natural processes. The depletion of an aquifer contributes to enforced scarcity and strengthens the claims of those with plenty of money on those who have little. Aquifers recharge at their own rate. Trees grow at their own pace. Oil and coal are created over millions of years.

Seventeenth-century Britain suffered what was called an "iron famine," which was accompanied by massive deforestation.[14] The production of cannon and ships exhausted not only Britain's iron mines, but its forests were used as fuel for the smelters, iron mongers, and blacksmiths.

> [T]he shortage of shipbuilding timber was first noticed during the wars against the French in the 1620s and the shortage became acute in the 1650s, particularly for specialized requirements such as masts. A first-rate, 120-gun ship needed a mainmast forty meters long and over a meter in diameter. Until the mid-seventeenth century the navy could rely on the oak forests of England, especially those of Sussex. In the late seventeenth century, the Admiralty belatedly introduced officially sponsored replanting schemes even though it would take a century before the trees could be used. In the meantime timber would be imported.[15]

each other and humans with sheep. They put birds and mice in bell jars and evacuated the air pressure to observe the results. These were graphic examples of Nature depicted as female and scientific experiments that considered animals as machines."

13. Ponting, *New Green History of the World*, 76–77.

14. Moore, "Silver, Ecology, and the Origins of the Modern World," 126. "Looking at England in the early seventeenth century . . . one ton of pig iron could be produced . . . from the 'natural increment' of 8–10 acres [of forest, for wood-fuel]."

15. Ponting, *New Green History of the World*, 276–77.

In the last chapter, we discussed land. How much land does it take to support an Indonesian versus an American? And we discovered that the American requires a great deal more land, but that the land was not always in the United States. In fact, of the total production of land as materials and energy used to support the American, a large fraction was outside the United States in places like Indonesia, which represents an *unequal exchange* of land by shifting the environmental costs, or *environmental load*. We'll use a term for this from here forward: *environmental load displacement*. When I drink my coffee, I have used money's abstraction-velocity (price) to consume land-based production outside my own nation, shipping it to me using fossil fuels, at a rate of exchange that is wildly unequal between Americans and the people in the coffee's nation of origin; and I displace the environmental costs (e.g., pesticide/herbicide pollution, etc.) to that same nation of origin.

Oil, gas, and coal began mainly as plants, which stored energy using photosynthesis, then were buried by geological processes. Through decomposition without oxygen, these materials were "cooked down" into a super-dense energy source. When we use oil, gas, or coal, we are using the land-based production of plants that occurred millions, even hundreds of millions of years ago.[16] We are using this land-based production up at a very fast rate, almost half in less than a hundred years. So we have not only displaced environmental loads in space (to other people), we have displaced the environmental load over time, by exploiting photosynthesis from the distant past, to build and sustain structures that will inevitably become obsolete when it is no longer economically feasible to extract and process this dwindling and ever more difficult to reach fuel.

Nowadays, almost all our machines are ultimately powered by fossil energy, with a fraction of electricity being produced by nuclear fission (which also uses a great deal of fossil energy to build the reactors and mine, mill, and refine the fuel).

This computer with which I type these words is a machine. It is a combination of nature (materials and energy), knowledge (technological

16. Inderscience, "How much oil have we used?" and International Business Times, "World Energy Day 2014." We have used approximately a trillion barrels of oil so far, mostly in the last hundred years. Best estimates are that we have around 1.3 trillion in remaining oil. The problem with simple arithmetic here is that the first trillion were the easiest to find and extract. So the cost in both money and energy to get the oil out of the ground and refine it were relatively low. Every new barrel will be more difficult and costly than the last in both money and energy, which is why we have begun widespread employment of an extraction technique called hydraulic fracturing to break up stone layers far below ground in order to suck up the oil that remains between the seams. All oil is not the same, and all extraction is not the same.

know-how), and (unequal) exchange (using general-purpose money). Thermodynamically, this computer consumes useful energy (negentropy) and leaves behind greater overall entropy. This computer I write on is a *structure*. It is a structure that dissipates energy. This is why Hornborg, using a term from Prigogene,[17] calls machines *dissipative structures*.[18] A human being is a *dissipative structure*. A machine is a *dissipative structure*. A city is a *dissipative structure*. *Order* in the form of negentropy goes in, and *disorder* in the form of greater overall entropy comes out. This is irreversible.

> Dissipative structures are systems that stay far from thermodynamic equilibrium by continually drawing on exergy (negative entropy) from the outside and exporting the entropy, or disorder, they produce in the process.[19]

This disorder in not "merely" thermodynamic, because thermodynamics are not mere. Every material phenomenon without exception obeys the Second Law. This disorder is manifested in the material environment. Computers have become irreplaceable in the current US and world economies. Computers are made from several essential and *imported* materials—cobalt from the Democratic Republic of Congo, iron from Brazil, palladium from Botswana, gold from Costa Rica, copper from Chile, selenium from the Philippines, zinc from Peru, silver and antimony from Mexico, chromium, manganese, and platinum from South Africa, and aluminum, arsenic, barium, cadmium, lead, and mercury from China. These are also the essential materials in every "technologically developed" nation's governance and management systems, in maintaining our energy and transportation grids, in education, and in high-technology weapons systems.

Jason Moore notes that the expansionary economic drive of capitalism, even in its earliest stages, has always been based on the exploitation of "cheap nature," and when that cheap nature has been used up at home, it has always driven capitalists and their governments to find more "cheap nature" abroad. There are two principle and related facets of American power that *assure* the reliable inflows of these materials: *financial domination* with *military power* as accelerator and backstop.[20] This power is employed not merely

17. US Department of Energy, "Ilya Prigogine, Chaos, and Dissipative Structures." Prigogine said that certain stable structures in nature (nodes), like life forms, are maintained "far from equilibrium," equilibrium being a state of rest or death, by a continual flow of matter and energy through them. These nodes take in "orderly matter and energy" and release dissipated matter and energy.

18. *Merriam-Webster Dictionary*: "'Dissipate' means 'to spread thin or scatter,' and in physics it means 'to lose (e.g., as heat) irrecoverably.'"

19. Hornborg, *Power of the Machine*, 42.

20. Moore, "The Capitalocene, Part II," para. 8. "Capitalists are victims of their

to ensure importation, but to acquire imports at *unequal exchange rates*. The inequality itself—apart from its actual history—is numerically demonstrated in two correlated statistical tables: annual per capita gross national income (GNI) and annual per capita energy consumption.

2014	Per capita GNI ($US)	Per capita energy consumption (kg/oe)
Botswana	7,240	1127.8
Brazil	11,530	1362.5
Chile	14,910	1806.7
China	7,400	1806.8
Congo	380	479.5
Costa Rica	10,120	1328.5
Mexico	9,870	1570.3
Peru	6,360	667.1
Philippines	3,500	577.8
South Africa	6,800	3645.1
United States	55,200	7164.5

Reference: World Bank[21]

As exchange detectives, then, who seek out nodes and flows, the technologies that more or less define our "stage of development"[22] are nodes that draw in flows of materials from far afield for their production, and for their operation and maintenance. These nodes "import" *order*, or useful energy (negentropy), for work (energy slaves) and "export" *disorder*. So our *technology* is the embodiment of (1) *unequal exchange* as a (2) *dissipative*

own success. To the extent that productivity advances in wide-ranging fashion, input costs rise, and one of two things must occur: boom turns to bust or new sources of supply are found. On a systemic level, however, new sources of supply are not easy to locate and put to work. Capitalist organizations are not well-equipped to map, code, survey, quantify and otherwise identify and facilitate *new* sources of Cheap Nature . . . If capital is not well-suited to do this, the modern state is. Thus at the heart of modern capitalism is not only state and geopolitical power but *geopower*."

21. http://data.worldbank.org/indicator/NY.GNP.PCAP.CD?locations=BW.

22. Further down, we will show how problematic this idea of development in stages actually is.

structure, which could not happen without the exchange velocity provided by (3) *general-purpose money*.

Your lithium batteries require cobalt. The Congolese cobalt mine employs a combination of fossil energy powered machines, cheap labor (child miners in this case), and deforestation to mine the cobalt. It results in sulfuric acid, arsenic and mercury in the surrounding air and water, cyanide as a waste product for milling, and the dumping of massive amounts of tailings onto adjacent land.[23] In the Democratic Republic of Congo there has actually been a series of civil wars for control of these valuable minerals. And one hour of minimum-wage American labor is $7.50 an *hour*, whereas the minimum-wage Congolese makes $1.83 a *day*.[24] This is unequal exchange expressed as an *appropriation* of time.

Out of Sight and Out of Mind

The *out of sight and out of mind* phenomenon works in an especially sly way with technology, or machines. We tend to think that technology itself has no moral content, and that any *moral* content is added only by how we use technology. I am thinking now of Harriette Arnow's classic novel *The Dollmaker*, in which Kentucky farm woman Gertie Nevels uses her pocket knife to open an emergency airway in her child's neck to prevent him dying of whooping cough. Later in the novel, after she and her family have been economically forced into city life and factory labor, and her husband Clovis is morally degraded by it, he uses the same knife to commit a murder. This is how we think of technology, because technology is dead, right? It doesn't do anything without our direction, therefore it can have no moral characteristics apart from how it is *used*. "The machine is represented as standing there, aloof and innocent, intrinsically devoid of significance."[25]

Industrial technology, however, is always a *node* for various flows of distant materials and energy, and therefore always has two faces: a clean, visible *order*, like your brand new computer inside its shiny, colorful box . . . and a dirty, even violent, and invisible *disorder* elsewhere, gained nearly always through unequal exchange, facilitated in every case by either direct plunder, general-purpose money, or both. We see the stone in the tramp's tricky soup as the basis of the soup. This is all rendered *out of sight and out of mind* by

---

23. Dumaresq, "Cobalt Mining Legacy."

24. *NationMaster*, "Minimum Wage: Countries Compared," http://www.nationmaster.com/country-info/stats/Labor/Salaries-and-benefits/Minimum-wage.

25. Hornborg, *Power of the Machine*, 115.

distance or by the fences around factories with no windows, yes, but also by language and by money itself, which reduces everything to a *price*.

This relation of the *apparent* to the *concealed* in technology is constructed by our language. Ellul, with all his insight, still used the term *autonomous* to describe technological structures.

Most economists actually deny that such a thing as unequal exchange exists, because classical economics sees everything only as the instance of a price negotiated by two "equal" parties.[26] Each thing is defined as a quantity of money for which it is exchangeable, and "the market" is an autonomous *mechanism* (instead of what it is, a carefully *regulated power structure* of exchange) that assumes everyone *consents* to every exchange because no one is holding a gun during the exchange. Their situations that lead them to the point of exchange are excluded from consideration by economics and liberal law, as if decisions are made in vacuums.[27] Things *appear* by themselves— based on this conceptual abracadabra, be it machine or market—leading us to conclude that they *exist* by themselves, that they are autonomous, when they are nothing of the kind.

Environmental factors are considered *externalities* to most economists, that is, all considerations *external* to price at the moment of exchange are dismissed outright.[28] The two main things that are always concealed by our loyalty to the apparent (within sight and therefore in mind) are environmental damage and relations between people characterized by the power of some over others.

Time and Space

"Development" and "progress." We think of these as part of the same phenomenon. Progress is like an arrow pointed at the heavens, up-up-up we go, toward some peak of perfection; and development is like the lateral spreading of a cornucopia of ever more technological goodies. Together

26. This argument is based on the claim that people make choices based on subjective, or "normative," values that cannot be reasonably compared. But for this claim to hold, one has to exclude the observable and quantifiable (read: "objective" or material) differences in invested time (labor) and space (land) that are the context of exchange. Classical economics can only "solve" this problem by arbitrarily declaring everything apart from the instant of exchange to be "external," or irrelevant, and by measuring only the quantity of money exchanged at that instant.

27. This exclusion, which is a form of *intentional ignorance*, is what I call the "libertarian fallacy."

28. Caplan, "Externalities," *The Concise Encyclopedia of Economics*, 2008.

they constitute a *way of knowing* that predominates the thinking of industrial-benefiting nations.[29] But there is another difference between these two
related ideas. Progress—an idea that really took root in the nineteenth century—is understood as a *process*. Development, on the other hand, is an idea
about structures. Development is a *product*, and it is understood to exist in
various *stages* at the same time. Sweden is considered a developed, higher-
stage, nation. Botswana is considered an undeveloped, or underdeveloped,
lower-stage nation.

When we talk about differences in development between Sweden and
Botswana, even though we speak of the difference across space—Sweden
and Botswana in 2017 are both co-located in time, but apart in *space*—we
talk about the "distance" (spatial) between them, developmentally, in terms
of *time*. Sweden is more modern, or advanced in metaphorical time. Botswana is *backward*. Sweden is in the twenty-first century, *modern*. Botswana is "stuck in the past." These may seem to be harmless figures of speech,
but they carry with them some malignant hidden assumptions.

First among those assumptions is that Sweden and Botswana are like
two separate runners on two separate lanes of a track, and one has simply
pulled out ahead of the other. But the palladium mined in Botswana that
is used for catalytic converters, ceramic capacitors, membrane reactors,
hydrogen storage, and jewelry in Sweden, is not used by Botswanans at all.
A handful of Botswanan intermediaries get rich, but the vast majority of Botswanans, especially the miners, remain desperately poor, and this is what
makes Botswanan palladium competitive with Russian palladium, for example, which is more abundant. So not only does Sweden get the benefit of
unequal exchange, using products made with Botswana's palladium; Sweden
gets palladium without the deforestation, soil destruction, or mining pollution, which it exports—using money—to Botswana. Sweden is not running
ahead of Botswana like a racer in her own lane. Sweden is in a *parasitic* relation to Botswana and the rest of the "underdeveloped" world, just as the rest
of the industrial-benefiting nations are parasitic on the lesser "developed."
Sweden is "in the twenty-first century" *because of* the "underdeveloped"
nations. If they were not locked into the exchange relations that require unequal exchange, neither Sweden nor any of the other "major" nations could
exist in their present forms.

Sweden is the thirty-first largest economy in the world (measured by
the movement of money). Its major imports are computers, petroleum,

---

29. It is harder today to refer to core nations as "industrialized" when the actual
industries are being sent abroad in search of cheap labor. But the formerly industrial
nations are still the principle beneficiaries of industrial production.

automobiles, medications, clothing, and food.[30] As exchange detectives, when we look at Sweden as an exchange node, we see these things flowing into Sweden (or Great Britain, or Australia, or Germany, or the United States), and we understand that if these flows were cut, an industrial-benefiting country would summarily fall into a deep social crisis. Imagine if we in the United States suddenly found all products made in China were priced up by 500 percent to pay American workers to make them? Walmart and every other big-box store would close.[31]

The incredible natural beauty of Sweden and that of other "first-world" nations has been compared to the wrecked and denuded landscapes of "third-world" nations, leading many people to conclude that higher levels of development will lead to greater environmental protection. This is a classic case of confusing *correlation* with *causation*. In fact, our beautiful forests and set-asides and national parks are a benefit of *environmental load displacement*, which means that the narrative here of cause-and-effect is actually a mystification.[32] Development does not protect the environment in first-world nations but destroys it in third-world nations. *Out of sight and out of mind.*

Even on smaller scales, we see *environmental load displacement* in support of technological "development." When big industrial concerns are built in the United Sates, they will typically locate near poorer communities who will bear the brunt of these industries' environmental damage. Given that poverty in the US is racialized, and that there is a racial caste system still in place even between whites and many nonwhites with similar incomes and net worth, racial minorities are the worst affected by industrial pollution.[33]

"Development" of every country in the world to the "stage" of Western Europe and the US would theoretically require four earths of arable land and an additional two and a half earth-atmosphere's to absorb the carbon emissions.[34] We base our popular judgements on the one supposed *stage* of technological development *following* the other, when in reality one exists parasitically and simultaneously *upon* the other.

Automobile

What an interesting word. Auto as in *autonomous* (self-propelled) and *mobile* as in motion, Autonomous motion. And yet we know from our prior

30. Organization of Economic Cooperation and Development, "Sweden" (2014).

31. Not an altogether bad thing.

32. The act of bewildering or perplexing.

33. Swift, "It's Not Just Flint."

34. McDonald, "How Many Earths Do We Need?"

study of the properties of energy that there is no such thing as matter in *autonomous* motion. The car appears to be moving by itself, and more so in the past when it was compared to a carriage pulled by a horse or an ox. In fact, before the term auto-mobile was popularized, these things were called "horseless carriages."

This term is a perfect example of what we've discussed about *out of sight and out of mind,* about how the "imaginary center" appearance of something has the magician's effect of concealing a menu of realities that brings that thing into existence and maintains it. It becomes a *way of knowing,* even though we know we have to fill the tank to make the car go, and even though we know the car is composed of many materials from many places, worked by many hands. It becomes a *way of knowing* that is a way of ignoring . . . or denying. This is why we can honestly say that classical economics is actually a systematic form of denial.[35]

There are plenty of studies that attempt to calculate the carbon footprint of the average automobile, which is a measure of what comes out on the entropy-end of automobile use. They can tell you what percentage of greenhouse gases come from automobiles generally. They can tell you how many hectares of mature pines are necessary to reabsorb the carbon from one kilometer of car travel. They can calculate the difference in total fuel kilocalories consumed by a gas powered, hybrid, or electric vehicle, whether using oil or coal. But as exchange detectives, we are looking at the car as a more extensive *node of exchange,* and in studying the car that way, we look not only at the exchange of negentropy (order) into entropy (disorder) during operation, we also analyze the construction and maintenance of the vehicle itself.

That car is made of steel, stainless steel, aluminum, copper, rubber, timber, cotton, leather, plastic, polyester, polycarbonate, polypropelyne, tungsten, and all those minerals and precious metals we listed earlier for computers, which have become components of automobiles. Labor consumes land for food, so the labor represents land production. Each of these materials is mined, or pumped, or harvested, or processed from what was otherwise extracted, which results in deforestation and erosion; and each of those materials consumed a quantum of energy—mostly fossil hydrocarbons, resulting in air pollution. Between each process (at each *exchange node*), there is transport of materials (and the transport vehicles are

35. Chakrabortty, "Mainstream Economics Is in Denial," para. 10. "Yet look around at most of the major economics degree courses and neoclassical economics— that theory that treats humans as walking calculators, all-knowing and always out for themselves, and markets as inevitably returning to stability—remains in charge. Why? In a word: denial."

exchange nodes). The finished products are transported to various assembly facilities (nodes), whereupon the components assembled are transported to the final automobile assembly plant (nodes), and finally the cars themselves are transported to retailers (nodes). Every bit of land/labor/time that went into the final product, as well as every bit of useful energy (negentropy), are now invisibly embodied in that automobile. Every hectare of land used to feed the workers becomes a node for inputs of fertilizers, pesticides, herbicides, water, seed, and petroleum for the machinery. The general transport systems that facilitate the flows between nodes—road, rail, ship, or air—are themselves nodes through which flow materials and energy (negentropy transformed into entropy). We haven't even begun to look at replacement parts, oil changes and other lubricants, refueling, specialty fluids, water and detergents for washing, waxes . . . the containers for the oil, the refinement and transportation of the lubricants, the pumps and sprayers for the water, the sewers to get rid of the dirty water, and so it goes. It is the interwovenness of the general self-organization around existing power structures that makes our job as exchange detectives—tracking flows and nodes of flow— impossible to finish. Nonetheless, we can give the lie to our day-to-day *way of knowing*, wherein we go to the car dealership, we see this shiny colorful machine, we exchange some money for it, and summarize the whole process with, "I got a good price on a car today." Exchange, using money, narrows down our larger reality into a tunnel vision focus on the instant of a money-exchange, to that thing called *price*.

Ramification

Obviously, there are complexities beyond simply flows and nodes. The reason we go back to capture inflows and outflows is so we can mentally map those realities that we have been trained by money-culture to refuse to notice. The reason maps are helpful, as graphic representations, is they can help us get to a place that we cannot readily see in an instant by showing the many relationships between material things and forces that are *mediated* by culture. We see from above with maps, so to speak, and we peer into the past for the restless ghosts that invisibly inhabit the present. Let's take this automobile, for which we have mapped a few flows, and follow it out.

Ramify (from the Latin *ramus*, meaning branch) means "branching out." When we speak of *ramifications*, we are describing those phenomena that "branch out" from a thing or an action—branching consequences. In this case, we want to study the ramifications of technology; and since we cannot possibly study every consequence, or ramification, we will focus on a few ramifications related to the last example we used: automobiles (or should we call them oil-mobiles, since we know they are *not* autonomous?).

Well, we have to talk about roads, don't we? Just for starters. Cars, even the high-clearance, four-wheel-drive behemoths, are not incredibly useful without roads. And roads undergo development alongside cars. The standard size of a road or even a parking space is determined by a window of standard sizes for cars and trucks. The US Interstate Highway system, built during the Eisenhower administration, was designed not to get you to Grandma's for Thanksgiving, but to speed up transport by tractor-trailer trucks. The bridge clearances are exactly high enough to accommodate those trailers. And we already talked about dead animals, emergency rooms, land seizures, destroyed habitat, and blocked foot traffic.

This one machine, the automobile, has caused us to quit walking, so we can infer some health issues. We travel on our behinds. We don't gaze around very much (and we ought not to text), because at the velocities we travel in cars, you have to focus on staying inside the lines to prevent crashing off the road, squashing pedestrians and critters, and colliding with oncoming traffic. We moved from cities to suburbs because of cars. Suburbs are specifically designed as a kind of high-end barracks for people who work in the city, but who commute there by car.[36] Markets have turned into car malls and car strip-malls with parking lots that take up more acreage than the building themselves. Service stations and travel plazas and motels (a neologism for *motor*-hotels) are ramifications of a society built around cars.

There are political ramifications. In North Carolina, when I lived there years ago, there was a State Board of Transportation with nineteen members. One was appointed by the General Assembly's Senate President Pro Tem, another by the Speaker of the House, and the rest by the Governor. A study of campaign contribution records showed a very strong correlation between appointments to the Board of Transportation and contributions to the Governor's election campaign. Roads were big bucks in North Carolina. The contractors who built the roads—some of whom were on the Board—got deals, a billion-dollars-worth. The land speculators who wanted to "develop" the areas around future interchanges got deals. The people who wanted to build service stations, travel plazas, strip malls, and subdivisions got deals. These were *political ramifications* of cars . . . and money.[37]

36. Semuels, "White Flight Never Ended." In the United States, the construction of suburbs was a direct result, encoded in policy, of white people fleeing the newly integrated spaces of the cities. The phenomenon was called "white flight." It was the replacement of *de jure* segregation by *de facto* segregation.

37. Hall, "How much for a seat on the Board of Transportation?" When a society depends absolutely on money, politics becomes absolutely about money, about *exchanges* of money.

In 1999, Hurricane Floyd hit North Carolina, then hovered over us,[38] dropping torrential rains on the eastern part of the state. We hit every 500-year flood marker, and whole towns were destroyed. Fifty-seven people were killed. Damages were around $7 billion. And we called this a "natural disaster." Which was only partly true. The hurricane itself was accelerated by climate change, but even more immediately, Eastern North Carolina had undergone a period of rapid "development," which meant hundreds of thousands of acres that had formerly been forest, grassland, or farmland—permeable surfaces—had been turned into roads and parking lots—impermeable surfaces, to support low-wage industrial corridors and outlet malls. So untold millions of tons of water that would have been slowed down in their return to watercourses were accelerated by asphalt and concrete.[39] This, too, was a "natural" ramification of cars.

Technology is not separable from nature, and it is never "innocent." Behind every piece of technology are relations between human beings and the alteration of nature which includes human beings, and this means the *existence* of the technology always confronts us with moral questions. What are the full, and not just monetary, costs to people, places, and things of this technology? Of making it? Of using it? Of maintaining it?

With any technology, if we study it, we will discover ramifications. Why is this important? Because our *way of knowing* in this era leads us to divide things into parts and study the parts, pulling things away from their contexts and pretending those contexts are irrelevant. This habit serves power, because it serves the status quo, which *is* the context.[40] It serves the status quo,

38. We were living in Raleigh then.

39. Hunt & Stevens, "Permanent Pavement Use and Research." "Traditional building has led to massive areas of impervious surfaces, such as roofs and parking lots. These impervious areas tend to be interconnected and result in increased downstream flooding and erosion. Simultaneously, the American appetite for mobility has enabled a pavement revolution. More roadways and parking lots have been constructed to accommodate vehicles. Traditionally, parking and driving surfaces are impervious by necessity. Large parking lots are constructed to allow for peak volume days. These lots contribute to downstream flooding and erosion because nearly all stormwater runs off. Many of these areas service traffic infrequently. One challenge facing engineers is to convert areas of low use from impervious to pervious surfaces to help reduce the amount of runoff. Some of these surfaces include driveways, fire lanes, overflow parking, walkways, drain pipes, and even small parking lots that receive daily traffic."

40. MacIntyre, *God, Philosophy, Universities*, 173–74. Even universities train the minds of students for de-contextualization. "[T]he curriculum has become increasingly composed of an assorted ragtag of disciplines and subdisciplines, each pursued and

because it conceals inconvenient consequences, as we can see from this very superficial look at the ramifications of cars. We depend on cars, not by choice but necessity now in the US, because our built environment is structured around this machine. For everyone who has a powerful vested interest in the status quo and its stability, it is better that people don't ask questions . . . about accident rates, health problems, air-land-water pollution, habitat destruction and species extinction, restriction of transit, noise, climate change, quality of life, or energy dependency. Context is always dangerous to power.

We are detectives on the trail of money, its true nature, about which we have already voiced suspicion. We have said that money is a "cultural construction," a sign, but that it has profound *environmental* consequences. We have seen now that without money, industrialism would not have been possible—the velocity of exchange and the reduction of everything to price are what make industrial society possible.[41] We cannot see money apart from its context, and we cannot understand context until we tear down the mental wall between nature and culture to understand money.

> It was only with the sunset and eventual disappearance of the sense of contingency, when the world fell from the hands of God into the hands of man, and all constraints on technological development began to fall away, that the tool could be unreservedly glorified, and the way opened for a fully technological society.[42]

taught in relative independence of one another . . . What disappears from view in such universities [is] . . . any large sense of and concern for enquiry into the relationships between the disciplines and . . . any conception of the disciplines contributing to a single shared enterprise."

41. Industrial society emerged as capitalist society, because the purpose of industrialization was, and remains, to mass produce commodities—things for sale—which was motivated by the desire to turn *some* money into *more* money, the basis of the capital accumulation process. State socialist societies that unsuccessfully imitated this process to pursue "development" were inevitably drawn into the capitalist world system because they imitated this process, which relies on general-purpose money, and were therefore drawn into the ecological and economic dynamics that inhere in money. Absent the profit motive, which was part of this system, these states could not compete over the long run, and collapsed.

42. Illich, *Rivers North of the Future*, 76.

7

Money

You are also to count off seven sabbaths of years for yourself, seven times seven years, so that you have the time of the seven sabbaths of years, namely, forty-nine years. You shall then sound a ram's horn abroad on the tenth day of the seventh month; on the Day of Atonement you shall sound a horn all through your land. You shall thus consecrate the fiftieth year and proclaim a release through the land to all its inhabitants. It shall be a jubilee for you, and each of you shall return to his own property, and each of you shall return to his family. You shall have the fiftieth year as a jubilee; you shall not sow, nor reap its aftergrowth, nor gather in from its untrimmed vines. For it is a jubilee; it shall be holy to you. You shall eat its crops out of the field. On this year of jubilee each of you shall return to his own property.

—LEVITICUS 25:8–13

WE ALL KNOW THAT money can be used as a weapon. This is not new. Even when Leviticus was written, probably around 700 BCE, people were using debt as a weapon to take land from others. We are going to show that this is just one problem with money. Modern, or general-purpose money has characteristics that destroy things even absent the element of intent. It is *inherently* dangerous, because it is an ecologically potent phenomenon; and that is why it is crucial that we understand it. Like explosives or powerful acids or sharp instruments, it may be useful, but our careless use of it can have terrible consequences.

Jesus and the Coin

I'm going to take liberty as the writer here, and begin this chapter with some biblical interpretation that might seem like a digression. Further along, I hope to explain why. But I do it now in the hope that, like a seed, it will sprout later in the soil we are preparing.

Many Christians will tell you that it is our Christian duty to pay our taxes. This claim comes from proof-texting Mark 12:13–17.[1] Jesus is quoted in English as saying, in response to a question about paying taxes to the Emperor, "Give to the Emperor the things that are the Emperor's," or "Render unto Caesar what is Caesar's." Just as we are emphasizing *context* to understand money, we need *context* to determine the true meaning of this passage.

To begin with, there are controversies about the Gospel of Mark related to when it was written, by whom, where it was written, and for whom. In this account, we will rely on Howard Clark Kee's extensive study of Mark, *Community of the New Age: Studies in Mark's Gospel*. Kee places the Gospel in or about 68 CE and believes, based on the "symbolic universe" of the Gospel's language, that Mark was written in northern Palestine for a predominantly Galilean audience, around two years before the actual destruction of the Second Temple by the Roman military.[2] There was a war between the Romans and Judean rebels that had broken out in response to longstanding tensions related to not only the Roman occupation of Palestine, but the depredations of Roman colonial surrogates among the Jewish elite *against the Jewish peasantry.*

This conflict, of course, is the very setting for all the Gospels, because Jesus of Nazareth lived in the midst of this tense military occupation and corresponding Roman counter-insurgency campaigns against Jewish partisan fighters. The cross, in fact, was the Roman punishment for political crimes, and it was used most liberally against those partisans or people suspected of supporting them.[3]

Economically, taxation from the Romans was combined with taxation from the temple, King Herod, the priests, and the Levites to appropriate the majority of money earned by the general population, who were peasants,

1. Proof-texting is pulling quotes out of context from Scripture and fallaciously presenting these detached phrases as evidence in support of an argument.

2. The temple was destroyed by fire, whereas the prediction of its destruction in Mark 13, "Mark's little apocalypse," has it destroyed by being pulled down "stone by stone." The assumption, then, is that Mark predates the temple destruction (in 70 CE).

3. Muzeum, "How the Romans Used Crucifixion," para. 1.

both landed and landless.[4] Landlessness was created principally by *debt foreclosure*[5], whereupon many landless peasants were driven by need into villages near wage work. Nazareth was such a village, and Joseph as well as Jesus and his brothers were *tektones*, construction workers, who probably worked four miles outside of Nazareth on the massive Herodian project to re-build the city of Sepphoris.[6] The standard daily wage was one *denarius*. This was Roman coin, and it was disliked by Jews because it was stamped with the image of the emperor, anathema given the Jewish prohibition against graven images.

Jesus entered Jerusalem during the reign of Tiberius. The coin had Tiberius's image and the inscription "Tiberius: Caesar and Divine Son." In other words, "Tiberius, Son of God." The Jewish "no other gods before me" rule in the Ten Commandments did not square with Tiberius's claim. It was for this reason, as we see during the cleansing of the temple, that there are *money-changers* in front of the Jewish temple, who would change the *denarius* for Jewish *shekels* to pay the temple tax, to prevent these "portable idols" that were Roman currency from soiling that holy ground.

In the narrative structure of Mark 11 and 12, we see Jesus challenged by those who were conspiring against him in a five-step story-convention. (1) Jesus is approached. (2) Jesus is challenged with a trick question. (3) Jesus answers a question with a question. (4) His opponents reply. (5) Jesus gives an unexpected answer to the first question that exposes his opponent's hypocrisy.

In Mark 11:27–33, (1) the Sanhedrin, or temple officials, approach Jesus. (2) "What kind of authority do you have here?" they ask, then follow up, "And where does that authority come from?" This is a demand for credentials. Jesus says, (3) "Answer one question, and I'll answer yours. Were John the Baptist's actions from heaven or humans?" He's putting them on the spot before a crowd that put a great deal of stock in John the Baptist, so they are afraid to answer Jesus's trick question. (4) "We don't know," they replied with a wary eye on the crowd. (5) "Well then," Jesus told them. "if you won't answer, neither will I." Bam!

Same structure in Mark 12:13–18. Pharisees and Herodians—an odd couple indeed who generally disliked one another, but both threatened by this renegade rabbi, they unite and (1) approach Jesus. After a bit of ironic flattery, they put the question: (2) "Should we pay taxes to Caesar?" Again, a crowd of people stands near, and they really *hate* Roman taxes. But the

---

4. Myers, *Binding the Strong Man*, 52.

5. See Levitical code at the beginning of the chapter.

6. Myers, *Binding the Strong Man*, 57.

officials are also nearby, and to speak against taxation would be a crime against the state. He's damned if he does, and damned if he doesn't. In the Greek, they use the term *agreúsōsin* to describe this interrogation, which means to hunt with traps. This term tells Mark's audience that Jesus is being hunted here. This is not some rhetorical question to set up Jesus as a lawmaker who tells you to be a good citizen and pay your taxes. This is an attempt to get Jesus killed. "Hand me that coin," Jesus replies, and when they do, he asks, (3) "Whose image is on that coin?" It is a *denarius*, and we know whose image is on it, as well as the inscription: "Tiberius: Son of God." In Mark's Greek, "inscription" is written as *epigraphe*. There is only one other place in Mark where this term is used: to describe the mocking conviction writ the Romans posted on Jesus's cross, "Jesus, King of the Jews." So Mark's Jewish audience hears this Gospel read, and they know the significance. (3) The Pharisees and Herodians reply to Jesus's question about whose image: "Caesar's." Jesus's reply (5) does not say "render," but *apodote*, or *re-pay*. "Re-pay to Caesar what is Caesar's, and to God what is God's." Repayment goes to the one to whom you owe your debt. For Jews, this is a stark choice presented between loyalty to Caesar and loyalty God. Bam again!

> [N]o Jew could have allowed for a valid analogy between the debt owed to Yahweh and any other human claim.
>
> There are simply no grounds for assuming that Jesus was exhorting his opponents to pay the tax. He is inviting them to act according to their allegiances, stated clearly as opposites. Again, Jesus has turned the challenge back upon his antagonists: What position do they take on this issue? This is what provokes the strong reaction of incredulity (*exethaumazon*, only here in the New Testament) from his opponents—something no neat doctrine of "obedient citizenship" could possibly have done.[7]

Money History

Your money belongs to Caesar, too. Look at it. It has a dead state official's face on it. And it is not actually *your* money. Let's see why.

Many people believe that Karl Marx first formulated the distinction between use-value (the useful quality of a thing) and exchange-value (monetary price). In fact, our first record of this distinction is from Aristotle.[8]

---

7. Ibid., 312.
8. Meikle, "Aristotle on Money."

Money didn't suddenly appear; it evolved. As far as we can tell, people used otherwise useful things as media of exchange, like shells, or cows, or measures of grain, in prehistory. These things were used like money, but at some point they became a "use-value" (the shells made a necklace, the cow made beef, the grain made bread) and they were consumed. Later on, things like rare shells, a luxury item, were used as something more resembling modern currency—or a universal exchange equivalent, though culture often restricted the *universality* of exchange by custom or law. With mining, precious metals, like silver and gold, which were still used as luxury items (jewelry, for example), were also used as currency because they were both coveted and portable. By around 1100 BCE, people living in what is now China were exchanging pieces of bronze shaped like the goods representing certain categories of exchange. By 600 BCE, we have the first historical evidence of actual coinage: King Alyattes of Lydia (modern Turkey) set up a mint—a stamping mechanism to flatten out weights of gold, embossing a design on the face.[9] It was only two and a half centuries between then and Aristotle's writing, by which time this system of currency had enveloped the Mediterranean and given rise to Aristotle's distinction, from his own observations of monetized trade, between *use-value* and *exchange-value*. Six hundred years later, we see Jesus and his enemies in this episode with a stamped coin.

Money has undergone a series of abstractions. Abstraction—*again*, for emphasis—is the process of pulling back from a specific instance of something into a category that encompasses varying specifics into sameness again. I am Stan. I am male. I am human. I am mammal. I am animal. I am life form.

Money began as something called specie, which is not a category of life in this case, but a category that differentiates material that can be used as-money-*or*-as-itself from money that is strictly an exchange equivalent. Shells or gold are specie-money. They can be used to make other things. From there, we see specie-backed money—usually paper. A piece of paper is *redeemable for* a specific amount of silver or gold, for example. The first paper money—or banknote—was issued around 618 CE by the Tang Dynasty in what is now China.[10] By the mid-seventeenth century, banknotes were

9. Burn-Callander, "The History of Money." This does not mean there was no currency before that. As we saw, when Leviticus was written around a hundred years earlier, there was some unspecified kind of money through which debt could be accrued.

10. *Time*, "Top 10 Things You Didn't Know About Money."

in common use among traders in Europe and between Europe and its new colonies. By the mid-nineteenth century, in the United States, banknotes were first issued as "legal tender," meaning this was the only acceptable currency with which to pay taxes, and that all state-sanctioned merchants were required to accept it in payment. These banknotes were backed by gold, meaning you could theoretically cash in the banknotes at the Treasury Department for gold. The gold-backing was dropped in a few cases during emergencies, like war, whereupon the currency became what we now call *fiat* currency, currency accepted on trust without the ability to redeem paper for precious metal. Gold backing was reestablished as soon as possible, because without the specie-backing, or redeem-ability in gold, these currencies could more easily plummet in value and become worthless if people became distrustful and lost confidence in them. (Money has a psychological character, too.) There was no *referent* (precious metal) for the *sign* (money) that could hold up the stop sign and say (pun intended), "The buck stops here." We will return to *signs* and *referents* momentarily.

With paper also came the danger of counterfeiting, so states established elaborately designed presses to make banknotes that were difficult to copy.

In the 1940s, through a long historical process between the Great Depression of the 1930s and World War II, a global currency *regime*[11] was established,[12] in which a review board established and periodically reviewed the gold value of the US dollar, whereupon other agreement-signatories' currencies were "pegged" to the dollar, or assigned a fixed exchange rate. X amount of currency A was exchangeable with Y number of US dollars. The dollar itself was fixed in value at one-thirty-fifth of a Troy ounce of 24-karat gold; and during the periodic reviews, an analysis was applied to ensure roughly equal buying power between the dollar and other currencies. In the 1970s, during an economic war *with its own allies*,[13] the United States unilaterally (and in violation of international agreements, i.e., the Bretton Woods Agreements)[14] abandoned both the gold standard and the

11. "Regime" here does not mean the same thing as a political *regime*, but a system based on centralized planning.

12. Ghizoni, "Creation of the Bretton Woods System." This financial regime was called the "Bretton Woods system" after the conference at Bretton Woods, New Hampshire, where the international conference was held in 1945 establishing these agreements.

13. Covered in detail in chapter 9.

14. This regime included the United States, all of Western Europe, the United Kingdom, Canada, Japan, and Australia.

fixed currency exchange rates; and US dollars have been fiat currency ever since.[15] Given the dominance of US currency worldwide, and the fact that international debts are settled with dollars, the fiat dollar has today become for all practical purposes the world's most general-purpose money. And we have arrived at the point now where money is electronically exchanged without even a piece of paper.

At each step along the way, the further generalization, or *abstraction*, of money has corresponded to the transformation of ever more persons, places, and things into *commodities*, or things for sale. This process of *commodification*,[16] in turn, has corresponded to similar abstractions of the things for sale. The person who hires out to sell her/himself as labor becomes a legal *individual*, without any defining characteristics. A specific parcel of land becomes *real estate*. A worker, a lamp, a book, a room, and a pet boa constrictor are all homogenized *by* and reduced *to* dollar values. General-purpose money abstracts many *unlike* items into a single category that makes them all the same: they have a *price*. Anything specific that was held sacred (land) is now no longer sacred (real estate). A forest becomes a collection of dissolved resources, freely exchangeable for . . . Coca-Cola.

Signs, Signs, Everywhere Signs

Money is a *sign*. Let's grab a couple of new concepts, then see why we say that.

Jakob von Uexküll was a German biologist in the late nineteenth and early twentieth centuries. He was vitally interested in how humans and other organisms *experience* their environments. You are reading this right now, so you are *experiencing* a stream of thinking that is translating idea-symbols (words) made of other sound-symbols (letters) that represent your language (symbolic representations), which can be written (textually expressed in phonetic codes) or spoken (vocally expressed by phonetic codes). You are perhaps hungry or sated, thirsty or quenched, warm or cold, in pain with a malady or comfortable in your favorite chair. In time, you will need to go to the bathroom and relieve yourself or to the kitchen to make some food. You will scratch an itch from time to time. You may be fantasizing about sex or a beach vacation or throttling your unpleasant boss. You may be annoyed with distractions, a rowdy child, or a noisy heating pipe. As you tire, you may feel

15. Lowenstein, "The Nixon Shock."

16. Prather, *Christ, Power, and Mammon*, 1. Prather cites theologian Karl Barth, who saw that "*commodifying* spirit" as one of Mammon's demonic perversions of God's world-ordering powers.

yourself yawn. This unified *emergence* of experience is what Uexküll called "self-in-world," or in German, *Umwelt* (pronounced OOM-velt).

Later on, during the twentieth century, a Hungarian linguist named Thomas Sebeok, teaching at Indiana University, took Uexküll's idea of the *Umwelt* and merged it with his own lifelong interest in something called *semiotics*, or the study of signs and symbols as well as the way they are interpreted. What Sebeok claimed was that all living things respond to signs. Language is just one form of sign-system, but bees communicate direction and distance to each other, plants take cues from soil temperature, etc., and for each organism each sign has a *meaning*. These signs and meanings connect everything with everything else. When two or more organisms are operating together through signs, like the flower's color and the smell of its pollen attracting the butterfly, you have a *semiosphere*, a semiotic world, or a world of signs, which joins one *world-in-self*, or Umwelt with the *world-in-self* of others, *like* others and *unlike* others.

So we are not only constituted by those material flows we spoke of earlier, as individuals with things going into the body and things going out of the body; we are likewise constituted—and *connected*—by flows of signs within *semiospheres*—sign-worlds full of meaning. Signs are received and interpreted, and then we signal outward again. A dog will wag its tail to invite you and raise its hackles to warn you. Sign. Interpretation. Response.

A sign has *meaning* because it *refers* to something. I say "book" (verbal sign) and I point at the book (somatic sign), and you know that it is *this book* to which I *refer*. We are brought together by signs through their *referents*, the things to which they *refer*. In the same way that we are shared through our physical environment, exchanging various materials, we are shared through our cultural environment by signs linking us to each other by referents. Simple signs like an odor or a color or a motion, then more complex signs like pointing at the book, and more complex signs still, like the word *book* which symbolizes the thing itself, or the highly complex *contents* of the book's story, or by a piece of music, a dance, a game, a law, a bureaucratic maze of procedures, etc. As a Christian, I am connected to other Christians through a *story*, and that story, as multiple and nested meanings, itself ramifies—or branches out—through other aspects of my life and the life of other Christians, because we try to "live into" that story.[17]

One of the main theorists of *semiotics*, or the study of signs, Charles Pierce, broke this down into a simple schematic. There is the *signifier* (I), the *sign* (point), the *referent* (to the book), and the *interpretant* (*you* infer what *I* mean). Right now, I am the *signifier*, the collection of textualized worlds

17. Human beings are uniquely *storied* creatures.

constitute the *signs*, the subject of money as an ecological phenomenon is the conceptual *referent*, and you—the reader—are the *interpretant*.[18] We share a semiosphere in the way we share a biosphere, or ecology, through a complex web of *meaningful* relationships.

Here is a forewarning as we continue our mission of detection. Remember the problem with two-ness or dualism? That mental China-Wall between the *subject* and *object* only scalable with mathematics, and how that same wall has been placed between *nature* and *culture*? We tend to believe, based on our mental habits from a dualistic culture, that the semiosphere—symbols, language, and other *cultural* constructions—are separated from *natural* phenomena—that aspect of being which responds with perfect theoretical predictably to natural laws. But what we are saying here is that the semiosphere and the biosphere share a reality and are thoroughly penetrated one by the other. With this held in our minds, let's move along.

The Catholicity of Money

Human economic exchanges are always somehow *regulated*, by custom, law, or both. Exchange has rules. The *regulation* of human social affairs, including exchange, is what we call *politics*. So where in a university we might find one department called Economics and another called Political Science, we are going to tear down a wall and acknowledge this overlap between regulation of social life and the regulation of economy (exchange) with the term "political economy." In the real world, you never have one without the other. So this is an arena where the (material) goods involved in *exchange* are both made and moved through a (cultural) matrix of signs (language, custom, covenant, habit, law). We might add to that, given that we are breaking down the imaginary wall between nature and culture, "political *ecology*."

Our modern *way of knowing* also leads us to draw a line between "religion,"[19] politics, and economy. These distinctions, however, are fairly

18. Every complex communication between people has in the background a view of reality. Every interpreter receiving the communication likewise has a background view of reality. In a pluralistic society, that background view may be different. When the background view of reality is different between signifier and interpretant there is a high probability of misinterpretation. This is why we are spending a great deal of time early in the book to establish the coordinates of a more or less common background view of reality.

19. I put *religion* in scare quotes because I question its *validity* as a category. It is an abstraction that ignores the vast differences between cultures and traditions, and it erases the specific content of particular spiritual or faith practices. When you classify a Christian church as a "religion," you are pulling it into a category where it has no meanings of its own (and "religion" as a category has *never* been well-defined). It is a category that attempts to dominate, or capture, the specificity of each practice or tradition or school of thought with a distinctly modern and encompassing anthropological

recent distinctions. Former *ways of knowing* saw these as aspects of the same thing. The sacred, the regulatory, and the forms of exchange were all fitted together in concept and practice. These aspects of social organization were united in a *symbolic order*, that is, by a complex system of signs that supported a shared way of understanding the world. These involved codes for relations between members of the group and codes for relations with outsiders. Notions of purity and pollution were mixed with and reflective of ideas about gifts, sacrifices, and worship. Exchange was regulated by concepts that "fit in" with these other ideas and practices.

Anthropologist Paul Bohannan studied the Tiv people of Nigeria between 1949 and 1953, and he found that they did not recognize money as we describe it, as one thing exchangeable for everything. The Tiv refused to use currencies in a way where the *sign* had no *referent*.

A sign is, in a sense, *stopped* by its referent, the way gold used to say, "Stop here," to a banknote. I say "book" as I point at that book, and the sign finds its resting place there. The sign cannot move over, under, around, and through the book, the lamp, the carpet, and the coffee cup.

For the Tiv, there were three separate "spheres" of exchange: subsistence, luxury goods, and marriageable women (however repugnant that may be). Brass rods or cattle were currencies for luxury goods. Grain for subsistence goods. Women for women. Brass rods could not be exchanged for women or subsistence goods, for example, and grain could not be exchanged for white cloth and other luxury items.[20] Apart from our disapproval of trading women, the point is that these separate spheres created referents for each currency—boundaries beyond which they were not allowed—that prevented one person obtaining enough brass rods to buy up other people's farm tools or food.

> [T]he . . . spheres of exchange among the Tiv would have entailed transactions and relations that could be viewed as metaphorical. It could, for instance, be argued that, for the Tiv, chickens were to cattle what utensils were to cloth; chickens and utensils belonged to the sphere of subsistence items, cattle and cloth to that of prestige items. Within the prestige sphere of the Tiv, brass rods functioned as a special purpose currency . . . The undifferentiated nature of modern money, by reducing

---

term. It is very difficult, for example, to cleanly differentiate, through strict definition, the category "religion" from "patriotism," even though we separate these concepts in day-to-day discourse.

20. Bohannan, "The Impact of Money on an African Subsistence Economy."

itself to tautology,[21] appears to preclude any such metaphorical messages.[22]

As a Christian, I subscribe to certain big ideas and generalities: creation, grace, sin, redemption. These, however, are embedded in a specific community and tradition, and they have *particular* meanings. Taken apart from that community and tradition, and taken apart from the rest of the conceptual architecture of that community and tradition, these ideas lose their peculiar Christian qualities. Within a tradition they are, in a sense, *located*. When Christians speak of small-c catholicity, they are not referring to the Church of Rome, but to a certain *universality*. Redemption, through Christ, is *available* to all, *universally* available, and therefore aimed at ever greater *inclusion* without greater abstraction.

Modern general-purpose money[23] is also very catholic. It aims toward ever greater generalization. But unlike a church, general-purpose money is not *embedded* in either community or a narrative tradition, with God as revealed through Jesus the Christ for its ultimate yet *specific* referent. Money is *without* a location or narrative, because it has no referent apart from itself. It is without differentiation, except in quantity—one dollar, two dollars, twenty dollars, a million dollars, all just dollars[24]—like music played with only one note. It is universal because it can go anywhere the way muriatic acid eats its way through grout, dissolving everything as it goes, breaking down what was stone-like into something that is sand-like, because there are no referents to say, "Stop here!"

Ancient Israelites had a law of jubilee, described at the beginning of this chapter, wherein every seven years, debts were forgiven; and every seven times seven (49) plus one (50), there was a Jubilee, and not only were debts forgiven, but all land lost through debt was returned to its original families. There was economic activity, but it was bound within and restricted by those other aspects of social organization that we moderns would not classify as

21. *Tautology* means circular reasoning or saying the same thing using different words. A tautology has no referent at which point it "stops." Modern, general-purpose money is a sign with no referent? Money equals price equals money. This is tautological, or *self-referential*.

22. Hornborg, *Power of the Machine*, 169–70.

23. Given what we learned about the Tiv, and what we will learn about other forms of money later on, we need to differentiate modern money as "general-purpose" from here forward.

24. We use dollars here, fully recognizing there are other currencies. This simplification is for clarity now, and in a later chapter, we will cover how currencies relate to each other.

economic.[25] Having recognized the ways in which monetary debt resulted in accumulation for some and ruination for others, they imposed a periodic stop-and-reset through Jubilee cycles. It was recognized that money needed to be *contained* by justice, not set loose in the market. Money was customarily *embedded*. Economic historian Karl Polanyi referred to "embeddedness" when he described how many economic practices are restricted by non-economic ones, like the Tiv relating one currency to subsistence and another to prestige goods.[26]

When we look at exchange historically, abstracting from specific cultures, we can still identify cross-cultural forms of exchange.[27] Subsistence, or "householding," is one form where production and consumption are in the same place, like peasants or old-time family farms. People can give gifts as they did in Potlatch cultures. People can barter, exchanging things for other things without money, as use-values.[28] People can consolidate their goods under a central authority that redistributes them, called redistributive economy.[29] We can engage in reciprocal exchange (not barter) using an exchange equivalent, money, that is restricted as the Tiv did. These forms of economy can be mixed together. The point is, what we now take for granted as an economy, where price is allegedly adjusted by "supply and demand," was not always so, and therefore is not inevitably so in the future.

Charles Peirce (1839–1914), the semiotician, developed a classification system for signs—any signal that refers to something and is received by an interpreter. Human signs, he said, signify three kinds of phenomena: *facts*, *qualities*, and *conventions*. I point to a can of paint and I say, "I want that paint." The term "paint" signifies the actual existing thing called paint, a *fact*. When I browse through the swatch booklet for various paint colors, and I find the one I want in a paint, I point to the swatch, and say, "I want this one." In this case, the sign—the swatch—is not paint, but a way to specify a *quality* of the paint, its color. When Harriet Tubman wrote, "Mrs. Stowe's pen hasn't begun to *paint* what slavery is," she wasn't referring to paint or the quality of paint, but to a more complex social issue, using certain speech

25. Myers, "God Speed the Year of Jubilee."

26. Polanyi, *The Great Transformation*.

27. Ibid., 41.

28. My sister cleaned a dentist's house in exchange for having her teeth cleaned.

29. In truth, in most redistributive economies, the authority responsible for redistribution made sure it received more than everyone else. Sin is universal.

conventions, like irony and metaphor. Or in another case, we read an oral thermometer at 101 degrees Fahrenheit, and that sign—*by convention*—tells us someone has a fever, a *fact*. These categories—fact, quality, convention— are what Peirce called sign "elements."

These *elements* then appoint *classifications* to signs. These classifications he called *index*, *icon*, and *symbol*. *Index* signs refer to natural things. *Icon* refers to representative things. *Symbol* relies on a socially shared understanding. An actual face is *indexical*. A portrait photo is *iconic*. A yellow happy-face emoticon is *symbolic*. And we can see that these categories, from index through icon to symbol become ever more abstract. Peirce called this "firstness," "secondness" and "thirdness."

> The first is that whose being is simply in itself, not referring to anything or lying beyond anything. The second is that which is what it is owing to something to which it is second. The third is that which is what it is owing to things between which it mediates and which it brings into relation to each other.[30]

These categories do not refer to the properties of the things themselves, but to our perception of the signs for them. Gold money is firstness. Gold-backed paper is secondness. Paper fiat money is thirdness. Electronic exchange redeemable for paper is a kind of second-thirdness? The point is, *all* these other signs—whether fact, quality, or convention; whether index, icon, or symbol—always have something to which they *refer*.

Except money.

Modern general-purpose money is not a *symbol*, because it stands for nothing. It is not a language. Money is not *to* a thing-for-sale as a word is *to* an object. Money doesn't relate to money itself like words, as describing differences and forms, because the only difference in money is *more* or *less*. General-purpose fiat money is not symbolic of anything for which it is exchanged. There are no cultural conventions that establish a symbolic relation. The red on the traffic light is understood in a cultural context. Prior to car traffic, or in the absence of car traffic, it has no meaning. We might be able to say that a pizza symbolizes a particular sum of money (even this is questionable), making money a *referent*; but we'd never say that a sum of money *symbolizes* a pizza.

So why does this sign stuff matter to us as exchange detectives?

Mainstream economics tells us that money is the measure of all things *without differentiation*. This is why we can exchange forestland for soft drinks, and it shows up only as a cipher (i.e., $). "Growth," for

30. Peirce, quoted in Hornborg, *Power of the Machine*, 165.

example, using only $ is how we measure the economy. "We had three percent growth [in $] this year." What does that actually mean? Does it tell us how many people are rich? Poor? Homeless? Does it tell us anything about food quality? About illness? The state of a power grid? The fitness of water to drink in Flint, Michigan? Births? Deaths? Soil health? Air quality? Types of employment? What are the economic preoccupations of you and your family right now?

Economists use a measure called *Gross Domestic Product*. This is an averaged calculation of how much profit there is overall, how much money is spent overall, and how much money is received in income overall. These are reduced to a single number; and that number represents only a bald *quantity* of ONE *quality*: $. Talk about abstraction! In 2015, that was around $18 trillion for the United States. It made no difference whether that money circulated through goat farms, resort hotels, convenience stores, or weapons factories. They are all reflected by the same code: $. One thing might be $$, and another more expensive one $$$$$$$$; but the code is otherwise undifferentiated. Even computer code, because it has to accommodate specific information, differentiation, and *context*, requires two. Even the simplest DNA requires four nucleotides. "We could regard money," says Hornborg, "as a communicative disorder."[31]

> The conceptual cornerstone of economic science [$] is thus as vague as the most abstract definition possible of the most elementary unit of communication. It specifies absolutely nothing about the substance of economic processes. The all-engulfing character of modernity is generated by this tendency toward abstraction—that is, by the use of signs (including concepts such as "utility") that can stand for anything to anybody. The core of our "culture" is a black hole; at the heart of our cosmology are empty signs.[32]

Why Semiotics?

Richard Dawkins is among those who propose something called *universal Darwinism*, which purports first of all that mathematically demonstrable scientific discovery constitutes an ultimate truth claim; that is, it can explain everything. Everything. *Universal Darwinists*, however, violate their own stated principle by jumping to the non-mathematically-demonstrable conclusion

31. Ibid., 170.
32. Ibid., 171.

that both nature and society can be explained using nothing but their "Darwinist" triad, i.e., *adaptation* (evolution) through *variation*, selection of the "fit," and *retention* (in biology, this means heredity).[33] They have taken an overly general account of natural selection and attempted a further generalization of that account to everything else: economics, psychology, anthropology, and linguistics. Linguistics, for our discussion, falls within the scope of *semiotics*—the study of signs—and we will show why *universal Darwinism* is inadequate to the task of understanding any of these things.

The linguistics—or study of language—of the *universal Darwinists*, whose obsessive motivating purpose seems to be proving a negative—that there is no God[34]—is called, unsurprisingly, "evolutionary linguistics." In evolutionary linguistics, the basic assumption is that a word or phrase, for example, is selected in the same way that nature selects for long necks on giraffes, through a process of variation (different lengths of neck), selection of the "fit" (longer necks get more food and live longer to reproduce more); and retention (the trait is stored genetically and passed on through reproduction of the "fit").[35]

What is assumed in this worldview is *materialism*, or the assumption of the material as the ground of all being. This is an aspect of the dualism we discussed earlier. The subject is unreliable, but the object contains the only discernable *truth*, discoverable through strict observation that is disciplined with mathematics. The Austrian philosopher Rudolf Steiner (1865–1925) explained how this was an attempt to break being into time *and* space (instead of time-space), separating them and making *space* the dominant partner.

> The concept of matter arose only because of a very misguided concept of time. The general belief is that the world would evaporate into a mere apparition without being if we did not anchor the totality of fleeting events in a permanent, immutable reality that endures in time while its various individual configurations change. But time is not a container within which changes occur. Time does not exist before things or outside of them. It is

33. Sydow, "Sociobiology, Universal Darwinism, and Their Transcendence."

34. There is a truism in logic that says, "You cannot prove a negative"; but this is not absolutely true. The exceptions are "proof of impossibility" (2 plus 2 cannot equal 5) and "evidence of absence" (There is no coffee in that cup). In this case, however, the claim "There is no God," falls outside of either exception, because God—at least as understood from the perspective of Christian philosophers like Aquinas—is prior to and transcendent of the Being within which we, as Being's time-space-matter captives, establish these kinds of evidentiary proofs.

35. Campbell, "Bayesian Methods and Universal Darwinism."

the tangible expression of the fact that events—because of their specific nature—form sequential interrelationships.[36]

For Darwin, as well as Newton, whose mechanical ideas Darwin adopted, and Dawkins with his posse of God-phobic materialists, the separation of time and space and time's subordination to space (materiality that "holds still" for observation), were necessary to reduce all reality to a sequence of simple, mechanical causes-and-effects, what Aristotle called "efficient causation."[37] The other three types of causation (see footnote) made them dizzy. The reduction of all phenomena to efficient causes is an attempt at *control* (an obsession most often associated with anxiety). If time is not a thing but an expression of shifting relations, then it, too, is wild. It needs to be domesticated by the material, locked into plots on a map. French philosopher Henri Bergson (1859–1941), who was vitally interested in the phenomenon of cinema, compared this attempt by materialists, to domesticate time, to films—which, though they appear to flow continuously, can be broken down into frames where all that disorienting motion can be frozen into the apparent three dimensions of *space*—height, width, depth.

> Such is the contrivance of the cinematograph. And such is also that of our knowledge. Instead of attaching ourselves to the inner becoming of things, we place ourselves outside them in order to recompose their becoming artificially. We take snapshots, as it were, of the passing reality . . . We may therefore sum up . . . that the mechanism of our ordinary knowledge is of a cinematographical kind.[38]

This materialist notion of language, then, not only cannot account for Taussig's Bolivian peasant-miners baptizing money, it cannot account for the immense complexity of a simple conversation between two Western metropolitan persons about a novel they both read. What is required is an *expansive and inclusive*, not a *reductive and exclusive*, approach to language that allows for context. When Ludwig Wittgenstein (1889–1951) formulated his ideas about language, which he compared to games, he pointed out

36. Selg, *Rudolf Steiner, Life and Work*, 1:174.

37. Aristotle defined four types of causation: material, formal, efficient, and final. Material causation was what made up something—this book is made of paper and ink. Formal causation is how something is formed—a daisy is a daisy and not a rose because of their specific and differentiated *forms*. Efficient causation is a sequence leading to a phenomenon—billiard ball moves, hits another billiard ball, energy is transferred, second ball moves. Final causation is a purpose or goal, what an action is aimed at—I am writing now for the purpose of "causing" a book.

38. Bergson, *Creative Evolution*, 332.

that language can mean "giving orders, and obeying them, describing the appearance of an object, or giving its measurements, constructing an object from a description (a drawing), reporting an event, speculating about an event, forming and testing a hypothesis, presenting the results of an experiment in tables and diagrams, making up a story; and reading it, play-acting, singing, guessing riddles, making a joke or telling it, solving a problem in practical arithmetic, translating from one language into another, asking, thinking, cursing, greeting, and praying."[39]

The *universal Darwinists*, in trying to break everything in the universe down to its evolutionary *utility*, evade these problems by claiming that they simply haven't yet identified the whole train of cause-and-effect. In other words, their theory is correct even though it hasn't yet been scientifically demonstrated to be so, because it is correct. Then they castigate faith as a form of unfounded belief without the least sense of irony. More to the point, when they speak of evolution as if it were reducible to their *vary-adapt-retain* triad, they fail to have noticed that human beings—with language in particular—have evolved to be "biologically determined *not* to be biologically determined";[40] in other words, we are *by our very nature* "constructed" by *culture*, which cannot, as the dualists would have it, be separated from nature any more than time can be separated from matter and space, nor can our semiosphere be deconstructed within the adapted framework of Newtonian (mechanical) physics.

> Wittgenstein's theory of language games can be instructive on several accounts when applied to semiotic discussion. Indeed, any interaction with signs, production of signs, or attribution of meaning owes its existence to its status as a move in a language game—that is, a conceptual architecture, a grammar, that we must uncover.
>
> Consider the Augustinian definition of the sign: something put in the place of something else (to which it is imperative to add: in a relation of meaning or representation). Wittgenstein tells us that of the elements that make up the semiotic relation (sign, modes of representation or signifying, the sign's referent, etc.), none exists outside a language game. In an interpretive act, nothing is "intrinsically" a sign: the grammar of the language game is what makes it possible to identify the sign, its way of being a sign and what it is a sign of.[41]

39. Wittgenstein, *Philosophical Investigations*, para. 23.

40. Goff, *Borderline*, 30.

41. Xanthos, "Wittgenstein's Language Games," sec. 2.4.

Hornborg shows how semiotics can account for similarities of communication across phenomena without resorting to dualism as an anti-anxiety drug or removing piece of reality from its context and thus destroying its *meaning*.

> From the point of view of universal [Darwinism], the specifics of local contexts of interpretation can be seen as *constraints* on reproductive success. Logically, the ideas, artifacts, and human persons that should be selected for are those that are least dependent on context [the opposite of natural systems *and* evolution] . . . Abstract language, universalizing knowledge, general-purpose money, globalized commodities, and cosmopolitan personalities all share one fundamental feature: they are free to transcend specific, local contexts. They are not committed to *place*. There is thus an inverse relation between experiential depth and spatial expansion, between meaning investment and market shares. McDonald's is testimony to the ecology of cultural diffusion.[42]

Let's do a summary/review/synthesis now.

Think of these things now: a computer, a horse, a vacation cabin, a fighter-bomber aircraft, a scented candle, a toilet, and a bushel of apples. You play games on the computer, you ride the horse, you sleep in and go fishing from the vacation cabin, you fly the fighter-bomber to kill and terrorize people, you set the mood in a room with the scented candle, you do what you do with a toilet, and you press the bushel of apples into a jug of cider. These are things you *use*. Each one is used differently from the other. To abstract them together, to encompass them, you would have to go very general (e.g., they are all solids, or each has weight, or each is visible). These are not useful distinctions for things that have different uses.

Money, however, is a sign that *can* abstract (encompass) them all, as we have learned, as a *price*. Each has a price, measurable by the same sign—money. Through price, money makes unlike things alike in this one key respect. What this depends upon absolutely is whether or not that thing is *for sale*. A thing that is not for sale has no price, and is not encompassed by price (money). But anything that is not presently *for sale* can be encompassed by price by putting it up for sale, or by "privatizing" it. The view of the beach may be free to all. But there are views of the beach that are *for sale*. Something happened to transform that view from priceless to with-price. It became a *commodity*, a thing-for-sale, and this is the encompassing

---

42. Hornborg, *Power of the Machine*, 166.

category associated with price. A horse and a beachside view which are not at all alike can be rendered alike in one respect; they each have a price.

Once money de-specifies things through price, money also has an effect that erases many boundaries: *velocity*. By attaching a price to *many different things*, which makes them exchangeable *by a single sign*, money puts exchange's pedal to the metal. That is why you can head into that big box store with nothing but money, and walk out with cherries from Chile, a fishing pole from China, pork chops from North Carolina, bird seed from California, and a magazine from New York City. Paraphrasing, "*One sign to rule them all, one sign to find them; one sign to bring them all and in the market bind them.*"[43]

If money is a sign, it is the most *abstract* of all signs because—as we keep harping on—it has *no referent*. Its referent is an empty abstraction called *value*, but that value is stated in quantities of money, making the relation between money and value a kind of circle, like a dog chasing its tail. Value is money is value is money . . . etc. It sits apart from other qualities in a way that allows money—certainly a sign, because it signals something, or we wouldn't use it—to get away with what other signs cannot.

If a human can be pulled inside the category Primate, and Primate can be pulled into the category Mammal, and Mammal can be pulled into Animal, the abstraction still refers back down the scale. But nothing compares to general-purpose money, which can, through price, create a category that pulls into itself vacation cabins, fighter-bombers, and apples. Price divides the world not into classes of things, but into two simplistic camps: commodity and non-commodity.

Solvent

We can see that money as the single measure of economy conceals much; and this concealment is crucial. Money conceals the destruction of a rain forest to grow cattle for a foreign market to acquire dollars to pay an international debt (there are those ramifications, read backward). But it not only *conceals* these processes, it *makes them possible where without money it would be impossible*, as we have seen, because it universalizes (abstracts, decontextualizes) exchange and thereby increases its *velocity*. More than concealing and facilitating these phenomena, however, the very nature of this code with neither alternates nor reference points runs *counter to nature*.

43. Tolkien, *Fellowship of the Ring*, 272. Paraphrase of Sauron's inscription on the Ring of Power: "One ring to rule them all. One ring to find them. One ring to bring them all and in the darkness bind them."

When we speak of *nature*, even though anything that happens in space-time is necessarily *natural* as it is constrained by natural law, we are generally thinking of how natural processes happen *apart from* technological intervention. The natural processes of the biosphere, or the totality of Earth's surface ecology, tend to stack and increase in complexity. By that, we mean that the natural processes of exchange progressively contribute to more life forms in more places in meshworks that are increasingly *complex* and self-regulating. Cells are components of organisms. Various organisms make possible a tree. Many trees and accompanying flora and fauna are components of a forest. More things relate specifically to one or more parts of the system. Each bit, then, is located, or *contextualized*. Each bit has *referents* within the overall system that say, "Stop. Here is where you belong. Here is where you can flourish and help the rest of us flourish."

If you sink an old ship in certain coastal waters, within a few years that ship will be transformed into a highly complex reef with many life forms. If you leave a field alone here in Southeast Michigan—which began as a mixed conifer and broadleaf forest—within thirty years, that field will be a forest again. In a sense, it *wants* to be a forest. Forest is its default position. Taken together and observed from the point of view of thermodynamics, these are counter-entropic processes, based on *extravagance* not scarcity. The systems are actually becoming more and more self-sustaining and self-regulating. They are consolidating more *negentropy*. They are becoming more complex, more *ordered* for overall flourishing, more *attached*, more *contextual*.

The way these natural systems sustain themselves is through increasing resilience, or by increasing their ability at many scales to survive shocks. Diversity is nature's main "strategy" for system resilience. If a farmer plants a field with a hundred thousand heads of nothing but cabbage, in very short order there will arrive a hundred thousand or more of some kind of bug that prefers eating cabbage to anything else in the world. This is why industrial monocultural farming requires so many flows of materials from *outside itself* to maintain production. The farmer has to purchase pesticides and herbicides and machines to spread them and fertilizers for the depletion of soil nutrients, etc.[44] This system has *no diversity*, and therefore has very *low resilience* (which leads to high maintenance using outside flows). In a highly complex forest, however, one form of bug cannot threaten the system, and in short order will encounter a limitation on its numbers in the form of a bird that likes to eat that particular bug or a wasp that like to kill its larva

---

44. This has what Illich might call an iatrogenic effect—the cure creates another illness. We already see "super-weeds" taking hold in monocultural farms, weeds that are developing resistance to herbicides, just as some bacteria develop antibiotic resistance.

to use as an egg incubator. The system can receive various insults, but it has diversity and flexibility to combat those threats.

This is one of the mechanisms whereby nature accords a higher priority to the survival of *relational* structures and their complexity than it does to individual parts of the structures; not by diversity *per se*, but through a set of relations between the various parts, each of which is *embedded* with the other. In fact, no ecosystem can be understood at all by separating each of its components and studying it as if it were independent of the system. Certainly, I can determine many facts about a pawpaw plant, and put them in a botany book with a picture of nothing but a pawpaw plant; but the plant itself requires various things from the soil, various companion plants to thrive, and even flies to achieve its pollination. It has a stinky flower that smells like rotten meat just to attract those flies (a trickster's sign). Natural systems thrive on *context*, or a web of relations.

General-purpose money, however, works directly against this via two linked, progressive processes, *disembedding* and *commodification*; and instead of extravagance (e.g., one plant producing thousands of seeds), money economics is based on enforced scarcity (the competition for a finite quantity of money). The more successful the increase of general-purpose money, the more unsuccessful are surrounding natural systems. The aggregate of all biomass is systematically displaced by a growing aggregate of technomass. It is a zero-sum game. If I win, you lose. Biological processes create increasing order (negentropy), whereas money-economies reward disorder (entropy).

Exchanges within a high-equilibrium (resilient) structure like a forest are not universal. They are *embedded* in the complex whole. The signals are not interchangeable. This signal sent out by the pawpaw flower doesn't facilitate exchange with everything else, but with flies. The gold in the ground along the Amazon River is *embedded*. The sandalwood tree growing in Indonesia is *embedded* in a forest. The oil sands in Alberta are embedded in a forested geologic structure. The only reason these things are extracted is to increase the accumulation of money, and if general-purpose money were not *universally exchangeable*, there would be no motive for the wide scale, systematic destruction of these extractions.

When a beach is open to the public, it is just a beach. When it is privatized and closed except when you pay admission, it has been transformed into a *commodity*—a thing for sale, a thing exchangeable for money. When I grow a surplus of tomatoes in my garden and give them to my neighbors, they are still just tomatoes. When I set up a stand to sell them, they become *commodities*—things for sale. The water in my well is water. The water in a plastic bottle at the corner store is a *commodity*. When I was young, the idea of buying bottled water would have been ludicrous. But as aquifers have been depleted or poisoned, and as water companies have been privatized, more and more drinking water has been *commodified*.

With precious few exceptions, every process now designed to accumulate general-purpose money contributes to *disembedding*, or uprooting; and every time the so-called market for something becomes saturated and quits producing profit, more and more things are *commodified*. It is like cancer spreading (growth!). Coca-Cola can be bought with the same general-purpose money acquired through the systematic destruction of a rainforest. In relation to nature and natural systems, profit always rewards most what is most wrong!

Markets and machines are *dissipative structures*. They take in, or eat, *order* created by nature—like *negentropy*—and crap out *disorder*, or *entropy*. We saw earlier that virtually *all* technology does this.

As we pointed out in speaking of general-purpose money's "catholicity," *general-purpose money is a sign with no referent*; there is nothing that says to it, "Stop here." Money allows things to be carved out from their natural setting (their context) in order to be sold as commodities. These biological systems, then, eventually collapse, because they have been *dissolved* into independent components (commodities) that can no longer *relate* to those things upon which they co-depend. The pawpaw has no ground frost to break its dormancy, no walnuts to kill out competitors or give them much needed shade, no carrion nearby to draw flies and pollinate it.

Scientifically, what a solvent does is (1) create a cavity between one part and its neighbors, then (2) remove that part through the insertion of the solvent. The more money that is accumulated, the greater the environmental destruction. The more money that is accumulated, the greater the dissolution of traditional communities which are constructed around and upon material-biological systems. We have been *disembedded* from family and place, ourselves now also commodities, for sale to the highest bidder, and re-embedded in an abstraction called "the market" that is on a path to the commodification of everything, that perversion of power that Karl Barth called the "commodifying spirit of Mammon."[45]

When you consider that cultures are determined by environments and environments by cultures, you begin to see how general-purpose money dissolves natural systems and cultures at the same time. Economics cannot account for this. Economics doesn't want to account for this. Economics is a form of propaganda deployed on behalf of people who benefit most from these processes through accumulation, and *context*—like showing the inseparability of culture-environment-economy—is always dangerous to power.

45. Prather, *Christ, Power and Mammon*, 1.

Entitlement and Accumulation

The most insidious social characteristic of money, especially general-purpose money, is that because it is a code without meaning, a value that can promiscuously attach and detach from anything that is for sale, money allows those with guile or power or both to accumulate wealth at scales not possible without money.

Almost 2,000 people worldwide, or .0005 percent of the world population, have assets exceeding a billion dollars. A billion dollars can buy 3,225,806,452 pounds of potatoes, 37,679 Ford F150 pickup trucks, 71,429 pounds of cocaine, 5,000 $200K houses, two Central American national telecommunications companies, 1,000 square miles of Wyoming, or 20,000,000 hours (1,538 average lifetimes) of high-quality private tutoring. Michael Bloomberg has forty times that amount, Warren Buffett sixty times, and Bill Gates seventy-five times, making them the most parasitic creatures on the planet.

Prior to the exchange domination of general purpose money and the total *monetization* of the economy, these kinds of fortunes were frankly not possible, not even to the most powerful people in the world. Nothing but money can hold this vast store of (abstract) value. No one can keep 3 billion pounds of potatoes or live in 5,000 houses or drive 37,679 trucks.

The means of accumulation are varied but very finite, the main thing being that this kind of *accumulation* of wealth in the money-form can only be accomplished by using money to acquire more money. At a certain hypothetical point, depending on the circumstances, it is no longer possible to increase wealth in its *concrete* forms. No reasonable quantity of actual *things*, like trucks or cocaine or pedicures, can do what money does as a sign—a marker of price-value—and moreover, as we showed earlier in the book, no actual *thing* can be exchanged with the *velocity* of money. You would not use pickup trucks to buy groceries or Ravensburger jigsaw puzzles.

To make sense of the term accumulation, we need to understand general-purpose money as an *entitlement*. Possessing money entitles one to time, space, matter, and energy. It allows me to appropriate these together. When a person goes into her or his local Kohl's and picks up a pair of comfy Chaps house slippers, they are appropriating time, space, material, and energy. The shoes are made in China, using leather, polyester, nylon, and plastic. What is embodied in those slippers are the labor of the factory workers, the food that fueled them (time, material, and energy), the land that grew the food (space and material), the time it took them to make the shoes, the oil to make the plastic (material), the cow it took for the leather, the food to raise the cow, the energy to process the cow, the labor of the people who transported them, the energy of transportation, etc. You get the picture. In each step of each process, there are people; each of those persons is in relation to other people. The worker has a boss, the farmhand works for a farm owner, and so forth. The magic of money is that when I drop into Kohl's and buy my comfy Chaps house slippers, barely even speaking to the checkout person (who is figuratively chained to a machine for eight hours a day—*technique*), the *relationships between people*, near and far, have been given the appearance of *relationships between things* (money and commodities). *Out of sight and out of mind.*

The more money one has, the greater the entitlements. The greater the entitlements, the more power that can be accumulated in the form of time, space, material, and energy. Bill Gates may not want a hundred thousand trucks, but if he felt he needed to, he could hire an army. People with a great deal of money have found it more efficient, however, to cultivate political leaders of their own choosing and frequently of their own class, giving them a degree of conceptual separation from direct accountability. These things are not very controversial.

What is controversial is to say that *accumulation by one always and inevitably comes at the expense of another.* This claim runs counter to two and a half centuries of propaganda disguised as economic theory which tell us we can all benefit together from the bounty of technologically-enhanced nature. But when I build the mental boundary around my Chaps house slippers, that boundary that says "property," I am excluding not just others who may want my slippers, but all those who I have appropriated *out of sight and out of mind.* I have managed to deny the ways in which my role in one exchange was parasitic on others. This reluctance to admit that one's desires and comforts might be parasitic is what accounts for the unwillingness of many people in the United States—and not just the rich ones—to acknowledge how we benefit within a world system; and it accounts for why we often *want* things to be *out of sight and out of mind.* Our lives are hectic enough and insecure enough; and we don't need to be implicated for greater sacrifice and responsibility. It is easier to say, "We are entitled" or, if that's too self-indicting, "This is just nature's way."

Modes of Accumulation

Hornborg describes five ways of doing things, or *modes*, to accomplish accumulation: (1) plunder accumulation, (2) merchant accumulation, (3) financial accumulation, (4) under-compensation (of labor), and (5) under-payment for potential (of materials and energy).[46] I would add Hornborg's own term, "environmental load displacement." Jason Moore names the basic accumulation *necessities* which correspond to these *modes* "the Four Cheaps": (1) cheap labor, (2) cheap food, (3) cheap energy, and (4) cheap raw materials, summing them up ecologically as "cheap nature."[47] Cheap is accomplished through a combination of *force, general-purpose money, unequal exchange,* and *dissipative structures.*

Plunder is fairly easy to understand. You have some money, and I want it, so I beat you and steal it. On a larger scale, we might discuss piracy on the seas, which has even been used as a weapon of statecraft. After wars, many losers have had their treasuries looted. The conquest of colonies and the enslavement of humans to exploit them for profit was plunder. Plunder is merely stealing—generally with the element of force.

Simple *merchant* accumulation is what we saw between Europe, the Mediterranean, and Asia for several centuries, where travelling merchants would buy cheap in one place and sell at a higher price elsewhere. In the markets around Haiti, where I have spent a good deal of time, the *march-ands* (market women) buy produce from local growers in bulk and sell it in smaller portions at a markup.

Finance, for our purposes, is a mode of accumulation based on *rent.* By that we do not mean what you pay to your landlord each month for an apartment, though that qualifies as a form of *rent.* Rent here is an economic term of art for *royalties* paid without anything actually being produced. Rent includes what is paid to use property, but also as interest on a loan—a royalty for using the money. Rent is the insurance premium. Rent is the dividend paid on a stock. Capitalists—or people who use money to accumulate more money—who accumulate using rents, or royalties when nothing is actually produced, are called *rentier* capitalists. Bankers are *rentier* capitalists. Insurance companies are *rentier* enterprises.[48] Day traders are *rentiers. Financial* accumulation is the mode of accumulation employed by *rentiers.*

Under-compensation is the means of accumulation that pays less for labor than the value that labor produces. This is the most common modern form of accumulation. A group of workers produces goods or services for which buyers pay X amount. The overhead of y is paid, leaving X-Y. The workers are paid X-Y-Z, and Z becomes surplus, which is appropriated by

46. Hornborg, *Power of the Machine,* 57–60.

47. Moore, *Capitalism and the Web of Life,* 17.

48. Lohmann, "Strange Markets." Lohmann describes insurance as "commodify-ing uncertainty." With the emergence of financial derivatives, the commodification of uncertainty reached new heights.

the employers or owners. We call this surplus value "profit." There is a high probability that you, the reader, work for some enterprise that thrives by paying you and your co-workers X-Y-Z. You produce, on average, less than you take home in monetary value. You are *under-compensated*. This can be a comfortable arrangement that is (hmm) relatively just; but the *structural reality* is that the owners always stand to profit *more* by paying you *less*. This is why so many industries have moved their operations to places like El Salvador or Indonesia. They can increase *under-compensation* and thereby accumulate more profit, or surplus. And once one does it, the rest must follow suit or fail.

Finally, there is *underpayment* for resources. In Pennsylvania logging companies bid the "stumpage price" to log an acre of trees on state land. The larger the company, the larger the operation, the lower the bid they can afford; so in 2008, for example, a big company could pay $300 (the "stumpage price") for an acre that yielded $1,800 in sales.[49] They do not pay for the loss of habitat, subsequent erosion, fire hazards from scattered wood-waste, water degradation, or aesthetic losses,[50] because these costs are not given a monetary value.

> Nature could not be rendered cheap until it was rendered external.
>
> —JASON MOORE[51]

This process of ignoring things that are not priced is called *externalization*. These non-money costs are *external* to all economic calculations. Externalization is just one way to pay less for a material than it actually has in productive potential.

The most popular car in the United States is a Honda Accord, which weighs 3,605 pounds. If you add two adult passengers, that adds at least 300 pounds, for 3,905 pounds. Averaging between city and highway driving it will travel around 31 miles on a gallon of gasoline. Measured in productivity. If gasoline costs three dollars a gallon,[52] that means we can push two tons thirty miles for three dollars at an average speed exceeding that of a human walking by a factor of more than ten. In the US labor market, as this is written, a crap job will pay around eight dollars an hour, which means that

49. Jacobson, "To Cut or Not to Cut," 6.
50. Environmental load displacement.
51. Moore, "End of Cheap Nature."
52. Gause, "Sultans of Swing?" As this is written, gasoline is cheaper because of a financial anomaly which includes a Saudi oil glut on the market to undermine its competitors.

gasoline costs what it would take to pay a person for less than twenty-three minutes of work—work which would obviously not be nearly as strenuous as pushing a two-ton vehicle. The reason we can get gasoline that cheaply is a result of many factors. The energy was stored up over millions of years. The land was appropriated to pump out the oil. Taxpayers footed the bill for basic transportation and communications infrastructure. Tax holidays were afforded the energy companies that extracted and refined it. And the United States Navy maintains six carrier strike groups, at $39 million per day, which roam the high seas to ensure the security of critical resources. The oil companies themselves are paying well below the actual cost of the product, economically as well as environmentally and socially.

The State

The topic of the Navy is a good segue here to talk about the role of the state in accumulation.[53] We have seen how money facilitates accumulation, and greater abstraction of money (general-purpose money) facilitates greater accumulation; but the political context is essential. The state is, for us in this period of history, the final authority recognized for a legal monopoly on force. The state enforces certain social conventions, including economic ones. To assess the roles of the state,[54] we will describe the context for the state in this historical period using what is called *world systems* analysis. Because even though some individual states have a powerful degree of political independence to decide for themselves, or autonomy, all states are now economically linked (in substantial part because of US dollars being the world-currency) to all the others.

The state prints money; and contrary to popular belief, money is *not* private property. When people say, for example, "I want the government to keep its hands off my money," they are claiming something that is not true. The money does not belong to them. Without the state, that money as they know it, "legal tender," meaning legal for the payment of taxes and exchangeable for all private transactions that are taxed, would not exist. The state issues the money through banks, printed by the state, and its purpose is to circulate in order to increase the velocity of exchange to sustain accumulation ("growth"). It is a banknote, and says so—"Federal Reserve *Note*"—and it ultimately belongs to the United States Treasury. It is signed by the Treasurer of the United States and by the Secretary of the Treasury. The individual notes even have serial numbers.

53. Moore, "The Capitalocene, Part II."

54. The nation-state, not the federally-consolidated (sub) states within the United States—a nation-state.

The United States is a *capitalist* state, even though there is no law or policy that states this explicitly. That is, this state's purpose is to ensure *accumulation* for members of the *business class*. Even the administrative and security responsibilities are fundamentally designed to support accumulation. Again, this is never stated explicitly, but can be inferred from the sum of its laws and policies and their intents. As a capitalist state, the United States, in coordination with its fifty sub-states and its external possessions, ensures profitability by *ensuring the conditions* for those *modes of accumulation* listed above, and ensuring the "Four Cheaps" to which Moore points: cheap labor, cheap food, cheap energy, and cheap raw materials.

The Indian Wars, the Mexican War, slavery, etc., were methods of state-sanctioned *plunder* to acquire land and ensure land productivity through one system of *under-compensation* (the slaves were not paid and were provided minimal subsistence housing and rations). The Spanish-American War was a war of plunder during which the United States added to its colonies (expansion). There is still a US military base on Cuba's Guantanamo Bay (now a US torture center) that was acquired during that war and never returned even after Cuba's independence. Puerto Rico is still a US "possession."

A capitalist state has seven key economic responsibilities to guarantee accumulation for the business class: (1) to ensure enough workers for production at rates that allow for profit; (2) to ensure that banks can provide finance capital for loans; (3) to ensure the externalization of costs adequate to protect overall profits, including publicly-financed infrastructure; (4) to ensure markets sufficient to absorb production; (5) to ensure expansion sufficient to compensate for saturated or lost markets, whether by financial or military means, or by opening new arenas of commodification ("privatization"); (6) to ensure enough general stability for business to flourish without major interruptions, and (7) to ensure an adequate supply of resources. Once these seven requirements are satisfied, then the coordinated activity between productive activities and financial activities can "grow" the economy. Failure to expand will eventually result in falling rates of profit as markets are saturated and-or "cheap nature" quits being cheap, and falling rates of profit will result in profit-based enterprises failing.

There are ideologues who describe something called *laissez-faire* capitalism, that is, capitalism that is purely driven by unfettered market choices with little to no plunder or coercion, but historically this is a fantasy. This is a totally ahistorical perspective that intentionally ignores past plunder that established present legal property relations, using highly abstracted, formal arguments to substitute an idealized reality for the actual messy one.

Laissez-faire capitalism has *never* existed, and it *cannot* exist for reasons we will explain when we return again to *the ecology of the money-sign*.

We have noted already that this expansion of fictional value through general-purpose money supports a form of development—industrialism—that relies now overwhelmingly on fossil hydrocarbons for fuel,[55] which refers us back to the Second Law of Thermodynamics, or Entropy Law, and to technology—which is comprised of materials from afar, acquired through monetary velocity, and which relies on more materials and energy from far afield for sustained operation, maintenance, and component replacement. The imperative of "growth," or *expansion*, means that materials and energy will be used up and force the appropriation of materials and energy from further and further away. When you look at the historic expansion of the United States and other early-industrialized and currently-industrial-bene- fiting nations who depended for development on colonies, you can imagine the process of expansion. We saw examples from the Roman and British empires in chapter 2 of how that exhaustion of resources nearby leads to expansion and exhaustion that inexorably spreads. This leads us to our next chapter on *development*.

55. Fossil-energy capitalism is not the only form of capitalism, but a recent ener- getic regime that catapulted industrial capitalism into high velocity. Slaves, wood, and coal provided the energetic basis for early accumulation regimes.

8

Development

Woe to those who add house to house and join field to field, until there is no more room, so that you have to live alone in the midst of the land!

—ISAIAH 5:8

Where do most radical thinkers stand on belief in human progress? In fact, they have not rejected it; they want to speed it up. The commitment to creating the Kingdom of Humanity, in a radicalized form, still undergirds the condemnation of capitalism. Almost all social readings are permeated with the unstated premise that our age is an improvement over all others.[1]

—KATHARINE TEMPLE, CATHOLIC WORKER

Production, Consumption, and Space

IF YOU COULD GO back in time to the mid-sixteenth century and land in what is now Eastern Virginia, you would encounter six tribes of indigenous people who collectively belonged to a political and trade network called the Powhatan Confederacy. They used beads and tobacco as forms of currency in some trade, but no one depended upon either for their livelihood. By and large, they lived through a combination of subsistence farming, hunting, and gathering. They also did some very limited mining of copper for bead-making and tools. Subsistence farms grew corn, beans, and squash as staple crops, supplemented by fruits, nuts, fish, and game gathered from the local environment. Houses were generally one room, constructed of saplings,

1. Temple, "The Myth of Progress."

leather, and bark. As with many other subsistence cultures, production and consumption overwhelmingly happened in the same place.[2]

Compare this to our own lives, where we consume what has been produced from all over the world, where general-purpose money has made this possible, and where our dependence upon money is nearly absolute. Further, let's revisit what we have learned as exchange detectives about flows and nodes, and be reminded that one of the mental tricks that this space-separation between production and consumption is *out of sight and out of mind*.

There is a common argument that neither the world system nor the ecological crisis we are experiencing is "capitalist," because the Soviet and Chinese economies were/are "communist." This is actually a deceptive argument, because both these economies, apart from their own rhetoric, employed the same *means* for development as capitalist economies, and were in fact both deeply dependent upon trade relations with named-capitalist economies. Deng Xiaoping of China is one of the founding fathers of neoliberal capitalism.[3] The world systems perspective looks at the world economy as a whole. And as Jason Moore, professor of sociology at Binghamton University, points out,

> It is difficult for me to read the Soviet project as a fundamental rupture. The great industrialization drive of the 1930s relied massively on the importation of fixed capital, which by 1931 constituted 90 percent of Soviet imports. The Soviets were so desperate to obtain hard currency that "the state was prepared to export anything and everything, from gold, oil and furs to the pictures in the Hermitage Museum." If the Soviet project resembles other modes of production, it is surely the tributary, not socialist, mode of production, through which the state directly extracts the surplus. Nor did the Soviets turn inwards after 1945. Soviet trade with OECD countries (in constant dollars) increased 8.9 percent annually between 1950 and 1970, rising to 17.9 percent a year in the following decade a trend accompanied by sharply deteriorating terms of trade and rising debt across the Soviet-led zone.[4]

2. *New World Encyclopedia*, "Powhatan," http://www.newworldencyclopedia.org/entry/Powhatan.

3. Kwong, "The Chinese Face of Neoliberalism," para. 3.

4. Moore, "The Capitalocene, Part II." This is difficult to fathom for many people, because we have been trained by schools and media to compare differences in outcomes to variations in stated ideologies—which between the West and the Eastern Bloc *were* very different—even when the material methods for achieving outcomes are far more similar. More "materialist" histories show that the collapse of the Eastern Bloc

One of the main errors of Marxism generally in its criticism of capitalism, flowing out of its early acceptance of a "progress" narrative,[5] was
its failure to account for industrial machinery itself as a flow-node that
concealed its background realities, what we have repeatedly referred to
here as the *out of sight and out of mind* problem. More importantly still,
Marxism failed to fully account for general-purpose money as an *ecological*
phenomenon that *disembeds*, or dissolves ecosystems and communities.[6]
So when we describe the *world* system as capitalist, we are saying that these
anti-capitalist projects, still embedded in a capitalist world system, failed
because of what they shared with capitalism itself. They continued to believe that they could cleanly separate culture from nature. One can very
easily argue that today's China is a capitalist powerhouse, regardless of what

---

was more an immediate outcome of economic warfare than failures of ideology; and
that these two different-sounding but materially similar structures were both inevitably
heading toward collapse, the West later than the East because it did prevail in economic
warfare which gave it a new lease on life (fresh expansion opportunities) for a period.

5. Day, Keri, "The Myth of Progress." Womanist theologian Keri Day says, "If competition and commodification constitute the inner logic of neoliberal capitalism, the
myth of progress is neoliberalism's legitimation." What we call the "myth of progress"
is the nineteenth and twentieth century idea that humanity is on a path to its own
self-perfection. For Christians, this is part of the Pelagian heresy: the idea that we
can work out our own salvation by our own wit and effort. The idea has always been
imperial, as the history of the Progressive movement shows, highly racialized (though
most self-identified "progressives" nowadays have abandoned the racial narrative for a
cultural one), and promoted as part of core-nation nationalism. Part and parcel of this
myth has been technological optimism, which carried with it both an ignorance of the
implications of the Second Law of Thermodynamics and the illusion that machines,
or technology, can be "innocent" of background social relations. Some will say that
this book is pro-leftist or pro-Marxist because it criticizes capitalism; but in fact—like
Mies and Illich—the perspective of this book is far more radical than Marx and does
not fit on that neat line that runs from right to left in the popular imagination. That
said, I must also include Alasdair MacIntyre's remarks—himself also a friendly critic of
Marxism—that although Marxism shares the same ethical conundrums as the liberalism it challenges, between duty-ethics and utilitarianism, equating Marxism with its
grotesque distortions by the Soviet Union and its imitators, is historically unfair: "[A]
s Marxists move toward power they always tend to become Weberians. Here I was of
course speaking of Marxisms at their best, say, in Yugoslavia or Italy; the barbarous
despotism . . . which reign[ed] in Moscow can be taken to be as irrelevant to the question of the moral substance of Marxism as the life of the Borgia pope was to that of the
moral substance of Christianity" (*After Virtue*, 261).

6. Though Marx (not to be confused with Marxism[s]) was the most influential
modern thinker in unpacking the contradiction between use-value and exchange-value, as well as how relations-between-people were concealed by the *out of sight and out
of mind* phenomenon (which he called *fetishism*) and represented as relations-between-
things. This author, for the record, rejects Marx-ISM out of hand *as a political program*,
while I accept and embrace many crucial insights from Marxist scholars.

they call themselves. It is an authoritarian (capitalist) market economy very much like Pinochet's Chile.[7]

This book's theses, while they incorporate some of the criticisms of capitalism laid out by Marx, constitute a criticism of capitalism that is far more radical than that of Marx. They do not simply reject capitalism. They reject the myth of progress as antithetical to the message of the Gospels and antithetical to human and non-human flourishing over the long term.

Centers and Margins

I live in a town of around 24,000 souls, the commercial center for a farming county, which also has a hospital and three small colleges. There were once a lot of union-wage factory jobs nearby in Toledo and Detroit that supplemented farm income, and this town then bustled with consumer activity. Factories, however, were shifted into regions around the world where accumulation could be increased through steeper *under-compensation*, that is, cheaper labor; and this town has many abandoned buildings and closed shopfronts. The farms have mostly been consolidated into giant monocrop operations leased by transnational corporations, and the farmers themselves raise these cash crops by strict rules, laid down by those corporations, with no more autonomy than a McDonald's manager.

If I go to a real estate site on the web and ask for houses that are priced above $300,000 (very high for this town), all but one of the listings show up on a map in the southeastern quadrant of town, with on midway along the east, and close to the country club. If you drive through our town from east to west along the main east-west thoroughfare, the houses and neighborhoods become shabbier the farther west you travel, and this end of town is also where most of the factories and warehouses, as well as toxic superfund sites are. Money as an entitlement helped create this map, which we might call a center-margin map. The center is where the good stuff flows *into*, and the margins are where the bad stuff flows *out-to*.[8] Those with more money-entitlements live in a kind of center in the east, and those with far fewer money-entitlements live in the west. Those in the west tend to work for those in the east. The east gets clean and pretty, and the west gets dirty and ugly. If you map where you live, you will find something similar; and if you live in a big city, you probably have a third region that is a throwaway region, with "surplus people," that is, people the economy doesn't want or need anymore—areas of extremely high unemployment, environmental toxicity, and

7. Gilson and Milhaupt, "Economically Benevolent Dictators."

8. Some scholars refer to this as a "core-periphery dynamic."

high crime. This latter is the margin of the margin, or the falloff region. In the triad between Miami, Santo Domingo, and Port-au-Prince, the United States is the center, the Dominican Republic is the margin, and Haiti is the fall-off zone. Within Miami itself, these three zones also exist—rich, working poor, and fall-off regions of hopelessness and high crime.

Centers exist parasitically on margins, and as margins are increasingly weakened by their parasites, more people enter fall-off zones, the center shrinks, and new margins, or parasite-hosts, are established closer to the center. This is why the once flourishing American "middle class" is now feeling the pinch. It is being marginalized, or parasitized.[9]

Center-margin can be mapped at differing scales. Mississippi is an extremely poor state compared to Connecticut, and the poorer states contribute indirectly to the well-being of the richer states, but inside each there are also center-margins by region, by county, by city. Center-margin is not a *place*, even though we can roughly map it; it is a *relationship*. Seen metabolically, as "the processes by which a living organism uses food to obtain energy and build tissue and disposes of waste material," the center-margin relationship is the result of the good stuff flowing one way and the bad stuff flowing the other way with the center as the exchange node. The benefits accrues at the center and the devastation and waste goes to the margin. Our mapping of flows as exchange detectives is what Helga Weisz calls "material flow analysis."[10]

What gets imported? What gets exported?

Import-Export

Saudi Arabia once supplied the rest of its region with wheat. Yes, wheat. Most people don't think of Saudi Arabia as a wheat producer, because it is largely desert. But beneath that desert is a massive underground network of aquifers, or underground lakes. While Saudi Arabia has between five and eight billion cubic meters of surface water, it has almost 2.3 trillion cubic meters underground.[11] These aquifers supplied the water for wheat production. By 2009, Saudi Arabia began importing more wheat than it grew for

9. The political hat trick of the business class that benefits from this marginalization is to convince that "middle class" that they are being parasitized by the poor. This is why reactionary movements, their animosity directed at scapegoats, are typically "middle class" movements.

10. Weisz, "Combining Social Metabolism."

11. Jeddah Regional Climate Center, "First National Communication Water Resources."

itself; and by 2016, it was importing around 99 percent. The saying went, they were "selling hydrocarbons to buy carbohydrates." This was a huge opportunity for Ag giants like Cargill in the United States, which could sell US taxpayer-subsidized wheat in ever greater volumes to the Saudis.[12]

The largest oil field in the world is Ghawar, in Saudi Arabia, and it produces around 65 percent of all Saudi oil. Ghawar production began to fall in the 1990s, and in 2006 it began falling precipitously. Pooled oil wells, underground oil lakes, with "sweet crude"[13] like Ghawar begin production under their own pressure; but over time, as the contents are pumped out, the pressure falls. The Saudi solution to that problem is water injection.[14] They inject large amounts of sea water into the margins of the fields in order to bring the pump pressure back up, salting the ground for centuries to come.

The revenues from oil have been used for "development," or urbanization, which has increased water demand, which has further depleted aquifers. The fallback position for the Saudis has been ocean desalinization; but desalinization relies on fossil fuels which is accelerating the depletion of the oil fields as well as creating greater strains on the national budget. Rationing has been enforced, which is contributing to greater social unrest.[15]

Headed by the largest and richest remaining hereditary monarchy in the world, Saudi Arabia routinely employs violent population control measures to its own people, including public beheadings, to ensure its own stability as an international energy hub. Moreover, it regularly engages in open bribery, and initiates as well as intervenes in conflicts throughout the region to secure that stability.[16]

As this is written the United States imports $53 billion a year in oil from Saudi Arabia, and in return exports $115 billion in weapons to Saudi Arabia, with whom the US is formally and informally allied in multiple military and diplomatic conflicts. A starker example of the regional import of order (negentropy) and the export of disorder (pollution, water depletion, authoritarian corruption, and war) would be hard to find.

12. Blas, "Saudi Wells Running Dry."

13. High-quality, easily accessible, low-sulfur oil.

14. Massachusetts Institute of Technology Press Release, "Carbon Capture and Sequestration Technologies," December 6, 2013.

15. Cooke, "Turmoil in Saudi Water Sector."

16. Wehrey, "The Authoritarian Resurgence."

The Trees

In February 1996, when Sarajevo, Bosnia-Herzegovina was the epicenter of the civil war resulting from Balkan politico-economic disintegration, the flows of fuels into the city were disrupted by ambushes and snipers along all the routes into the city. The temperatures dropped, the snow accumulated, and within days, people began cutting down the trees in the parks to obtain firewood.[17]

In the 1990s and 2000s, I spent a good deal of time in Haiti and the Dominican Republic, which share the same island, Hispaniola. Haiti had been internationally gang-raped since the colonial period, including massive deforestation to harvest precious hardwood and clearing land for sugar, coffee, and sisal. The Dominican Republic suffered some of those extractive depredations, but it became a client state of the United States and a tourist destination, while Haiti was exploited and left along the figurative roadside. One of the policies of the Dominican government was to subsidize bottled gas for its citizens to prevent them cutting the forests that attracted tourists. Haiti had no such policy, especially since it was subjected to a series of political coups that disrupted any political continuity. If you look at a satellite photograph of the Haitian-Dominican border, you can actually see the border in the contrast between the forested Dominican Republic and deforested Haiti. Thermodynamics on high-altitude display.

In the absence of any fuel supplies or subsidies, Haitians largely rely on charcoal to cook; and cook they must, because their staple grain is rice. Charcoal is produced by cutting woody material, even brush, and subjecting it to a flameless underground burn. The demand for charcoal, and the small amount of money available to charcoal producers—extremely poor, low-status, hardworking people called *chabonye*—has created a condition wherein the brush and trees are being cut at earlier and earlier stages, accelerating the desertification—or transformation to desert—of Haiti.

The relative affluence of Dominicans compared to Haitians has also created a situation in which Dominican sugar and tobacco growers employ Haitian laborers at rock-bottom wages and in slave-like conditions; and Dominicans have been socialized to dislike and disrespect Haitians almost as a lower life form. Ramification.

Higher rates of deforestation often correspond to lower "levels of development." We saw earlier in the book that this is a source of confusion, the belief that the more industrialized and "advanced" nations have superior environmental practices, when in fact they have simply displaced their

17. Guccione, "Life After Death," para. 9.

environmental loads to the margins. How long would it be, in the northern half of the United States, if fossil energy flows were stopped, before we cut the park trees for firewood before burning our own furniture?

In 86 BCE, Rome had a million inhabitants. By the fourth century CE, it had a million and a half. Wood was used for buildings, heating, cooking, baths, cement, plaster, glass, cart-making, and ship-building. Wood was depleted locally, then the harvesting activities spread, first to 100 kilometers, then 500, and the rivers were then put to use to float timbers from further afield. Harvests spread to Sicily, to the Apennines in the north, to Macedonia, to Asia Minor, to Egypt, to Gaul, to the Black Sea, and the Iberian Peninsula. Many of these areas remain deforested to this day. Rome was the *center*, and the exploitable, extractable *margins* radiated outward.[18]

A quarter of Brazil's Amazonian forests have been lost. In 1970, that number was one percent. Amazonia is now very close to a "point of no return" for ecosystem collapse. The acceleration of deforestation in Brazil's Amazonia has been caused in large part by timber for export, beef for export, soybeans for export, and sugar for ethanol to offset petroleum shortages.[19] China buys Brazilian timber to make products, using its own cheap labor, to sell in the United States, in order to accumulate US dollars. Brazil exports more beef on international markets than any country in the world.[20] McDonald's is one of the main beneficiaries of Brazilian soy, which is a Cargill feed[21] for the grow-fast-to-slaughter chickens used in its chicken nuggets.[22]

This is the reason we need *world* system analysis and the tracking of flows and nodes. When a tree falls in the forest, it is heard around the world. Deforestation is nearly always a product of *environmental load displacement*; and that means the benefit goes one place and the cost goes another. This is never an equal exchange. The average Brazilian earns about a quarter of what an average American does. More than 26 percent of Brazilians live on less than two dollars a day.[23]

18. Williams, "The Role of Deforestation."

19. Allen, "Deforestation's Challenge."

20. See the website of the Brazilian Beef Exporters Association: http://www.brazilianbeef.org.br/.

21. Cargill is a giant American agricultural corporation.

22. Vidal, "The 7000km Journey."

23. UNDP, *Human Development Report 2007/2008*, "Economic Statistics." http://www.nationmaster.com/country-info/stats/Economy/Poverty/Population-under-%242-a-day

War on Subsistence

Capitalism not only has frontiers; it is fundamentally defined by
frontier movement.

—Jason Moore[24]

In chapter 5 on technology, we pointed out how "development," which is
difference over space (Brazil in 2017; the United States in 2017) is spoken of
as a difference over time, or "in stages." We showed how this misrepresenta-
tion serves—like the recipe for "stone soup"—to fix our gaze on one point at
a time as a way of making us ignore contextual *relations*.

> The current fashion . . . is to dissolve any distinction between
> the modern and the premodern as a modern fabrication . . . The
> rather remarkable implication is that, in the course of the emer-
> gence of urban-industrial civilization, no significant changes
> have been taking place in terms of social relations, knowledge
> construction, or human-environmental relations. The closely
> knit kinship group, locally contextualized ecological knowledge,
> attachment to place, reciprocity, animism: all of them are sud-
> denly dismissed as myth. With the displacement of the old nar-
> rative, represented most forcefully by Karl Polanyi, emerges the
> new but implicit message that we have always been capitalists.[25]

The Polanyi who blew up this "implicit message" wrote a book called
The Great Transformation, the publication of which was eclipsed by the end
of World War II. The narrative of economics, and even the narrative of pop
culture, is that everyone has always been essentially the same; and that the
emergence of a market-dominated society was the result of removing the
dead weight of authority and superstition from the past. In fact, nothing
could be further from the truth, as Polanyi showed with his history of the
violent and intentional process over decades to impose the so-called "self-
regulating market" on the whole of society.

We have been covering two key Polanyian concepts in this book so
far: the *multiple forms of exchange* (reciprocity, redistribution, householding, etc.), and the phenomenon of *disembedding*, in Polanyi's case of people
being disembedded from non-market relationships like family, home town,
etc., and *re-embedded* in strictly market relationships. Polanyi was a Hungarian intellectual living in Germany, before Hitler's rise in 1933 convinced

---

24. Moore, *Capitalism and the Web of Life*, 115.
25. Hornborg, *Power of the Machine*, 235.

him to become a scholar in residence at Bennington College in Vermont. He later taught at Columbia University.

In *The Great Transformation*, he described the two-pronged process of *enclosure* and *regulation* that was employed by modern states to remove people from non-market driven communities and networks, especially those that gave people a degree of independence from the need for money to survive. People did not voluntarily leave their subsistence farms in the countryside to live in the city and work for wages in a factory. In fact, they fought that at every turn. They had to be legally and forcibly removed from the means of subsistence, especially land, in order to economically conscript them into emerging "labor markets."[26]

The "Inclosure Laws" of Great Britain were originally a system of combining many small farms under the control of many families into large holdings by one person (and evicting the rest) in order to support the wool export trade.[27] One main result of historic enclosure was forcing former inhabitants of the countryside into the city slums with a new dependency on wage labor to survive.[28]

The term "enclosure" is now used as a catch-all for any legal-policy or economic action that transfers small holdings and-or public commons into large private enterprises. Privatization is a form of enclosure. Intellectual property laws are forms of enclosure. Enclosure might be defined for our purposes as any law that privatizes commons, that which is free and open to the public. The result always increases dependency on money, market relations, and those who have the most money.[29]

Ecological feminists Maria Mies and Veronika Bennholdt-Thomsen called modern development, based on enclosure, "the war on subsistence."

> In the North and, since 1945, increasingly in the rest of the world, everything that is connected with the immediate creation and maintenance of life, and also everything that is not arranged through the production and consumption of commodities, has been devalued. This includes all activities whose object is self-provisioning, whether in the house, the garden, the workshop, on the land, or in the stable. What doesn't cost or doesn't produce money is worthless. This devaluation of self-provisioning work cannot be understood, if measured only quantitatively. It

26. Polanyi, *The Great Transformation*.

27. Shiva, "Sacred Cow or Sacred Car?" Sir Thomas More described Enclosure pithily: "Sheep eat men," he wrote. Vandana Shiva rounded up to the present: "Cars eat men."

28. Fairlie, "A Short History of Enclosure in Britain."

29. Ovetz, "Privatization."

indicates at the same time the degradation and contempt of the person who does this work . . . This barrier of disgust,[30] which today surrounds all unpaid, essential-for-life subsistence activities, has no relation to the content of this work. Such activities are suddenly recognized as decent professions, not only for women but also for men, if they are carried out by industrialized, waged labour . . . High esteem for wage labour obviously rests on the high evaluation of money and on its myth. Not the image of money as a simple medium of exchange or measure of value, but of the money that creates ever more money which then becomes the basis of life, security for life and the hope of32 progress, emancipation, culture, and the "good life" . . . *He/she who does not work for wages cannot live.*[31]

Enclosure of Language

Ivan Illich likewise identified "progress" or "development" as a systematic war on subsistence. Illich had a unique way of referring to subsistence activities. He called them "vernacular." With regard to language, the term *vernacular* means the way that ordinary people speak which may not conform to more formal grammatical rules. Illich described vernacular community and vernacular practices as those that were rooted in *householding* forms of economy, in friendships, and in the most common forms of local social reciprocity. The vernacular semiosphere corresponded to vernacular meanings corresponded to vernacular practices and relations, each mutually reinforcing.

What is interesting about Illich is that he again describes the loss of the vernacular to a process of "radical monopolization," or *enclosure*—cultural, political, and economic—through increasing *institutionalization*, as the hallmark of modernity; but he again traces its gestation and development back into his own church. Christianity in power, the church as an institution, practiced a form of *enclosure* of the church as a people of God. Moreover, he directly associates the imposition of "grammatical" language with the emergence of the imperial nation-state that has overseen a 500-year "war on subsistence." Imposed language and grammar was a form of *semiotic enclosure.*

30. Disgust is culturally constructed and serves to emotionally police social boundaries, those boundaries between what is considered clean and unclean. When I was an urban high school student in the sixties, one of the most common insults thrown at people who appeared unsophisticated was to be called "farmer."

31. Bennholdt-Thomsen and Mies, *Subsistence Perspective*, 17.

When the Western Roman Church was in power and faced with a unstable political ecology within which to exercise that power, the church began treating sin as a question of law. It was "criminalized," in Illich's words,
which gave the Church the juridical aspect of what would eventually come
to be that of the modern nation-state. It attempted, as we noted in the first
chapter, "to insure, to guarantee, to regulate Revelation," to enforce by law
the radical freedom that was gifted to humanity by the Incarnation. In other
words, it "institutionalized" grace, and thereby perverted it.[32]

By 1492, when Isabella of Castile had married Ferdinand II of Aragon
and consolidated their rule over Spain in a series of bloody wars and po-
groms, Isabella consented to financing an ill-conceived expedition by Cris-
tobal Colon (Christopher Columbus) to open a westward seaway to South
Asia. Colon, who had wildly overestimated the distance to the horizon used
this miscalculation to determine he would reach India in around 2,400
miles across the Atlantic Ocean. In the same year, she was approached by a
scholar named Elio Antonio de Nebrija who had composed a book of Span-
ish grammar, who suggested to her that the standardization of language
within her nation-state and throughout her future empire was as essential
as arms. He told her that "language is the consort of empire." Illich tells
these parallel stories, in spite of the fact that Isabella did not comprehend
what Nebrija was saying about language, just as Colon never realized that
Hispaniola, the island he first landed upon that eventually became Haiti and
the Dominican Republic, was not in India. Illich simply uses this story to
show two aspects of the modern empires, which would center on nation-
states, which indeed did come to work in tandem.

As Christendom gave way to secular modernity, the empires of Europe
did indeed require both arms and standardized language to establish their
power. Nebrija understood better than Isabella that the "loose and unruly"
vernacular speech of the heterogeneous peasantry made them more difficult
to rule and bend to the purposes of the state. The authoritarian church, who
had called itself the Mother of its members, lost ground to the state, and
the state adopted churchy terms to supplant the church. This was where
the term "mother tongue" originated, the nation-state as the new Mother,
and its language standardized to bleed off the subversive potential of vernacular tongues which contained within them vernacular ideas, values and
relations. Language was *enclosed*, and the first grammar books as well as
the first schools were designed to stamp out vernacular languages and with
them vernacular allegiances.[33]

32. Illich, *Rivers North of the Future*, 80–94.

33. Illich, "Vernacular Values." This *enclosure of language* may seem a digression

Encompassment

These changes corresponded in time and place to a changing political economy. Subsistence, and what Mies calls "the subsistence perspective," came to be an obstacle to expansion and commodification as well as a threat to the imperatives of nation-states that increasingly depended upon and became subordinate to those who had most successfully accumulated money. A community that produces all it needs for food, fuel, clothing, and shelter is not populated by people who willingly work in factories or take up arms for the state. Their environments provide them with most of what they need, abundantly in many cases.

Empires are comprised of consuming-parasitic centers and exploitable-host margins, margins that must expand as resources are exhausted. The need for more arms, more ships, etc., leads to the intensification of exploitation, the competitively driven search for greater production and velocity, and thereby for more of that essential disembedding and accelerating sign: money. The peasants must be removed from the land, the land converted to wealth accumulation, and the subsistence economies broken up to provide labor to the mills. And the language must be conformed to a way of thought that forecloses subversion. We will see in a later chapter how this war on subsistence was vastly accelerated around the world after World War II.

Dependency

We've circled around this; now let's lay it out. We are more engaged in subsistence living—understood in a good way—when production and consumption are *closer together in space*.

This is also and ultimately the only way we can dramatically reduce our utter dependency on general-purpose money, *by bringing production and consumption closer together in space*. Right now, my dependency and yours is based on the threefold reality that (1) all our goods and all our built environment are organized around the need for materials, land, labor, and energy that are often thousands of miles distant, requiring fossil energy for

---

in our study of money; but remembering for a moment that money is a semiotic phenomenon, as are languages, the abstraction of money corresponds to the abstraction of language because both are mutually reinforcing species of power. Language exerts a powerful effect on the "way we know." It is not surprising, then, that just as money has become completely self-referential (a sign without a referent), our public discourse, represented most clearly in the media but also in the academy, has also become increasingly self-referential.

extraction and transportation; (2) these goods and this built environment, including the technology, cannot extract these materials, land, labor, and energy from their original contexts without the solvent of general-purpose money; and (3) we ourselves, given the specialization of our built environment and our work, no longer have the capacity to survive without money. The simplest thought exercise here is to try and imagine surviving through today without it, through the week, through the month. What was done to those English peasants between the twelfth and twentieth centuries, which eventually wiped them out as a class that practiced *subsistence*, has been done to all of us. We have been *enclosed*.

Once you are in the position where you must have those dollars to live, you have become dependent upon those who have dollars to spare. Money, which serves them as an entitlement, now entitles them to your time, land, and sweat. This immediacy of need, the very fact that we can no longer survive without serving those with more money than we have, forces us into the manifold moral compromises that thoughtful people struggle with every day. I hate automobiles. They are destructive, dirty, dangerous, and expensive. As an American, living in the built environment that I do, I cannot at this point in time afford not to have an automobile. This dependency is what traps me in the many forms of complicity that whisper to me every day, "You are a hypocrite." We are captives to our domination over others, subjugated within the same structures. The power of Mammon *constructs* injustice; and the idolatry of Mammon maintains it.

These forms of dependency are *designed* as such, and not some socio-evolutionary accident. This precise system is maintained and protected by those in power, because they are fully aware that this is the architecture of their power. Dependency is nested, dependencies within dependencies within dependencies. Just as an unhappy wife might be trapped in marriage to an unsavory husband by her need for protection from other men or her inability to earn enough to survive, the unhappy worker in the miserable factory or stooped in a hundred degree field is trapped by dependency. The mid-level manager is trapped into being a prick to his subordinates—even when he hates it—by dependency. The postcolonial nation is trapped by the need to get dollars to pay international debts by dependency, and so on.

This is not saying each person is independent of every other person. We know this is not true. *Interdependency* is built into human nature. We are defined by that *vulnerability*. But we are not speaking of the covenantal relationships, the voluntary cooperation, the necessary divisions of labor arrived at under no duress and with the common good clearly in view.

Understand that the dominant class is dependent as well. We pointed out earlier that *the rich exist parasitically on the poor*, and the center nations exist parasitically on the marginal nations. A parasite *depends* on its host. The key thing to look for is not *interdependency*, but mutual dependency on an axis of *domination and subordination*.

Labor

In looking at nodes and flows, thus far we have set aside a key node of exchange: labor. We have spoken of labor, about how cheaper labor allows factory owners, for example, to increase the rate of profit. But we have not looked at the laborer in detail as a node of exchange.

When I worked as a stonemason's assistant once, the three of us on the team built patios, walls, stone fences, steps, bridges, artificial streams, and so forth. We would all drive out and meet at the job site, lunches packed, Thermoses filled with coffee, gallon jugs filled with water, dressed in clothes that had been abraded by stone, stained by soils, repeatedly washed, and peppered with frays and holes. The boss, Brook Burleson—who was also an artist, I have to add, and a very decent boss—drove in with his battered F-150 full of tools, and sometimes we had pre-positioned a big Deere backhoe on site if we were shifting stone that was too big to lift, roll, or lever. When I woke in the morning (I was in my fifties and a bit too old for the job, frankly), my hands would neither open nor close all the way, stiffened by the strain of gripping a strike hammer for hours. After four ibuprofen and a few minutes of hammering again, my hands would warm up and begin to flex. The sweat would begin to flow. We downed water, and carried stone, cut stone, placed stone, then downed more water. The stone arrived on pallets mostly, unless it was a very large or very special piece of stone, delivered by a wholesaler. We sharpened chisels on a grinder. We went through cheap gloves at a rate of a pair every three to four days. Stone is abrasive. We had sand brought in for footers, lumber and stakes for guides and forms, rebar, and sometimes concrete grout (Brook liked dry stack, but would mortar in a pinch).

As labor nodes, we were exchanging food, water, coffee, and gloves, but also as "production nodes," electricity, grinder-wheels, stone, sand, lumber, gasoline, backhoe parts, and so forth. Laborers are nodes for exchanged and transformed materials. The stone might come from Georgia or Vermont. The gasoline from Saudi Arabia or Texas. The coffee from Africa or Latin America. The food from California or even there in North Carolina (if it was pork—fed on grain grown in Kansas). The electricity came from uranium mined in New Mexico. The sand came from Virginia. The gloves were manufactured in China (of course). The lumber from Tennessee. Brook was neither a greedy man nor a big capitalist. He liked working stone. But his ability to make his owner's share, which was seldom more than around $20 an hour, was based on how much the client was willing to pay (which was based on how much other masons would accept for the same work, though Brook was admittedly in demand for his artistry), how much it cost him to pay Enrico and me, how quickly we worked, and how much those materials cost.

When this analysis is expanded globally, however, and does include the big capitalists—as a group that also runs things politically—then we can begin to see labor-generalized as a category-node, through which materials-generalized are a flow-category. For the big capitalists to accumulate, they need to pay labor as little as possible, as we have seen earlier; but they also need access to cheap non-labor inputs that add to the cost of production.[34] More than direct inputs, the cost of "social reproduction" of the labor force—its food and housing and clothing—depends on "cheap nature" inputs available from the larger economy.

Waste

General-purpose money has the ability to increase the velocity of exchange, and it can dissolve things into parts for use elsewhere; but it cannot make water or land or clean air. In fact, that monetary velocity and dissolution is fundamentally based on using up water and land and clean air. What is profitable is almost always wasteful. The greater the level of development, the greater the quanta of waste . . . even when that waste is transferred *out of sight and out of mind.*

Profit is wasteful during and after production. The difference in exchange that happens at the point of production and during sales of production is a protected category, measured abstractly in money alone, which externalizes (conceals) the very material dissipation, dissolution, destruction, and reduction of the natural tendencies toward variation, "stacking," and complexity. Order is reduced to disorder.

> Capitalism is not a system of efficiency, and can only be identi-
> fied as a system of profligacy and waste. Such wastefulness is,
> moreover, immanent to capital; it is bound up with the constitu-
> tion of capital itself, and not only its palpable consequences for
> the biosphere and for particular landscapes.[35]

34. Cunliffe, "British Imperialism and Tea Culture," ch. 1, para. 10. Sugar from the West Indies and tea from India fueled the English industrial revolution by providing cheap calories and stimulants to factory workers.
35. Moore, "The Rise and Fall of Cheap Nature."

9

Case Study: Finance, Food, Force & Foreign Policy

Where are the rulers of the nations,

and those who lorded it over the animals on earth;

those who made sport of the birds of the air,

and who hoarded up silver and gold

in which people trust,

and there is no end to getting;

those who schemed to get silver, and were anxious,

but there is no trace of their works?

They have vanished and gone down to Hades,

and others have arisen in their place.

—BARUCH 3:16–19

Churches . . . have their problems with a Jesus whose only economics are jokes. A savior undermines the foundations of any social doctrine of the Church. But that is what He does, whenever He is faced with money matters. According to Mark 12:13 there was a group of Herodians who wanted to catch Him in His own words. They ask "Must we pay tribute to Caesar?" You know His answer: "Give me a coin—tell me whose profile is on it!" Of course they answer "Caesar's."

The drachma is a weight of silver marked with Caesar's effigy.

A Roman coin was no impersonal silver dollar; there was none of that "trust in God" or adornment with a presidential portrait. A denarius was a piece of precious metal branded, as it were, like a heifer, with the sign of the personal owner. Not the

Treasury, but Caesar coins and owns the currency. Only if this characteristic of Roman currency is understood, one grasps the analogy between the answer to the devil who tempted Him with power and to the Herodians who tempt Him with money. His response is clear: abandon all that which has been branded by Caesar; but then, enjoy the knowledge that everything, *everything* else is God's, and therefore is to be used by you.

The message is so simple: Jesus jokes about Caesar. He shrugs off his control. And not only at that one instance . . . Remember the occasion at the Lake of Capharnaum, when Peter is asked to pay a twopenny tax. Jesus sends him to throw a line into the lake and pick the coin he needs from the mouth of the first fish that bites. Oriental stories up to the time of *Thousand Nights and One Night* are full of beggars who catch the fish that has swallowed a piece of gold. His gesture is that of a clown; it shows that this miracle is not meant to prove him omnipotent but indifferent to matters of money. Who wants power submits to the Devil and who wants denarri submits to the Caesar.[1]

THIS CASE STUDY WILL attempt to integrate the concepts we outlined in preceding chapters on nature, knowledge, exchange, technology, money, and development. We will also discuss the outlines of financial practice. The focus of the case study will be the foreign policy of the United States with regard to money/finance, food, military force, and energy. The hope is that we can show how an exchange detective can follow the flows, so to speak, as a way of penetrating beneath day-to-day mystifications of our environment, locally and globally, and bringing to light those aspects of the environment that are most often *out of sight and out of mind*.

It was during the 1970s and early 1980s, that global economic forces were shaping a new form of international economy and corresponding changes in United States foreign policy. In 1973, as a protest against the US rescue of Israel from an impending defeat by the Egyptians in the Yom Kippur War, Arab nations implemented an oil embargo against the US, creating day-long gas lines that broke up only when filling stations pumped out their last drop of gasoline.

Oil prices rose dramatically, creating a tremendous windfall profit for oil producing states. Oil was denominated in US dollars, and those

1. Illich, "The Educational Enterprise in the Light of the Gospel."

additional dollars were "recycled" through Wall Street (the world center of gravity for speculative finance), the only market large enough to absorb the mountains of money being accumulated by the same oil producers who were withholding gasoline from the US[2]

Wall Street does not sit on money. Wall Street firms are *rentier* capitalists, that is, they accumulate money through royalties like interest on loans or stock dividends or financial "derivatives"[3] instead of production; and so the glut of petrodollars from the Arab oil states was converted into vast "development" loans for poorer countries, especially in Latin America.[4] These loans, not unlike the financial derivatives stirred with subprime mortgages that would crash the economy in 2007, had *adjustable interest rates*. The people making the loans were allowed to raise the interest rates during the life of the loan. Latin American governments have taken huge loans for "development."

During Jimmy Carter's presidency, beginning in 1974, the United States suffered something the economists' faulty models could not anticipate: simultaneous lack of "growth"—*stagnation*—and rapid loss of purchasing-power-per-dollar—*inflation*, which came to be known as *stagflation*.[5]

2. Robinson, "The Rise of the Petrodollar System."

3. Derivatives are contractual bets taken on fluctuations in the market.

4. Oweiss, "Petrodollars: Problems and Prospects."

5. Amadeo, "What Caused Stagflation?" The reason economic models could neither predict nor account for stagflation is because *the models are wrong*. The fact that they could do neither is exactly what proved them wrong. Those same models are still being used today even by the US Federal Reserve, in spite of the fact that in the wake of the 2007 meltdown, this model continues to fail.

The United States' Central Bank is the Federal Reserve. It is run by bankers, with a chief appointed by the state. In recent decades, the "Fed," as it is called, has tweaked the US economy by using the Federal funds interest rate as a tool to *create unemployment*. Bankers dislike inflation—X amount of money losing its relative purchasing power—because banks and other lenders thrive on debt repayment, which drawn out over time means that each passing day reduces the purchasing power of the money owed them. They have long enshrined their class-warfare from above in this economic pseudo-science, which leads them to conclude that inflation is caused principally by workers receiving too much money, which is a double-problem.

First, it means workers have more to spend, which they believe stimulates sellers to charge more for goods, which leads to inflation. Second, and perhaps more importantly from a class standpoint, when workers are fully employed and there are more jobs than people to fill them, the workers are in a stronger *economic* position vis-à-vis employers. Employers have to compete, via higher wages, to convince workers to choose them. This translates into greater *social* and *political* power for the working class vis-a-vis the employing class. When money is more available (via lower interest rates), more people build more businesses—so the *economic* logic goes—and therefore create more jobs, which expands profits overall, but also sets up that seller's market for workers. More jobs for the same number of people. So when the economy becomes "overheated," that

Federal Reserve Chair Paul Volcker responded to this with something called the "Volcker Shock," that is, since inflation was the greater danger to the rentier capitalists, he raised the interest rate from 7.5 percent to 21.5 percent, doubling US unemployment rates, while making large creditors whole.[6] These elevated interest rates were passed along, via Wall Street

is econo-speak for inflationary, the Fed raises interest rates, cutting off the creation of new jobs until unemployment reaches a certain threshold that transforms the worker-friendly market into an employer-friendly market again.

This "logic" has dictated that the Fed raise interest rates until unemployment is acceptably high, then droop the rates if unemployment threatens to slow profitability when unemployed people begin to hoard their money in order to pay for things like food, running water, and electricity. Balance between *inflation* on the one hand and *stagnation* on the other, which are seen as antithetical—one can only exist apart from the other.

This idea is still the "economic wisdom," even though this "logic" has serially failed, sometimes producing the unthinkable *stagflation*, combined inflation and stagnation, which has not disabused economists of their "theory" even after proving them wrong. In the last instance of failed economic "theory," after 2007, it has failed so spectacularly that the Fed has been forced to leave interest rates below one percent for the last ten years. Given that the Fed, in this regard at least, is a one-trick pony, one might say we are stuck in a chronic crisis. What they know how to do does not work.

Behind this superficial account of the Fed, however, there are a number of historical and economic complexities, not the least of which has been late capitalism's transfer of political power from industrial to financial capital. Industrial capital cobbles together some money, buys its infrastructure, hires workers, and makes widgets or bricks or computers or whatever. Then it sells its stuff at a profit, pays off its loans, and lives happily ever after (until the market is saturated, or a new widget comes along, or raw materials run out, and it's over). Financial capital does not accumulate money from making anything. It accumulates money as royalties—rents and interest and so forth. Financial capital loans money to industrial capital, but it also engages in all kinds of financial gambling, some riskier than others. The stock market, derivatives markets, etc., are casinos. This can create dramatic instability, as we learned from the Great Depression, whereupon the state implemented a policy of financial-pole repression, beginning with the enforced separation of savings and loan institutions from speculative financial enterprises. That wall between the two poles of capital was eventually eroded, and Bill Clinton drove the last nail in its coffin with the repeal of the Glass-Steagall Act during his administration. By then, the finance capitalists, headquartered at Wall Street, had pretty much taken over the government and the global economy, which they repeatedly crashed through financial bubbles without any consequences. In fact, they had become "too big to fail," and taxpayers bailed them out. The last crash was 2007–8, which is ongoing, and the much-hyped Obama slow-recovery—during which the interest rate remained near zero—was accomplished using a scheme called *quantitative easing*. This has served only to reflate the bubble that popped ten years ago, ensuring that the next crash will be a whopper. Economic historians, honest ones at least, like Peter Gowan or Michael Hudson or Susan Strange, will tell you that the US and global economy has blundered from one crisis to the next ever since the tail end of the US invasion and occupation of Vietnam.

6. Silber, "How Volker Launched His Attack."

institutions using those arbitrarily *adjustable* interest rates, to the Latin American countries that had received the aforementioned development loans—the *center* exporting its crisis to the *margin*—creating a crisis in Latin America. This Volcker shock doctrine lasted from 1979 to 1982.

When President Ronald Reagan was in office in 1982, Mexico announced that it was going to default on its Wall Street loans—that is, refuse to pay what was unpayable—stranding Wall Street with more than $100 billion in losses.[7] This was seen by Washington—joined at the hip with Wall Street—as a profound crisis. Not for the first time, and certainly not for the last, the US government stepped in to bail out Wall Street's finance capitalists. This was technically a bailout loan to Mexico, but the urgent intent was to ensure that Wall Street didn't take a bath on the Mexican default. The vehicle for loans to cover the previous loans to Mexico was the International Monetary Fund (IMF), an international institution formed in the latter years of World War II, in which the US exercises a very dominant role. But this time, the bailout loans had something attached to them in addition to interest, called "conditionalities."[8]

These conditions were actually ultimatums—"do this or else"—that (1) Mexico's internal markets be opened to US-based investors, including US multinational corporations, (2) that labor and environmental standards be rolled back to increase the rate of profit in order to pay back the restructured loans, and (3) that regressive tax structures be implemented that shifted the burden toward the bottom in Mexico . . . all to assist in the payback of the loans. A *structural* imperative, though not one of the specified conditions, was also that Mexican enterprises—in particular, Mexico's agriculture—be converted from production for local consumption to export products to get more of the US dollars required to service the restructured but now vastly expanded external debt.[9] Dollars were the world's dominating currency,

7. International Monetary Fund, "Tequila Hangover," 455–96.

8. Ruggiero, "Latin American Debt Crisis." The debt crisis was global, including Eastern Europe, but the size of Mexico's debt was the existential threat to Wall Street.

9. Liu, "Dollar Hegemony." This arrangement was named "dollar hegemony" by Chinese economist Henry C.K. Liu. "World trade is now a game in which the US produces dollars and the rest of the world produces things that dollars can buy. The world's interlinked economies no longer trade to capture a comparative advantage; they compete in exports *to capture needed dollars to service dollar-denominated foreign debts* and to accumulate dollar reserves to sustain the exchange value of their domestic currencies. To prevent speculative and manipulative attacks on their currencies, the world's central banks must acquire and hold dollar reserves in corresponding amounts to their currencies in circulation. The higher the market pressure to devalue a particular currency, the more dollar reserves its central bank must hold. This creates a built-in support for a strong dollar that in turn forces the world's central banks to acquire and hold more dollar reserves, making it stronger. This phenomenon is known

a general-purpose money like no other in history, now exchangeable for goods anywhere in the world, and required for the international payment of debts and for petroleum. Mexico's business class, through debt, was being *enclosed*, and in turn, they *enclosed* Mexico's peasantry to convert small holdings into monoculture export crops.[10]

Using similar crises, the IMF proceeded over the next few years to impose these "conditionalities"—called *structural adjustment programs*, or SAPs—on the majority of nations of the global margins, effectively undermining their national sovereignty inasmuch as the IMF, the World Bank, and the World Trade Organization, all US-dominated pre-market institutions that manage the so-called "free" market, came to dictate the economic policies of these structurally-adjusted nations.[11]

While these were originally emergency measures used to take advantage of Mexico's crisis, the Reagan administration soon realized that they had stumbled onto a model that could be employed around the world to open previously protected home markets to US investment under conditions that were very advantageous to US investors. Moreover, it was a way to capture the political leadership of debtor nations in a dollar-dominated system, which would come to be known as *neoliberalism*,[12] which is ideo-

as dollar hegemony, which is created by the geopolitically constructed peculiarity that critical commodities, most notably oil, are denominated in dollars. Everyone accepts dollars because dollars can buy oil. The recycling of petro-dollars is the price the US has extracted from oil-producing countries for US tolerance of the oil-exporting cartel since 1973."

10. Santa-Cruz, *Mexico-United State Relations*, 45–48.

11. Shah, "Structural Adjustment—a Major Cause of Poverty."

12. Harvey, *Brief History of Neoliberalism*, 2. Associated with the economic policies shared by Ronald Reagan (US), Margaret Thatcher (UK), Augusto Pinochet (Chile), and Deng Xiaoping (China), neoliberalism is described by David Harvey thus: "Neoliberalism is in the first instance a theory of political economic practices that proposes that human well-being can best be advanced by liberating individual entrepreneurial freedoms and skills within an institutional framework characterized by strong private property rights, free markets, and free trade. The role of the state is to create and preserve an institutional framework appropriate to such practices. The state has to guarantee, for example, the quality and integrity of money. It must also set up those military, defence, police, and legal structures and functions required to secure private property rights and to guarantee, by force if need be, the proper functioning of markets. Furthermore, if markets do not exist (in areas such as land, water, education, health care, social security, or environmental pollution) then they must be created, by state action if necessary. But beyond these tasks the state should not venture. State interventions in markets (once created) must be kept to a bare minimum because, according to the theory, the state cannot possibly possess enough information to second-guess market signals (prices) and because powerful interest groups will inevitably distort and bias state interventions (particularly in democracies) for their own benefit." This is actually the "globalization" (expansion on a global scale) of what we described in chapter 7

logically insupportable if and when there is official acknowledgment of *unequal exchange.*

This is a flyover at several thousand feet, and we are necessarily overlooking many of the details of this process, but we need to establish a kind of historical context wherein *neoliberalism* can be understood. Once we understand neoliberalism's outlines, we can begin to analyze a great deal about US foreign policy, which has been largely formed by the imperatives of neoliberal policy since the 1980s.

Genealogy

Neoliberalism itself—the world financial power structure in place as this is written, one that maintains American power—is now in a fresh crisis, because the same financial establishment that was turned loose on the world by the emergence of neoliberalism has both worn out its welcome around the world—creating great popular resistance to its demands—and creating tens of trillions of dollars of fictional value from runaway speculation in a series of so-called financial "bubbles." By fictional value, we mean money that is not matched in value by actual commodities within the market.[13] Money then becomes not just that destructive "sign without a referent" that dissolves ecosystems and communities; it becomes an entitlement that obeys what my friend Dennis O'Neil calls "the cartoon law of gravity": like Wiley Coyote, it is running along, shoots over the cliff, then suddenly realizes there is no ground underfoot, whereupon is drops disastrously.

The US-dominated financial system, called the "Dollar-Wall Street regime" by Peter Gowan and Susan Strange,[14] also found a way to exercise

---

on "Money": "A capitalist state has seven key economic responsibilities to guarantee accumulation for the business class: (1) to ensure enough workers for production at rates that allow for profit; (2) to ensure banks to provide finance capital for loans; (3) to ensure the externalization of costs adequate to protect overall profits, including publicly-financed infrastructure; (4) to ensure markets sufficient to absorb production; (5) to ensure expansion sufficient to compensate for saturated or lost markets, whether by financial or military means, or by opening new areas for commodification; (6) to ensure enough general stability for business to flourish without major interruptions, and (7) to ensure an adequate supply of resources."

13. When the mania that inflates these bubbles disappears and reality sets in, these "bubbles" "pop." People who had a million dollars yesterday in so-called financial assets find themselves holding worthless paper, or worthless shares on a computer today. The problem is that with the wall torn down between savings and speculation, the banks where average people have their savings have had those savings gambled on these potentially worthless assets.

14. Gowan, "Ways of the World."

managerial control over first world economies like Western Europe and emerging market economies like China and Brazil. This power was exercised not in the US role as *creditor*, but paradoxically in the US role as *debtor*, which requires a bit of an explanation.

This story actually begins at the end of World War II and continues to the present. The Soviet Union—itself savagely wounded by the war—attempted to secure a post-war partnership with its capitalist war allies in order to regroup.[15] More than 27 million Soviet citizens had been killed, and cities as well as farms were in ruins all the way to Stalingrad. Tensions and mutual suspicion, as well as a struggle between the US and the USSR over the governance of postwar Europe led to hostility.[16] The Truman administration opted for the National Security State as an industrial strategy that could capitalize on the ramp-up for the war, and it needed an enemy to justify the expenditures of what Eisenhower would later call the "military-industrial complex." The overtures from the USSR for a post-war peace were rejected in favor of official hostility by Truman. This provocative posture locked Western Europe into a military alliance with the US, called the North Atlantic Treaty Organization (NATO), and put an official stamp on the US foreign policy of Soviet "containment."[17]

This inaugurated a long period of proxy wars, the first in Korea, later in Vietnam. The US was enjoying the fruits of post-war dollar dominance, Keynesian high employment,[18] and a robust trade surplus. But the militari-

15. Moore, "The Capitalocene, Part II." "It is difficult for me to read the Soviet project as a fundamental rupture. The great industrialization drive of the 1930s relied—massively—on the importation of fixed capital, which by 1931 constituted 90 percent of Soviet imports. The Soviets were so desperate to obtain hard currency that 'the state was prepared to export anything and everything, from gold, oil and furs to the pictures in the Hermitage Museum'. If the Soviet project resembles other modes of production, it is surely the tributary, not socialist, mode of production, through which the state directly extracts the surplus. Nor did the Soviets turn inward after 1945. Soviet trade with OECD countries (in constant dollars) increased 8.9 percent annually between 1950 and 1970, rising to 17.9 percent a year in the following decade—a trend accompanied by sharply deteriorating terms of trade and rising debt across the Soviet-led zone. Need we recall that the 1980s debt crisis was detonated not by Mexico but by Poland in 1981."

16. Zickel, *Soviet Union: A Case Study*.

17. University of Virginia—Miller Center, "The President and the National Security State."

18. Economist John Maynard Keynes, seen as the architect of FDR's "New Deal" economics, promoted near full employment, with government assistance in job creation, to ensure adequate demand for products.

zation of US domestic and foreign policy simultaneously created a mounting national debt. The United States was indebting itself to other "developed" nations, borrowing money from Europeans to finance its military adventures in Asia, then printing extra money at home to make up the difference. Because the dollar's value was fixed for redemption at 1/35th of an ounce of gold, the US could print money without fear of draining the dollar of its value, which was then being used for investment in Europe.[19]

In the classical theoretical market, the value of a currency is determined by how it balances against a total aggregate of commodities. Too few units of currency and prices fall. Too many units of currency and prices rise. The latter is inflation—the enemy of loan sharks and bankers because it reduces the future purchasing power of collected principle and interest. So the dollar was losing purchasing power *on the market*, because it was being printed faster than actual commodities were being made, even as it remained exchangeable for European currencies at the same fixed rate. If you held Deutschmarks, for example, and the DM traded at four to one with a dollar—4 DM=$1—and the purchasing power of one dollar would buy four widgets on Monday but only three on Tuesday, then everyone in Germany being paid one dollar on Monday was losing a widget-worth of buying power during the exchange on Tuesday. But they had to accept this exchange as if it still bought four widgets whether they liked it or not.

The United States was printing more money, the dollar still fixed to gold, and the Europeans were watching their markets flooded with *overvalued* dollars, which they were then forced to accept. The market may have been saying that a dollar should be redeemable for francs or marks or pounds at one rate, but the post-war currency-control regime determined that Europeans had to continue to give away purchasing power with every currency exchange for devalued dollars. The US was *exporting its inflation* to Europe by repaying its military expansion debts to European lenders in dollars that exchanged the *same* while buying *less*.

When the first Special Forces advisors went to Vietnam in 1957, the system that appeared so robust on the surface was already creating the conditions for its next crisis. The Europeans, buying gold elsewhere at well above the $35 per Troy ounce, held onto their dollar denominated assets, hoping to redeem their dollars at something approaching their initial investment later. But by 1967, with the Vietnam War driving the US deficit to record levels, France realized this was a bad gamble and started cashing US dollars in for US gold, draining off the US gold stocks. France had called the US bluff. The Keynesian system of tightly controlling *rentier* capitalists,

---

19. Hudson, *Super Imperialism*, 141–54.

which included fixed currency exchange rates pegged to a gold-backed dollar, began to collapse in the face of the US decision to expensively militarize
its domestic and foreign policy.

On March 31, 1968, millions of Americans heard Lyndon Johnson an-
nounce on television that he would not run again for the presidency, and
that he would not substantially escalate the Vietnam War after the strategic
setback of the Tet offensive nearly two months earlier. Unperceived by the
public at large, the point finally had been reached at which depletion of
the US gold holdings had abruptly altered the country's military policy. As
financial historian Michael Hudson noted, "The European financiers were
forcing peace on us. For the first time in American history, our European
creditors had forced the resignation of an American president."[20]

When the 1968 elections arrived, we saw a scenario that is familiar to
us today. Democrats could not publicly argue for an end to the war, because
withdrawal would mark the destruction of the myth of US military invincibility. The options available in response to the collapse of the US Gold Pool
were (1) withdrawal from Vietnam, (2) continue the war and accept further
losses of gold and with it the erosion of US global power, or (3) force the
abandonment of the entire Bretton Woods regime[21]—the post-World War
II international financial regime—beginning with the gold standard. Because the Democrats had alienated a huge fraction of their base by refusing
to *oppose* the war, Republican Richard Nixon was elected. In 1971, Nixon
selected Option 3. He abandoned the gold standard for the US dollar. *Now
the dollar was truly a fiat currency, truly a sign without a referent.*[22] This was
a staggering checkmate against the US's alleged global allies. They then had
to do something with their trainloads of dollars (and dollars owed to them
by the US) to prevent the dollar's uncontrolled devaluation.

Quoting Hudson:

> By going off the gold standard at the precise moment that it did,
> the United States obliged the world's central banks to finance the
> US balance-of-payments deficit by using their surplus dollars to

20. Ibid., 248–61.

21. "Bretton Woods Agreement," http://www.investopedia.com/terms/b/bretton
woodsagreement.asp. "The Bretton Woods Agreement is the landmark system for
monetary and exchange rate management established in 1944. It was developed at
the United Nations Monetary and Financial Conference held in Bretton Woods, New
Hampshire, from July 1 to July 22, 1944. Under the agreement, currencies were pegged
to the price of gold, and the US dollar was seen as a reserve currency linked to the price
of gold."

22. Hudson, *Super Imperialism*, 263–76.

buy US Treasury bonds [loans to the US Government], whose volume quickly exceeded America's ability or intention to pay.

Twenty-five years [after WWII], the United States [discovered] the inherent advantage of being a world debtor. Foreign holders of any nation's promissory notes are obliged to become a market for its exports as the means of obtaining satisfaction of their debts.[23]

As the old saying goes, "if you owe the bank a thousand dollars, you have a problem. If you owe the bank a million dollars, the bank has a problem."

Nixon had not only erased volumes of US debt held by allies and forced perpetual European support for US military expenditures with the threat of tearing everyone's financial house down, he had opened the door for *rentier* capitalists to escape the limitations put on them during the New Deal. That is precisely why Peter Gowan referred to Nixon's risky destruction of the Bretton Woods' gold standard and subsequent abandonment of fixed currency exchange rates as the "global gamble."[24]

Hot Money

Susan Strange referred to the new way as "casino capitalism."[25] The *rentier* capitalists were free to gamble without constraints; but more importantly, the US government, in collusion with Wall Street, had inadvertently discovered a new weapon to use against recalcitrant "allies."

We need to divert here for a moment to take up a new term: "hot money."

We've already shown that fiat money has no referent, and that this increases the reach and velocity of exchange. Karl Polanyi warned that money was a dangerous thing to turn into a commodity itself,[26] but with multiple currencies, and the ability of people to accumulate money by gambling on shifting exchange rates, money itself *is* bought and sold on global markets.[27] When I was in El Salvador in 1985, even though the offi-

23. Ibid., 240.

24. Gowan, "Ways of the World." Nixon dropped the fixed exchange rates less than two years after abandoning the gold standard.

25. Strange, "What Theory?"

26. One of the main conclusions of Polanyi's book, *The Great Transformation,* was that market centrality in the economy will aim at a totalizing process of commodification.

27. This is called "currency speculation," the source of George Soros's spectacular wealth.

cial exchange rate was four *colones* to one dollar, the demand for dollars by
people involved in international trade—legal and illegal—was so great that
one could sell dollars for *colones* on the street through a mafiosi-network
of street-corner money-changers for 8-10 *colones* per dollar. Who is going
to exchange them at the bank for four to one? People do the same thing
on world markets. They look at whole national currencies, at whether they
expect them to go up or down against dollars, and they buy or sell accord-
ingly. Speculators can also buy national bonds and other variable-interest
instruments in order to cash out during the rise and fall of that asset's value.
With derivatives, you can even bet on whether these assets will rise or fall.
This money that chases across the globe looking for a good bet and a fast
return is called "hot money."[28]

We've covered fairly thoroughly how general-purpose money acts as
an exchange-accelerator and an ecological solvent. Illich pointed out how
Jesus suggests that if you worship money, you worship power. Now we need
to understand how general-purpose money operates in enormous concen-
trations in the citadels of power, in a world where money-dependency has
captured most of the population, through a successful war against subsistence . . . through global *enclosure*.[29]

The division of *money-as-a-use-value*, that is, money to accumulate
more money, *investment*, can be understood as two poles, like the North
Pole and the South Pole, between which everything else happens. At one
investment pole, you want to accumulate money by making things to sell.
Let's say you buy a cookie factory. You borrow your investment money,
pay for the physical plant and your initial supplies, and you hire some
workers. You expect, based on your business projections, that in five years,
you will have paid off your loans on a schedule that keeps your enterprise
afloat in the meantime with a little for yourself along the way. The bank
gets its principle with interest (the *rentier*'s royalty). The cookie factory is

---

28. Pettinger, "Hot Money Flows."

29. Araghi and Karides, "Land Dispossession and Global Crisis," para. 2. Araghi
and Karides describe modern enclosure with five characteristics: "(1) the transformation of a complex system of customary rights to land usage to legal and written titles
to land ownership, (2) the transformation of the concept of property from jurisdic-
tion over ambiguously defined areas to concretely defined (and enclosed) physical
spaces, (3) the rationalization of the use of such demarcated landed property as a form
of capital and at the service of 'primitive' and expanded capital accumulation, (4) the
increasing privatization of the earth's surface through dispossession and displacement
of peasants and Indigenous populations, and (5) **destruction of nonmarket access to
food and self-sustenance** and creation of a (mobile) global working class that is massively concentrated at the urban centers of the world economy (and often living a life
under a regime of 'forced underconsumption')."

the productive pole of investment. The other pole is when you are a day trader. You go in each day and buy shares of this or that, which has value that may fluctuate, and your idea is to buy one hundred shares of XYZ at a dollar apiece, in the belief that this enterprise will gain value. The next day, your XYZ shares are trading at $1.50 each, and you sell, making fifty dollars. This is gambling, in a real sense, but economists like to soften the edges with the term "speculation." This is the speculative pole of capital. These two poles—productive and speculative—can work together, because the financial/speculative pole often bets on stocks and so forth that are invested in some productive activity.

What we discovered during the Great Depression (1929–39)[30] is that people like to gamble more than they like to work, something every casino owner already knows; and when you let the "cool money" of enterprise investment mix too freely with the "hot money" of speculation, the hot money takes over. Money is not infinite, and when everyone seems to be accumulating quickly, there is an incentive to get into the market "while it's hot" to accumulate while you can, "while the gettin's good."[31] The speculative pole siphons off investment in the productive pole and comes to dominate the market, because more and more people with power and money are part of the speculative pole. A kind of herd mentality takes over. Speculative markets in particular are psychological markets that can do things utterly at odds with the material reality around them. This is what fueled the Tulip craze in seventeenth-century Holland, where the public value of tulips and tulip bulbs were caught in a competitive price tsunami that led to one type of tulip—arguably one of the easiest to grow—being sold for the price of four oxen. Later economists would use a metaphor for these sudden and inexplicable flows of hot money into a fictional space of overvaluation—bubbles.[32]

30. The longest and harshest economic downturn in US history—one that dragged down a good part of the rest of the world. Rampant speculation led to a massive stock bubble that burst in October 1929, causing half of all US banks to fail, wiping out the life savings of millions, creating mass unemployment as people quit spending, and vaulting Franklin Roosevelt into the White House. The Roosevelt Administration's policies included a legal firewall between speculation and savings institutions called the Glass-Steagall Act.

31. At the beginning of 2007, flipping houses had become all the rage, as housing prices were bid up daily in an "overheated" real estate market. By the end of the year, the bubble burst, and many were stranded with debts that exceeded the actual value of their real estate.

32. Mitchell, "Financial Speculation." Mitchell: "When [investment] becomes bad—when it becomes speculation—is when ever-increasing sums of money are invested in derivative products promising substantial returns *that are not supported by the actual underlying earnings*. At this point, money that could be invested in the productive economy is diverted to the purely derivative economy—the speculation economy—where it continues to recirculate until the inevitable crash" (italics added).

Financial speculation bubbles keep growing as long as everyone is willing to pretend that this fictional value is real, until a few people stop and say, "Hey, this can't last forever, so I'm selling this shit while I can." This becomes a kind of psychological contagion, or that "cartoon law of gravity." Everyone starts selling, the value of the tulips or stocks or bundled financial packages plummets, and before everyone can get out the doors with their parachutes, it spirals down out of any control and mushrooms into flame and smoke against the unforgiving ground of reality.

The New Deal's Glass-Steagall Act prohibited savings and loan institutions from working under the same roof with speculators, because during the Great Depression, this speculative crash wiped out the banks and with it most peoples' life savings. During the Clinton administration, this Act was repealed, and we have had serial bubble crises since.[33] Hot money from Wall Street is now running the government.[34]

With that short overview, let's return to our narrative during the Nixon administration.

New Regime: Debtor Imperialism

Long story short, the US dollar was the dominant currency, and if you were a nation other than the United States, you needed to protect your own currency from fluctuations and even speculative attacks. This new reality obliged central banks abroad to hold US dollars—in the form of US Treasury Bonds—in reserve, as a defense against problems with their own currencies.[35] These nations then became US creditors—the US owed them money. Treasury Bonds are IOUs from the US Treasury Department saying you have loaned money to the United States. But these new creditors were then the banks who—as in the banker joke—had the problem. Every holder to this day of US Treasury Bonds knows that the total debt owed by the United States is *categorically unpayable*. So to this day, no one—including China, about which there is a great deal of financial fear-mongering—can afford to begin selling off dollars and risk crashing the dollar's purchasing power, nor can they demand their money back at once. Too many nations hold too many dollars to "sell the dollar down" without cutting off their noses to spite their faces.[36] The US has neither the capacity nor the intention

33. Kelleher, "The Lessons of Repealing Glass-Steagal."
34. Taibbi, "A Rare Look."
35. Hudson, "New Financial World Order."
36. Long, "Who Owns America's Debt?"

of paying back those loans. The naked emperor is "wearing your clothes," and you damned well better act like it.

China holds over a trillion dollars in US Treasury Bonds. Japan holds $1.1 trillion. Ireland holds $275 billion. Brazil holds more than $258 billion.[37] The list goes on. If China were to initiate—as some China-phobes suggest—a cash-out of its Treasury Bills, and that cash-out caused a run on the dollar destroying half its value, China would lose half a trillion dollars in purchasing power. This is a game of chicken that the US has, so far, won every time.

The key to dominance in the world of the late twentieth and early twenty-first centuries has been *dependency*, again, and interdependency, but of a very unequal nature. There is that bad marriage. The husband depends on his wife for the management of the household, for a lot of unpaid labor, and for the care of children, and the wife depends on the husband for economic security; but in the event of a divorce, we find that the wife comes out much worse than the husband, giving the husband a threat to hold over the head of the wife. They depend on one another, but that interdependence is not synonymous with equal status or parity of power. It is *mutual dependency on an axis of domination and subordination.*

This is how US foreign policy is constructed for the most part, as interdependencies in which the US is always the dominant partner. And there are few things that human beings depend on more urgently than food; which brings us to a subject that is mixed up with finance, but not the same as finance.

Reorganizing Nature

Wall Street is a way of organizing nature.

—Jason W. Moore[38]

Money is not theoretically necessary for life. Human life sustained itself before general-purpose money. Human life cannot be sustained, however, without food. We will take a bit of time here to go into the topic of food, and therefore into chemistry and biology.

One of the chemical components of our world that is necessary for most plant growth, therefore necessary for food, and therefore necessary for our survival, is *nitrogen*. Oddly enough, after Timothy McVeigh blew up a federal office building in Oklahoma City, everyone—even

37. US Department of Treasury.
38. Moore, "Wall Street."

non-farmers—came to know that fertilizer is made with nitrogen.[39] Yet
nitrogen is the most abundant element in the atmosphere, so why should
anyone have to "produce" it industrially as a fertilizer? We live our entire
lives literally swimming in the stuff.

As it turns out, atmospheric nitrogen, like atmospheric oxygen, is a
conjoined twin. It consists of two, attached molecules: N^2, as it were. Plants
have to break this down into single molecules, then mix it with other stuff
in order to turn sunlight into food. The process is called biological nitrogen
fixation.[40] Prior to human intervention, this fixation process was accomplished by prokaryotes (or non-nucleated bacteria) and diazotrophs (or
ammonia-making bacteria).

World War I saw the widespread introduction of a new technology:
the machine gun. The adherence to pre–machine gun tactical doctrines
led to huge armies being mowed down like grass, then trapped facing
each other from pestilential trenches. One of the bright ideas for taking
advantage of this horror-film stalemate was the idea of killing the enemy
with poisonous gas.

During the war, Fritz Haber, a German-Jewish chemist, was appointed
director of the Berlin-based Kaiser Wilhelm Institute for Physical Chemistry. One of his jobs became the development of chemical weapons. He
would eventually invent a chemical called Zyklon B, a cyanide derivative,
which would later be used to help exterminate millions of his fellow Jews;
but during WWI he was preoccupied with chlorine and ammonia for the
development of poisonous gases for the battlefield.[41] His other preoccupation was artificial nitrogen fixation. He learned how to do that by combining hydrogen and N^2 under *heat and pressure*, using an iron isotope and
aluminum oxide as catalysts. He had already patented this process before
the war; but it would take Carl Bosch, the eventual cofounder of I. G. Farben
(the company that manufactured Zyklon B) to commercialize the process,[42]
which would eventually establish the basis for the population explosion
from 1.6 billion in 1900 to more than 7 billion today. What he had made was
chemical fertilizer, and it meant that even exhausted land might continue
to be "productive."[43] The food that feeds that additional 5 billion people is

39. Linder, "Oklahoma City Bombing (1997)."

40. Wagner, "Biological Nitrogen Fixation."

41. Bowlby, "Fritz Haber."

42. *Encyclopaedia Britannica*, "Haber-Bosch Process," https://www.britannica.
com/technology/Haber-Bosch-process.

43. This can be accomplished without chemicals using biodynamic methods, but
that is not our topic here.

largely produced with the assistance of chemical fertilizers and chemical poisons also used in warfare.

"Heat and pressure" to split nitrogen are not some seemingly infinite essence like space, nor are they immediately available like atmospheric nitrogen. They are transient phenomena that must be concentrated through some *procedure*. Haber was looking at a crisis created by the depletion of guano—bat and bird droppings used as fertilizer—mostly collected from the islands off the coast of Chile;[44] so he fell on a scheme that depended on another exhaustible resource, but one in greater abundance than the remaining guano: fossil fuel. This worked like a charm.

By post-WWII, American farmers were using prodigious quantities of chemical fertilizer across prodigious expanses of arable land, along with nerve gas, or *organophosphates*, as insecticides, expanding their harvests far beyond the American public's capacity to consume.[45]

The American manufacturing base had also expanded during the war, and given that the United States did not suffer the devastation that Europe and Asia did during the war, the US emerged from the war as a uniquely powerful actor. The other variable in the expansion of food production was the thoroughgoing *mechanization* of agriculture,[46] another net consumer of fossil energy. The United States began to build farm machinery; and as part of its goal of maximizing profit for farm machinery industries, as well as agricultural chemicals, it began to promote something called "developmentalism" for the so-called underdeveloped nations, which we described in chapter 6.

In 1943, the Rockefeller Foundation, Ford Motor Company, and the Mexican government established a joint venture called—in English—the *International Center to Improve Corn and Wheat*. Standard Oil—a Rockefeller company—was manufacturing fertilizer, and Ford was building tractors.[47] This was the beginning of the organized effort by first world corporations, with the active support of the US government, to push agricultural commodities into these so-called "underdeveloped" nations as part of their *war on subsistence*. By 1959, they had opened rural development academies in Pakistan, and by 1963 in the Philippines. These academies were performing research and development on high-yielding cultivars of wheat, corn, and rice. By the time of the Nixon administration, 120 of the largest agribusiness multinationals had established a joint program with the United Nations

44. Leonard, "Guano Imperialists."

45. Biddle, "Nerve Gases and Pesticides."

46. Machines that were, and are, themselves dissipative structures.

47. Foster, *Vulnerable Planet*, 93–94.

Food and Agriculture Organization (UNFAO).[48] The transformation in agriculture that followed was called the *Green Revolution*, a term coined in 1968 by US Agency for International Development Director William Gaud.

If ever there were a "revolution from above," this was it. And it did accomplish a great deal. Caloric intake from cereal grains worldwide increased 30 percent per capita by 1990, and the prices of grains fell. The availability of more staple grains also supported a doubling of world population between 1960 and 2000.[49]

Yet these very general statistics do not tell the whole story. Jason Moore gives us some context with his aforementioned description of those four "strategic commodities" necessary to keep all capitalist regimes afloat, the "Four Cheaps": cheap labor, cheap raw materials, cheap energy, and cheap food. If some or all of these commodities suddenly rise in cost, profit margins are threatened. Upswings in any or all of them are sometimes called "signal crises," because they *signal* the problem ahead if business and the state cannot get those costs back down.[50] For a fresh upwave of accumulation, big business needs more cheap labor, and more cheap labor requires more cheap food.

One early condition of World Bank development loans was that recipient nations industrialize their agriculture.[51] Smallholders were pushed off land (*enclosure*) to make way for large monoculture fields. Mechanization cut the number of necessary field workers to a fraction, and a process began whereby millions of formerly rural people—who were monetarily poor, but capable of self-reliant subsistence agriculture—were pushed into cities, where they came to rely more directly on the mass-produced staple cereals, *which they now had to buy*, and where they provided a windfall to urban manufactories of desperately cheap labor.[52]

Peripheral nation agricultural production was being exported, in order to get precious US dollars for use in international markets and to service external debts. The agri-barons of the periphery were not feeding their own

48. Islam, "Agro-imperialism," para. 5.

49. Hazell, "Green Revolution: Curse or Blessing?"

50. Moore, "Cheap Food and Bad Money." Moore writes, "Capitalism is therefore not a social system, much less an economic one. It is, rather, a *world-ecology*. Capitalism does not 'have' an ecological regime; it is a world-ecological regime—joining the accumulation of capital and the production of nature as an organic whole. While ecology is often used interchangeably with nature and environment, my redeployment is to offer the concept as a relation of human and extra-human natures, the *oikeios*. Relations between humans are messy bundles of human and biophysical natures, and are bound, at every turn, with the rest of nature."

51. "The IMF and the World Bank: Puppets of the Neoliberal Onslaught."

52. Kwa, "Agriculture in Developing Countries."

countries but engaging in monoculture for export, like coffee, sugar, and bananas (ergo the term "banana republic").[53]

Urban hunger is a specter that most leaders understand only too well. I witnessed two food riots when I was in Haiti, and I can say they were among the most memorable experiences of my life. Political leaders know very well that mass urban hunger is a recipe for political destabilization, and they avoid it at all costs. Because many of these nations were exporting crops, they fell short in providing basic nutrition to their own growing urban populations.

The United States, however, was uniquely positioned to take advantage of this situation, because the agricultural subsidies of the New Deal, originally meant to rescue family farms, had been carried forward to the benefit of large agribusiness corporations that were tossing the American family farm into history's landfill. Price supports for US grains, as well as cotton, peanuts, and tobacco, meant that agribusiness could produce as much grain as possible, and for every bushel produced the government would pay them a subsidy.[54]

This, along with the arable landmass of the American Midwest, quickly led to massive overproduction of US cereal grains in the face of periodic shortages around the world, which gave US agribusiness unprecedented pricing power in global grain markets. As the United States sought a way out of its occupation of Vietnam in the early 1970s, the dominance of US grain production in the world was used as a foreign policy weapon that rewarded clients and twisted the arms of nations that appeared reluctant to follow the American diktat.[55]

Grain was on a lot of political minds those days. Hubert Humphrey, the 1968 Democratic challenger for the presidency, had allegedly received an illegal campaign contribution of $100,000—a fact that would emerge during the Watergate hearings.[56] The same contributor would also give the Nixon administration $25,000 to assist in its cover-up of the Watergate break-in. These were not insubstantial sums then, as they may seem now. Not many people had then heard of this fountain of largesse, whose name was Dwayne Andreas.[57] Andreas pushed through a historic grain sale to the Soviet Union

---

53. Petras, "The Great Land Giveaway."

54. Paarlberg, "Tarnished Gold," para. 20. Even before this program bloated into a massive and perennial corporate giveaway, the supported crops were *preferentially limited* to cotton, corn, wheat, rice, peanuts, and tobacco.

55. NACLA, "The Food Weapon: Mightier than Missiles."

56. Schneider, "Dwayne O. Andreas," para. 17.

57. Carney, "Dwayne's World."

for the Nixon administration, worth $700 million, with his company as the middleman. That company was named Archer Daniels Midland.[58]

It was the next year, however, when Green Revolution food production was exposed to another vulnerability, the aforementioned Arab oil embargo. It is here that we can see how the requirement for cheap food to sustain accumulation and the history of the Green Revolution as an instrument of US foreign policy combined with the emergence of neoliberal finance that gestated during the Nixon administration.[59]

By 1973, the US was running not a trade surplus but a *deficit* of $6.4 billion.[60] Even more momentously and permanently, US domestic production of sweet crude oil had peaked in 1972 and was now in a decline that would increase US dependence on imports of this commodity into the foreseeable future.[61] Oil remained the principle feedstock of American domestic agriculture, and of the Green Revolution that was forcing the

58. Bovard, "Archer Daniels Midland—a Case Study," 16.

59. Moore, "Cheap Food and Bad Money," 231–32. Moore explains how the loss of exploitable frontiers for "cheap nature" forced the dominant class, whose rates of profit were falling as cheap resources began hitting their limits, began turning inward from productive capitalism (making things) to the dominance of finance capital (rentiers), which takes rent-returns on investment from existing wealth. "Neoliberalism's financialized and coercive strategies of redistribution are now looking like a case of killing the goose that laid the golden eggs. There are, it seems, few golden eggs left to appropriate. This extractive strategy revived accumulation, but it did so by cannibalizing the accomplishments of the Fordist-Keynesian order. On the one hand, finance capital achieved its hegemony at a moment when the system's capacity to restore the Four Cheaps was weaker than ever. On the other hand, the hegemony of finance capital has exhausted capitalism's greatest source of dynamism, found in successive scientific-technological revolutions that have labor productivity, and subordinated extra-human nature in its pursuit. This double exhaustion of productivity and plunder strategies is not coincidental with the hegemony of finance capital, but the condition of its birth. Neoliberal capitalism, it seems, has been cooking goose for dinner."

60. Dale, "US Trade Deficit," para. 7. A trade deficit is when a nation is importing more than it is exporting, never great news for that nation's manufacturers.

61. Zhou, "US Oil Production," para. 2. This peak was in "sweet crude," and the decline was not reversed until hydraulic fracturing technology was widely employed during the Bush and Obama administrations. "Fracking," as it is called, does not extract sweet crude, but oil trapped between rock layers. It has created a fresh spike over the last eight years. However, these wells pollute water and destabilize local geographies, even causing earthquakes. Moreover, the average "fracking" well itself peaks within eighteen months, then goes into permanent decline. The burst of "fracking" activity is certainly temporary, and once played out it will return the US to pre-fracking levels and foreign dependence. See Magill, "Fracking Boom Leading to Fracking Bust." Beginning in June 2014, the Saudis flooded the market with oil to drop the price worldwide, in a double-strike against US domestic producers and Iran, which has led to temporary but historic lows over three years—as this is written—in prices at the pump. LeVine, "Oil War with the US."

more marginal and dependent nation-states into a new order of financial colonialism. At the same time, the US became increasingly dependent on fossil energy imported from abroad, not merely to power its machines and transport, but to eat and to maintain the power of the US over food markets worldwide. Even the Soviet Union had been pulled into the American grain-trade orbit by Nixon, proving Kissinger's thesis that the food-weapon was "more powerful than missiles."[62]

The increasing dependency of marginal nations on American agricultural goods, as well as American support for the industrial capitalist model being adopted for marginal nation export agriculture, would lead to decreases in marginal nations' per-capita food production as well as financial and ecological bankruptcy.[63]

Nixon broke up the old order; but the new order was not firmly established until the Reagan administration. In the interim, after a period of three years' stewardship of the White House by the immanently forgettable Gerald Ford, the next elected president would have a dual-resume: a naval officer and an agribusiness CEO: Jimmy Carter.

Now a powerful social critic, Jimmy Carter was then a southern agribusiness plutocrat posing as a good ol' boy (a peanut "farmer"). Under Carter, an interesting thing happened. Something Southern folk in my family used to call "white liquor" or "white lightning" became legal and began magnetizing massive cash flows from US taxpayers in the form of corn subsidies. Corn liquor has been produced for many years by rural scofflaws. My own father did a short stretch in the hoosegow when he was discovered with a car trunk full of it in the 1930s.

But when Nixon was taking money from Dwayne Andreas, the CEO of the sugar and corn conglomerate Archer Daniels Midland, ADM was concocting a new scheme that would simultaneously justify more "farm" subsidies to agribusiness and claim to address the energy crisis of 1973, which was also such a windfall to Wall Street. The scheme was to make massive quantities of corn liquor, which is of course flammable, and re-christen it "ethanol." This was proposed as an "energy independence" measure[64] for the United States. It is made, naturally, with sugar and corn. ADM found a friend in Jimmy Carter. Carter called the energy crisis the "moral equivalent

62. Donley, "The Inside Story."

63. Wise, "Who Pays for Agricultural Dumping?"

64. Murphy, Hall, and Powers, "New Perspectives on EROI—Ethanol," Abstract. The actual EROEI of ethanol averages 1.07, which is barely a break-even. This does not account for anything except energy required to make more energy; so what is excluded from this calculation is soil destruction, water use, pollution, land set aside that could produce food, or the cost to taxpayers of corn and sugar subsidies.

of war," and his administration exempted ethanol-spiked gasoline from a federal fuel tax.[65] Carter began a loan program to build ethanol plants, which was halted by the Reagan administration for a while, until "farm" lobbyists paid serial visits to Capitol Hill, whereupon the Reagan administration recanted.[66] Neither party would challenge agribusiness subsidies; and both parties finally became avid ethanol boosters.[67]

It was this influence, in conjunction with neoliberal "free trade" policies that allowed US grain producers to begin a process called *agricultural dumping*. Dumping is introducing a surplus into a foreign market *below market value*, which results in local producers' inability to compete. Taxpayer-subsidized US corn, for example, is still routinely dumped into foreign markets at prices as low as 30 percent of market value. This leads to bankrupted local markets, and a growing and increasingly poor urban population that becomes hostage to money dependency in an imperial food market.[68]

A Mexican farm family who grows traditional corn is wiped out by genetically modified, chemical-industrial corn that is subsidized by a foreign power. The family loses their land to debt, moves to the city, where they may or may not find work *to get money* to feed themselves, and barring that, they may take the risk of illegal migration to the north to find work in the United States. One seldom hears about neoliberalism or agricultural dumping when the subject of extralegal immigration comes up in the United States; but the connections are clear. United States policies created the conditions that made mass migration inevitable. After many NAFTA[69] provisions went into effect that allowed US dumping in Mexico, between 1997 and 2004, taxpayer-subsidized US corn exports increased by 413 percent, while Mexican corn production fell by 50 percent based on a 66 percent devaluation of Mexican corn. In the same period, US soybean production increased by 159 percent, and Mexican soybean production decreased by 83 percent based on a 67 percent devaluation. Mexican pork production fell by 40 percent, corresponding to a 707 percent increase in US exports. Pork itself is not directly subsidized, but the corn that feeds industrial pork is. It is not a coincidence that NAFTA corresponds to the most massive wave of Mexican immigration to the United States in history.[70] No one leaves behind family and familiarity without a very compelling reason.

65. Goldenberg, "US Corn-Belt Farmers."
66. Brower, "Pulling Strings on Capitol Hill."
67. Beckel, "Senators Supporting Ethanol Subsidies."
68. Wise, "Agricultural Dumping under NAFTA."
69. North American Free Trade Agreement.
70. Wise, "Mexico: The Cost of US Dumping."

So the combination of developmental imperatives to mechanize and *enclose* agriculture for monocrop production, as well as agricultural dumping by the United States has created a situation where most of the rapidly urbanizing world is now dependent on US grain or US seeds and chemicals in order to eat.[71] US foreign policy pertaining to food had become what both Maria Mies and Ivan Illich described as "a war on subsistence." The androcentric cliché for holding power over others, "having them by the balls," might better be replaced by "having them by the bellies."

US international power politics combines the neoliberal debt traps with food monopolization as an effective mechanism of indirect control over a good deal of the globe. This is not, however, sufficient to exercise the kind of total dominance the US would require to halt the very real decay of US power that results from various kinds of imperial overstretch[72] and the world-ecology of neoliberal capitalism inevitably aims at its own physical limits. The debt regime is not sustainable. The energy regime upon which the current system depends is not sustainable. The material resources upon which economic expansion is based are finite. And the tolerance of others is reaching its limits.

The fallback position of any imperial power, when indirect controls are no longer effective, is direct control in the form of violence. That is one of the reasons the United States—with some of the best naturally defensible borders in the world, and an impossibly large land mass for any would-be invader—maintains a military force that is more expensive than the combined military forces of Russia, China, Saudi Arabia, the United Kingdom,

71. Referencing Jason W. Moore again, this is not only unsustainable, this cheap food will inevitably decline, because what land is available is being damaged by the methods required to get current yields, and the aquifers that supply irrigation to this form of agriculture are being depleted. Moore's caustic remark, that they have not only killed the goose that laid the golden eggs and are now cooking the goose, is very applicable.

72. Janaro, "The Danger of Imperial Overstretch." *Overstretch*, sometimes called "over-reach," refers to the dynamic we described in earlier chapters wherein the obligations of expansion combined with the reality of resource exhaustion send center-nations further and further afield for new exploitable margins to continue supplying/appeasing the political base in the center. At some point, when those resources are exhausted, expansion is reduced to maintenance, then over time, contraction, whereupon what were formerly semi-margins or even the weakest sectors of the centers are transformed into exploitable margins. From the hypothetical moment when that expansion stops, the center, or imperial core, begins an irreversible process of decline. This can be seen in multiple related spheres, economic, military, and political. One might map the beginning of our own period with the decline—and serial crises—of the US economy, which inaugurated neoliberalism, followed by the military disasters in Iraq and Afghanistan, and culminating now with the election of Donald Trump.

India, France, Japan, and Germany.[73] If you include the Department of Energy budget's nuclear weapons, as well as foreign intelligence budgets, our
war spending exceeds the rest of the world.[74] Calling the War Department
the Department of Defense is perhaps the most ironic example of PR-speak
you might ever hope to encounter. The US military is almost exclusively
dedicated to missions of occupation and aggression abroad.

Moreover, the force component of US foreign policy is not merely the
uniformed services; it includes a shadowy and well-financed covert operations component that allows military actions by US-directed surrogates to
provide an element of plausible deniability to US actions that might undermine our own official ideological claims of commitment to principles
like "freedom," "human rights," and "democracy." This covert establishment
employs 83,675 civilians, 23,400 military, and 21,800 paramilitary contractors, at a cost of $52.6 billion annually.[75]

Neoliberal theology asserts the primacy of the private and the value of
small government; but neoliberal practice has been massively underwrit-
ten by the state. The assurance of the market economy—as Karl Polanyi
pointed out almost 70 years ago—requires a network of overpowering financial and regulatory institutions. Without the state's affirmative actions
on behalf of the international business class, this class and its power would
collapse. Begin by thinking about how those six carrier strike groups from
the US Navy are required to ensure the flow of fossil hydrocarbons into the
high technology centers.

The failed attempt to conquer Iraq in 2003, while it certainly involved
oil, was also part of an effort to maintain a forward deployed US military capable of strategic intervention far from home. The Cold War had ended, and
the disposition of US military forces had become obsolete.[76] They needed
to be redeployed from positions that were calculated to contain the USSR
into positions that would give the United States more capacity to intervene
in energy-rich Southwest Asia, to put the imperial hand—as it were—on
the spigots of global *negentropy*. The failure to secure that political objective—given that military success is not based on tactical but on political
outcomes—means that the US objectively lost the war in Iraq.[77] The goal of

73. Peter G. Peterson Foundation, "US Defense Spending Compared to Other
Countries."

74. Alvarez, "US Department of Energy Atomic Defense Budget."

75. *Washington Post*, "The Black Budget."

76. Global Policy Forum, "Permanent Bases."

77. The bases were built, several as large as small cities, but they were abandoned by
the United States Armed Forces during the general withdrawal.

the Iraq invasion was permanent bases; but instead the Bush administration managed to win the Iran-Iraq war . . . on behalf of its nemesis, Iran.

The Obama administration further decided that the next best thing is to put forward bases near the Middle East and in the Asia-Pacific Theater to contain China;[78] and the Obama administration vastly expanded the role of the covert operations forces, as well as armed mercenaries, in its expansion of the Afghanistan War to five additional countries, as well as increasing its covert operations against Iran.[79]

Obama's administration was instrumental in the execution and consolidation of the coup against the democratically elected president of Honduras in 2009,[80] just as the Bush administration was in the failed coup against the democratically elected president of Venezuela in 2002,[81] and its successful coup against the democratically elected government of Haiti in 2004.[82] In two cases, the offending parties—President Chavez of Venezuela and President Zelaya of Honduras—were guilty of defying the Washington Consensus, that is, of *opposing neoliberalism*. President Aristide had merely *criticized* neoliberalism.[83]

More than strategic interests drive the reliance on military operations. Dollar hegemony, described above by Henry C.K. Liu, caused a "strong dollar" overseas, which inhibits the purchase of American goods abroad. The expansion of the military-industrial complex through huge defense contracts has served as a counter-balance to this deficit by acting as a surrogate export market for manufacturing that remains inside the United States.

The reason the taxpayers are not bailing out Lockheed Martin, Northrup Grumman, Boeing, General Dynamics, Raytheon, KBR, SAIC, Dyncorp, Hewlett-Packard, and a host of other major American corporations, including General Electric, Motorola, Goodrich, and Westinghouse, is that the margin of earnings that ensure their continued viability as capitalist enterprises comes from DOD contracts. If war spending were ended tomorrow, the United States would experience a dramatic loss of jobs across

78. The most dynamic capitalist state in the world as this is written, and therefore the United States' most formidable competitor for what remains of the world's "Four Cheaps." Even now, however, China is beginning to experience falling agricultural output, post-peak resource extraction, ever higher percentages of imported energy, and labor resistance.

79. Sutter et al., "Balancing Acts."

80. Weisbrot, "Clinton Admits Role."

81. Vulliamy, "Venezuelan Coup."

82. Sachs, "Bush Ousting Aristide."

83. Weisbrot, "Obama's Latin America Policy."

a wide spectrum of Congressional districts that have hitched to the DOD pork wagon.[84]

American foreign policy is amphibious. It operates through both the wet depths of public institutions and the dry lands of private institutions, and it includes a powerful and effective public-private perception management apparatus.[85]

One of the key advantages of the public-private partnership is that foreign policy is insulated from accountability to those below those institutions on the social hierarchy. The boundaries are blurred, via contracts and memoranda of understanding, between the US public sector—with its administrative apparatus, and its military and intelligence establishment with their vast budgets—and the private sector, composed of publicly funded "non-governmental organizations," think tanks, foundations, and an army of horizontally-integrated perception managers.[86]

Those perception managers use mass media as a conformity-producing web of influence that reaches right into the living rooms of a US culture that has 2.24 television sets per household, running an average of six hours and 47 minutes a day, 2,476 hours a year. To appreciate the latent power of television, realize that the average college class has a student in tow for three hours a week, approximately 45 hours for an entire course, excluding out-of-classroom study.[87]

The limits of public discourse are established *de facto* by a media that operates on the same liberal market principles as the people who own them and exercise dominance within the government and in those sectors sometimes called *civil society*. The media, the governing apparatus, and civil society are in fact three faces of the same dominant interests.[88]

In saying this, I am obliged to clear up a common misunderstanding of what this means and what we mean to say. It is easy to jump from the very general outline we have presented of three aspects of US foreign policy—finance, food, and force—to the conclusion that we mean to say, or that these facts tend to support the idea that, there is a conscious group of powerful conspirators who direct the world. On the contrary, we want to emphasize that this way-of-the-world has evolved through a series of contingencies, and that its stability is maintained precisely because it is

84. Reich, "America's Biggest Jobs Program."
85. Parry, "The Victory of 'Perception Management.'"
86. Tracy, "Perception Management in the United States."
87. Herr, "Television & Health."
88. Durish et al., "Civil Society, Cultural Hegemony, and Citizenship."

what some complexity theorists call *self-organized.*[89] Its most powerful actors are in many ways as constrained, or more constrained, by neo-neo-liberalism—or whatever you choose to call this particular period—than most of us are. We each play our parts, and while some situational conspiracies have always been part of the terrain of politics, they are limited in scope, reactive, and far less determinative of large-scale outcomes than, say, changes in the built environment, demographic shifts, institutional inertia, supra-personal power-structures, or *the power of general-purpose money as an ecological phenomenon.*

Remember, in our saga about the birth of neoliberalism, there was no straight line, but a confluence of events and contingent decisions: the French buying US gold, Nixon dropping the gold standard, the Egyptian war for the Sinai, the American decision to airlift TOW missiles to the Israelis, the decision of Arab oil producers to embargo oil to the US, the US balance of payments deficit, Nixon dropping fixed currency exchange rates, rising oil prices creating petrodollars, the petrodollar tsunami being converted into opportunistic development loans, the Mexican threat of default, and so it goes. These were not grandiose plots, but actions and reactions, each producing a number of unintended or unanticipated consequences, which stimulated new actions and reactions.

The belief in a conspiratorial view of history seems to me to be a psychological reaction to the fear of chaos. If the world is not as one would like it, at least a conspiratorial view of history suggests that history as a process is still subject to human control, and that once we wrest control from the unjust conspirators, the world can be made right again.

If there was an overarching cause for these developments, it is not conspiratorial, but the raw reality of a finite world facing a regime based on the ceaseless expansion of monetized accumulation. Money chews up ecosystems and communities, but there are very real limits to how far this combined process can go before it undermines the basis of its own existence. The seeming unpredictability, this sense of instability that compels some of us to reach for order in chaos with a history of conspiracy, has been produced by the current political milieu, one wherein neoliberalism has disembedded economies from local control and re-embedded them in national and transnational

89. This is particularly important in understanding the way that general-purpose money and the built environment that it corresponds to secure certain seemingly inescapable defaults in social organization. *Self-organization* is the sum of countless micro-decisions taken each day by every person on earth, decisions constrained by "the way things are." These decision are driven by short-term necessity, and are therefore "immunized" against attempts at longer term challenges to systems as a whole. Self-organization is the overall order that is reproduced by the sum of local interactions.

institutions, and those institutions are themselves now experiencing a loss of control in the face of unanticipated changes.

Structural adjustment programs have become political lightning rods that are igniting mass unrest around the world.[90] Green Revolution agriculture has spawned megacities that are entropic black holes, teeming with hopelessness and crime.[91] The US military, long considered the guarantor of last instance for the world order, has proven to be both the least cost effective institution on the planet[92] and a perennial source of new resistance and unintended outcomes. In Iraq and Afghanistan,[93] the myth of US military invincibility was shattered; and the costs of the Southwest Asia wars have bled the US Treasury white. Offshoring of US industry and the political empowerment of rentier capitalists—Wall Street—that was accomplished through foreign policy, has transformed much of the US domestic population not merely into wage workers marketing themselves as commodities, but debt slaves.

The oft-seen bumper sticker summarizes it: "I owe, I owe, so off to work I go."

Consumer debt in the United States is above $12 trillion.[94] In 2016, the average American household owed $16,000 to credit card companies, $27,000 in auto loans, $48,000 in student loans, and $169,000 in mortgages.[95] US household leverage, the ratio of debt to disposable income, was 55 percent in 1960. By 1985, that number was 65 percent. By 2012, household debt was 133 percent of household disposable income.[96] People don't understand *why* these things are happening, but they experience them nonetheless. And in a society with racial and gender castes supporting accumulation, the political response—not unheard of in history—is to fall in step behind an obscenely wealthy, dim-bulb carnival-barker like Donald Trump.

When the crisis of fictional value, made possible only with general-purpose money and expanded by Wall Street speculation came home to roost, trillions in bailout money were printed and awarded to Wall Street, while Main Street was left holding its debts.[97] Wall Street, according to the experts

90. Guimond, "Structural Adjustment and Peacebuilding."

91. Davis, "Planet of Slums."

92. Shaughnessy, "One Soldier, One Year." The actual cost of one US soldier per year is around $850,000 as of 2012. That cost is rising. This does not even begin to count waste, fraud, and abuse in the military.

93. Nader, "Imperial Failure: Lessons from Afghanistan and Iraq."

94. Liesman, "US Household Debt."

95. Kirk, "American Debt Crisis."

96. Glick and Lansing, "US Household Deleveraging."

97. Melendez, "Financial Crisis Tops $22 Trillion."

who work the Wall Street-Washington nexus, was *too big to fail.*[98] Generations into the future are now saddled with paying for these bailouts.[99] We are being structurally adjusted, which has always been a euphemism for *privatizing the gains and socializing the losses.* We are being transferred from the outer edges of the center to the inner edges of the margins. This has always been—given the nature of the global capitalist ecology—inevitable.

98. Boone and Johnson, "Way Too Big to Fail."
99. At least until the whole structure collapses, which may be sooner than later.

10

Merged Understandings

Watch carefully then how you live, not as foolish persons but as wise, making the most of the opportunity, because the days are evil.

—EPHESIANS 5:15–16

WHEN WE SPEAK OF inevitability with regard to the expansion of global margins and the contraction of the global centers, we base this conclusion on a study of flows, transformed through some nodes and sold through others. We have seen how economic "growth," depending as it does on constant increases in "productivity" requires both the under-compensation of labor and the constant flow of sufficiently cheap materials through labor-as-nodes for transformation into commodities. We have seen how economics "externalizes" non-monetary relations. And we have seen how the capitalist state secures the bases for profitability, including through the conquest—military or financial—of marginal areas to feed the centers, and including direct subsidies as well as hidden subsidies for accumulation infrastructure. We have seen how Moore's claim that—so far in history, at least—accumulation regimes require the "Four Cheaps," or that accumulation regime gets into big trouble. Food feeds people, and people work on fossil-energized machines, and food requires land and water and energy inputs, and machines require those distant mineral inputs, which require labor . . . and around and round we go. What the ecology of capitalism does is the same two things price (value) does: destroys distinctions between variables and transforms order into disorder—thermodynamic, geographic, and social. As we have entered into a long period of "underproduction,"[1] capitalism has entered into a kind

1. Overproduction is what happens in the market, when commodities outrun the market's capacity to absorb them. Underproduction is the mirror image of this—hinted

of autoimmune disorder in which the whole process is being subsumed into a dynamic of expanding financialization. As the material economy is exhausted and the service economy is saturated, accumulation increasingly expands value through speculation, inflating bubble after bubble of fictional value, until the "cartoon law of gravity" kicks in, and the bubbles burst. This is why economic models no longer work. This is why Keynesian economics will not work, except as a transitional safety net on the way to a complete redesign of the built environment. This is why the tried and true methods of the Fed no longer work.

Financialization does not respond to the former diktat of "supply and demand." Rather than capitalism achieving longer waves of accumulation (always punctuated by crises), we have entered a period of very short waves predicated on the continual reflation and deflation of "bubbles" of fictional value. Real estate is now bundled with pension funds and pork futures. Homogenization by portfolio.[2]

In the last chapter, we saw how there are many complexities in the way this inevitability will unfold, because many actors will try various strategies to either survive crisis, exploit crisis, or—in the case of the big business class—try to reestablish accumulation on new post-crisis footings.

As this is written, I cannot anticipate what we will encounter on the terrain of an ever more turbulent politics in the United States. If he hasn't been impeached, we will be living in the hopefully brief period of a Trump presidency; and if not, perhaps we will be stuck with a President Pence. In either case, we are living in the aftermath of an abrupt and perilous shift in American politics. In a real sense, we are seeing an outcome of the progression of

---

in earlier chapters when we said that the market plays by the opposite rules from physical nature. Underproduction exhausts its own inputs. A crisis of overproduction is market saturation. A crisis of underproduction is the dwindling of material resources for production that begins with higher prices that cut into overall profit and ends when the cost of those resources drops the profit rate below zero.

2. Moore and Ahsan, "Interview." Jason Moore says, "The problem of capitalism today is that the opportunities of appropriating work for free—from forests, oceans, climate, soils and human beings—are dramatically contracting. Meanwhile, the mass of capital floating around the world looking for something to invest in is getting bigger and bigger . . . capitalism . . . will feed into an increasingly unstable situation in the next decade or two. We have this huge mass of capital looking to be invested and a massive contraction of opportunities to get work for free. This means that capitalism has to start paying its own costs of doing business, which means that opportunities for investing capital are shrinking. There's all this money that nobody has any idea what to do with." What Moore does not say here, but which is implicit in his argument, is that the value of this free-floating money is not matched even by commodities now in circulation, which is why the return on investment is sought through the cannibalistic process of hyper-speculation in a period of under-production.

crises described in the preceding chapter. Understanding how money functions as a socio-environmental solvent is the main door we want to walk
through in this book, but we also need a provisional account of how that
kind of laboratory-like, analytical conclusion clarifies the way things happen
outside the lab, as it were, when this dynamic we have identified is manifest
in a world of immense complexity and shifting contexts.

Nesting

Where is each of us embedded? Who lives in your household? What are
the relationships of dependency there? The lines of authority? The division
of labor? The state of health of each? The psychological state of each? The
special needs of each? What responsibilities and worries does each member
have? Are some household members risk-takers and others risk-averse? Are
some neat, others messy? Some hot-natured, some cold? If there is conflict,
how is conflict resolved? Where do the members of that household go to get
the inputs for the household and its members—money, food, services, tools,
maintenance supplies, fuels, etc.? Where do the household outputs go—
trash, spent fuel, sewage, labor, money? What are the lines across which no
one will venture, the commitments, duties, obligations that tie each member
to the other? To other family and friends outside the household? What coping mechanisms does each member have, or the household as a whole; and
are any of those coping mechanisms based on consumer products? These
are the kinds of things that *embed* us, as imperfect and vulnerable "thinking" animals. This aspect of human existence is not generally understood as
political—because we still mentally segregate our lives the way we mentally
segregate the subjects we study in school. But every political structure is
based directly on what goes on in households, which are—in a sense—a
basic social-political-economic-ecologic unit, like a cell is to tissue . . . then
the tissue is to organ, organ to organism? Nested.

  This household—and there are many different kinds now—and its activities in what we have learned to call the "private sphere," combined with
work and the acquisition of consumer goods—multiplied many times and
constrained by our social-political-economic-ecologic environment—is the
basis of social *self-organization*. Those locally observable activities are connected to those duties, obligations, and habits in the household at the same
time they are connected by law, custom, and a built environment. We need
to think of these things together instead of separately.

  Self-organization means *spontaneous order*. That does not mean that
this ordering of societies is not without authority and intentional direction,

but that no one has the capacity to micro-manage all of society, so the members of a society, the households of that society, learn to "get by" using what is available to do the best they know how with what they have. Over time, all these singular and small-scale activities become synchronized through little adaptations. Once that synchronization becomes relatively stable across the whole society, we can say it has become self-organized. In the current social-political-economic-ecologic environment, this self-organization has taken place around the demands of a business class in power—so, around regimes of constantly expanding, money-based wealth accumulation. The rules and roads and communications lines, combined with our adaptation to them, make self-organization the automatic control mechanism that does most of the work on behalf of this regime. Ideology—or indoctrination, if you prefer—sets up a little policeman in our minds that reinforces the control built into the environment; because ideology simultaneously conceals and reproduces power. Between environment and ideology, most of the control function is taken care of, leaving only the remaining frictions along the edges of that stability as the purview of armed forces—police or military. So long as the society at large remains stable and those who dominate that society get what they need to maintain their domination—in our case, based on expanding accumulation—politics is a pretty boring affair, sometimes devolving into minor squabbles and self-serving positioning.

But the dominant class of people in a society are not the only ones with a vested interest in stability. Once a society is self-organized, people lose the aptitudes and means to "get by" any other way. So instability creates anxiety not just for the dominant class, but to nearly everyone else below them on the politico-economic ladder. When the last financial bubble burst, combined with the money lost by bankers and bond traders were pension funds, college savings, and retirement accounts. If the electrical grid goes down, corporations lose money, but Grandpa's oxygen machine stops, too. We are nested.

For most people, nested as we are and focused primarily on the duties and obligations we have to those closest to us, politics has a dual aspect: on the one hand, we have our immediate interests, and on the other—which seems almost a universe apart—we have our *ideas* about politics, which we pick up mostly from state schools and audiovisual media. Personal interests come into play, but these emerging concerns are cast onto a screen of a pre-existing indoctrination. Someone reaching retirement age becomes vitally interested in collecting on the Social Security into which she's paid her whole life. And a young person can easily become convinced by demagogues that he or she is paying for that Social Security (they are not, the recipient paid into it for years), and be convinced to vote for someone they

perceive to be representing their interests by trying to privatize or gut Social
Security. Immediate interests distorted by indoctrination.

A person might be supportive of a party based on an ideology they
learned at home growing up or from work or from one's social circle or out
of perceived interest—Republicans fight "socialism" by going after welfare
cheats, or Democrats fight "protectionism" by supporting "free trade" agreements. These latter ideas are produced more by in-groups and corporate
media, and, when questioned, the overwhelming majority of people cannot
articulate the actual policies being debated in any detail whatsoever, resorting to impressionistic sound bites and bumper-sticker gotcha-logic they
hear on a television "debate."

In the early twenty-first-century American form of social nesting,
the household has been largely disembedded from the surrounding community. Members often do not know neighbors, that is, those who live
very nearby, but instead move between the household, work, consumer
spaces, and affinity groups based on memberships, hobbies, or similar
ideas. Even churches have been pulled into this nesting logic. This results
in most people being isolated in a kind of smart-home, an electronically
equipped living space filled with convenience appliances and entertain-
ment media. Consequently, our "windows" on the outside world become
a series of audio-visual broadcasts, including mesmerizingly attractive,
psychologically researched "electronic hallucinations,"[3] that are designed
by those very people who sit at the top of the social-political-economic
heap. These hallucinations are paid for by advertising revenue from likewise rich and powerful concerns that have no vested interest in people's
perceptions becoming deeper, more integral, more complex, or even less
selfish (advertising appeals to selfishness and even touts it as a virtue). This
is a recipe—along with the loss of skills and practices apart from highly
specialized, money-dependent, self-organized culture—for seemingly inescapable dependency and near absolute conformity.

In the larger context of things where partisans on both sides of any
well-known public debate are still committed to capitalism in some form
or another, the organs of mass communication and mass conformity—conservative through liberal—are owned and operated by the very people who
have the greatest stake in capitalism. Pay attention to who pays their bills
through advertisements. Their ability to choose how a debate is framed, to
select which arguments are heard on what is allegedly "both sides" of an
issue (there are only two sides, after all, and reasonable people always sit
halfway between them), is an exercise of power on behalf of the very social

3. Hedges, "Retribution."

class that is propelling us toward a combined catastrophic crisis. Language carries meaning; and when you are the one who chooses the language, this is a crucial exercise of power. You are implanting one set of meanings that can actually foreclose many others. This gives mass media the capacity to convince most of us simultaneously that climate change is real—we are in the "Anthropocene" era, an ecological issue—and that higher numbers on the New York Stock Exchange are indicative of "economic health," an economic delusion.

In the deep background, however, things are constantly changing—things based on laws of nature that cannot be broken by propaganda—and those changes eventually result in disruptions and instability. The disruption, loss, or threat of loss of this strange form of stability, then, is what we characterize as a *crisis*. Things don't work the way they ought to, self-organization doesn't seem so smooth. Anxiety creeps in, followed by anger—focused or unfocused—and conflict is never far behind. We see it now in the resurgence of the hyper-nationalist, white-victim masculinity[4] that catapulted Trump into the White House.

Crisis

Crisis is variously defined, but we'll cobble together a definition here that applies to societies, big modern societies like ours, plagiarized from Yeats: crises are periods in which "things fall apart." Our systems and procedures no longer work. Our analyses and theories and purported solutions no longer work. Our *ways of knowing* no longer work.

We are living through a period of nested crises. There is a general crisis of ecology, in which climate change is just one emerging catastrophe among several. Nested within that, there is a crisis of economy, in which capitalism itself is unsustainable, because the ceaseless expansion of capital (which is a socio-ecologic *relation*) runs up against both ecological and social limitations. Nested within that is a crisis of stability, which includes wars and displacements, but also a general feeling of anxiety, insecurity, and simmering anger. This latter crisis is what became manifest in the 2016 US elections,

---

4. Goff, *Borderline*, 118. "The faster the social change, the more deeply is this destabilization felt on the skins, in the bellies, and in the very psyches of individuals. It is this disequilibrium—global, financial, social, and sexual—that has given rise to strategies that have shifted the discourse from the public to the private, from the social to the individual, and which has allowed those with the most material power to redefine themselves, in the resultant confusion, as victims. Just as the rich have redefined themselves as the victims of the poor, men shift premises to construct themselves as the victims of masculinized women."

when both establishment parties experienced profound challenges to their power. Running through all these crises are the moral impasses that incubated within modernity, and which modernity hasn't the means to reconcile. And for those who are churched, we hear with some frequency that there is a "crisis in the church." How could it be otherwise?

We are going to look more closely now at the various aspects of this general crisis, bearing in mind that general-purpose money (in the service of the business class that rules through it) facilitated the crisis, pulled us into a dependency that makes it difficult to see, much less remedy, the crisis, and which—by its very nature—sets up a kind of socio-ecological default that will defy remedies that do not change the nature of money itself as a species of power, as one of "the powers," as a *sign* that dangerously roams the world without a *referent* to stop it. We are going to look at the big picture of accumulation against the big picture of the "cheap nature" that sustains it, and how it is disappearing, precipitating that crisis. We are going to link the power structures of accumulation to this crisis of the disappearance of "cheap nature," and we are going to further link these macro-elements to the curious interface of social norms, the psychological *umwelt* of persons, and the dynamics of class, race, and gender. Then we are going to attempt an analysis of the Trump phenomenon, to which I believe the church must urgently respond, and therefore respond most appropriately based on the best provisional account we can give of that phenomenon.

Summarizing. The "capital" in capitalism is a set of socio-ecological relations that are *mediated by the monetary market* (with general-purpose money) and circumscribed by the institution of private property. "Capitalization," then, means pulling anything into that set of market-mediated social relations that wasn't there before. Before there were coal-burning engines, a seam of black stone in a West Virginia mountain was just part of the mountain. Then it was capitalized when the coal was transformed into a commodity, a thing-for-sale.

Given that social and natural phenomena are aspects of the same dynamic, we can rightfully claim that capitalization pulls culture-nature into market-mediated relations in the same move. Any society where capitalization has become the predominant preoccupation of the state, apart from war, can rightly be called capital-ist. The purpose of capitalists is to accumulate wealth in the form of money.

The power-structures of capitalism are designed to sustain accumulation, the first of which is general-purpose money. Accumulation is
accomplished by increasing return-on-investment. When the capitalist
class—those who have accumulated sufficient monetary wealth by control-
ling production and finance to exercise dominating political power—encounters roadblocks to accumulation, they are forced to make changes to
"re-start" accumulation. When they can no longer re-start accumulation,
capitalism will falter and perish.

In our account of "cheap nature," we have incorporated the insights
of geographer Jason Moore. What we have identified in earlier chapters as
"price," a form of value apart from the specific use-value of a thing-for-sale,
which Moore refers to in his tradition's idiom as simply "value."

> What we are seeing today is the "end of cheap nature" as a
> civilizational strategy, one born during the rise of capitalism
> in the "long" sixteenth century (c. 1450–1648). An ingenious
> civilizational project has been at the core of this strategy, to
> construct nature as external to human activity, and thence to
> mobilize the work of uncommodified human and extra-human
> natures in service to advancing labor productivity within com-
> modity production. The great leap forward in the scale, scope,
> and speed of landscape and biological transformations in the
> three centuries after 1450—stretching from Poland to Brazil,
> and the North Atlantic's cod fisheries to Southeast Asia's spice
> islands—may be understood in this light. Such transformations
> were the epoch-making expressions of a new law of value[5] that
> reconfigured uncommodified human and extra-human natures
> (slaves, forests, soils) in servitude to labor productivity and the
> commodity.[6]

Earlier in the book, we noted that "civilizational" centers accumulate
from margins, and that those margins, once exhausted, have to be extended.
Over time, the center over-extends, the civilization falters or falls, then contracts. Christopher Chase-Dunn and Thomas Hall call this—as seen over
time—a civilizational "pulse." Looking at capitalist accumulation, then, a
revolutionary shift from accumulation-by-land to accumulation-by-money,
profit taken from the "point of production" by *under-compensation* of labor

---

5. Moore is criticizing and "correcting" Marx's "law of value," which showed profit
solely extracted from commodity production through "surplus value," or paying workers less in wages than the value they produce for owners. Moore's "new law of value,"
as we will see, goes wider and deeper than the appropriation of value at the "point of
production."

6. Moore, "The Capitalocene, Part II."

can only work if there are sufficiently cheap flows going through that point of production and through that laborer as flow nodes: raw materials, energy, and food, for example.

Expansion is driven by both the imperative to constantly renew the production process and competition from without. The cheapest things are at first the easiest things (those nearest and requiring the least refinement). As time goes by, those things nearest and requiring the least refinement are exhausted, and those further afield are sought and exploited. The pulse moves outward. But at each stage, the exploitable "natures" themselves become more difficult to get and often more difficult to refine. The money collected from sales (or rents, that depend ultimately on sales) diminishes as more money is laid out for labor, raw materials, energy, and food.[7]

This dynamic of diminishing returns sends the capitalist to unexploited regions, which Moore describes as *frontiers*. And when we think about it historically, "frontiers" were always those places where people from the centers confronted people/nature in the margins in the search for fresh, "free" resources. This is why Moore says that the "new law of value" has to show that accumulation occurs in two places at once: the *point of production*, through under-compensation of labor, and the *frontier*, where "cheap nature" is still available through plunder and structurally or militarily-enforced unequal exchange.

Moore documents how every major crisis in accumulation since the "long" sixteenth century corresponds to a bottleneck in the flows of one or more of those aforementioned "Four Cheaps": labor, raw materials, energy, or food. And every overcoming of each crisis was based on the conquest of a fresh frontier—spatial or technological—to resume this fourfold cheap flow through the productive nodes.[8] The Green Revolution we discussed in the last chapter was a refreshed access to cheap food and cheap labor. "Food and climate," writes Moore, "finance and energy represent not multiple, but manifold, forms of crisis emanating from a singular civilizational project: the capitalist world-ecology." A project that elevated Mammon as the single grand mediator of all relations. Moore writes that the capitalist epoch ushered in by Mammon amounts to the "co-production of earth-moving, idea-making, and power-creating across the geographical layers of human experience."[9]

---

7. Moore's "Four Cheaps."

8. Cheap food flows through the laborers themselves, holding down their basic survival costs, to allow for greater under-compensation at the productive nodes—what Moore calls the "cheap food/cheap labor nexus."

9. Moore, *Capitalism in the Web of Life*, 2–3.

If Moore is on to something, and I think he is, then what do we make of the fact that UNFAO statistics show a near doubling of the Food Price Index over the last seventeen years;[10] or that labor compensation rates are rising;[11] or how China holds 80 percent of the world's critical tungsten reserves,[12] with the United States as the largest end consumer; or even how our current oil price drop is not indicative of a supply overage but a long-term supply crisis;[13] or how corn has become not just a publicly subsidized, energy-sink food source, but now also animal feed, fuel, industrial material input, and weapon of financial warfare.

Helga Weisz, head of Transdisciplinary Research for the Potsdam Institute of Climate Impact Research and Professor of Ecology at Humboldt University in Berlin, uses the metaphor of *metabolism* to track flows and nodes, as a way of getting closer to the idea of a capitalist world-ecology and further away from models that see society and nature as two, separate, yet interacting, forms of being. She does so in the context of *world systems* theory, which we saw earlier, an acknowledgement that we live in an economy that includes many nation-states, or an *interstate politico-economic regime*. In biology, metabolism means "the processes by which a living organism uses food to obtain energy and build tissue and disposes of waste material."[14] In social studies, metabolism means paying attention to inputs and outputs, or flows and nodes. World systems analysis looks at those flows, those inputs and outputs, across the world. According to Weisz:

> World-systems theory regards the expansion of the industrial capitalist system as intrinsically connected to a spatial separation, on a global scale, between the early and the later stages of the industrial production process, and between production and consumption in general . . . lead[ing] to a globally uneven distribution of the costs and benefits of the use of material and energy . . . I argue that an integration of social metabolism and input-output analyses provides a conceptually sound approach to account for ecologically unequal trade between national economies or world regions.[15]

10. Food and Agriculture Organization, "World Food Situation." http://www.fao.org/worldfoodsituation/foodpricesindex/en/.

11. Bureau of Labor Statistics, "International Comparison of Hourly Compensation."

12. Silberglitt et al., "Critical Materials." Tungsten is a crucial element in steel alloys, various electronics, and hardmetal tools, including oil and gas drills.

13. Maryknoll Office of Global Concerns, "Peak Oil, Low Prices."

14. *Merriam-Webster Dictionary*, s.v. "metabolism."

15. Weisz, "Combining Social Metabolism."

Dr. Weisz has just summarized one metaphorical way that exchange detectives can explain not only environmental damage but extreme social inequalities, facilitated by money as an ecological phenomenon. But Moore cautions that this is just a point of departure. His argument is subtle, especially if one is not already conversant in these kinds of flow analysis. The "metabolic" pathology, or "metabolic rift" account of the capitalist world-ecology still clings to the vestiges of that Cartesian culture-nature split, even as it tries to escape from it. This is not surprising. "Even when our philosophical position regards humans as part of nature," Moore points out, "the narrative rules, methodological premises, and theoretical frames of world-historical scholars often remain within the confines of a modernist view of nature as external. This may explain some measure of the profound undertheorization of 'ecological crisis,' and the widespread weakness of critical scholars to explain how nature matters to capitalism, not merely as output, but as constitutive relation."

In a very real sense, capitalism does not *cause* ecological crisis; it is *constituted* by it, because profit demands the *inescapable* transformation of *order* into *disorder* at the *frontiers*. If there is a crisis that encompasses all those nested crises, it is a crisis of capitalism. This is not to claim that these other aspects of the capitalist crisis are only dangerous to capitalists. Because capitalism—like the money that is its essential sign—is an *ecological* phenomenon, the collateral damage from this crisis will hit everyone, the most vulnerable first. Many are already there.

Moore says that "metabolic rift" theorists do what we have done earlier in the book, as a way of wading from the shallow to the deep end of the pool. We spoke of "ecological footprints." But when you think about it, we have *culture* (one thing) making a footprint on *nature* (another thing). And this is our common way of thinking, even by most environmentalists. "Debt leads to deforestation," says Moore. "Neoliberal programs drive cash-crop monocultures. Industrialization causes CO_2 emissions. Are these not reasonable causal statements?" Culture does not act *on* nature. The structures that are constitutional of both *ramify*. CO_2 emissions are an inhering reality that *constitutes* industrialism. Moore's point is that capitalism has "not *caused* a metabolic rift, it *is* a metabolic rift."

This is important to us, especially in the last chapter, where we will discuss what can be done, because it has implications for what we can do, and what those things-we-do can do. What it tells us right off the bat is that if capitalism is constituted as ecological crisis, then we will be categorically unable to overcome this crisis as long as our political-ecology is mediated by general-purpose money as capital in "the market." Neoliberalism *is* monoculture. Industrialization *is* CO2 emissions. Debt *is* deforestation. Capitalism *is* a frontier headed into the slaughterhouse.

So what are the states of the frontiers? Are there frontiers remaining? This has profound implications. Where will "cheap nature" be found next? If the only frontiers are financialization, "intellectual property," and military Keynesianism, then the capitalist world-ecology is in very dire straits. Because whatever these are, they are not cheap labor, cheap food, cheap energy, or cheap raw materials. They are instead a kind of world-historical autoimmune disorder, that process of self-cannibalization. We are eating the goose that laid the golden eggs. What the dominant class can no longer acquire through under-compensation in the productive process, it will seek in increased rents. This is why the average household debt in the United States has risen to more than $132,000.[16] *You* are the new frontier for accumulation. And there are limits to everyone's patience. This has implications for would-be peacemakers, and not popular or easy ones.

16. Woolley, "Do You Have More Debt?"

11

Church

By the abundance of your trade
You were internally filled with violence,
And you sinned;
Therefore I have cast you as profane
From the mountain of God.

—Ezekiel 28:16

Nekeisha Alexis-Baker, a Trinidad-born, Mennonite writer and activist, speaks to our worship of Mammon, but also the ways in which church has been pulled into that worship.

> Still the church as a whole has not been able to name [the market] as a false god, in large part because the church doesn't acknowledge its claims of holiness. The end result has been that the church has either attempted to peacefully co-exist with market capitalism, relegating our Christian beliefs to Sunday morning, while we invest in Wal-Mart, shop at the Mall of America, and work on Wall Street the rest of the week. Or the church has emulated the market's evangelical success, building "mega-churches" with roller rinks and fast-food restaurants, proclaiming a health and wealth gospel, and churning out widgets in the name of Christ. Both responses cause the church to lose its focus and its message of salvation. There is a reason why malls can contain Christian bookstores, chapels, and designated prayer rooms, and François and Marithé Girbaud feel free to portray Jesus' Last Supper with female models in expensive designer

clothes: Christianity in its current form is not a threat to the market's growing reign.[1]

In Ivan Illich's interviews not long before his death, he broke a self-imposed silence about matters theological, and made explicit the relationship between his long standing criticism of institutionalization as a social concern and his criticism of the ever more institutionalized church. He related a story about Jean-Guenolé-Marie Daniélou, a Jesuit priest who had been for some time in China, and who decided to make a foot pilgrimage from Beijing to Rome. Daniélou encountered a series of stages in the hospitality he received along the route. In China, the mere declaration that he was a faith pilgrim netted him some food and a bed for the night in someone's home. When he reached the zone of Eastern Orthodoxy, he was sent to the priests' houses or a parish hostel. By the time he reached Poland, which was Catholic country, he was given money to rent a cheap hotel.[2] Illich relates this story as a living example of the transition from personal hospitality—like that encountered by the mugged Jew and his Samaritan rescuer—to an ever more impersonal form of charity, one that eventually took form as institutional intervention via hospitals, mad houses, homeless shelters, and food pantries.

Jacques Ellul, noting the impersonality of modern money:

> Money has become *impersonal* because it increasingly seems as if the use of money is not an individual act, does not signify personal control, but instead results from distant and complex interactions of which our acts are merely echoes. No longer is there any real relation between an individual and his money, because this money is abstract and impersonal. Consequently, moral problems concerning money no longer seem to exist.[3]

Ellul called the political urge to correct injustices through social engineering, through the imposition of allegedly corrective systems, hypocrisy and cowardice, particularly from Christians, precisely because this institutional approach to charity is a mirror reflection of the impersonality of modern money. It is a cop-out. I can continue to use money they way I do now, especially if I am committing that money to a cause for *system* change, because when we accomplish this or that bit of social engineering, people won't need the charity of others. Moreover, once the *system* is changed,

1. Alexis-Baker, "Market Capitalism."
2. Illich, *Rivers North of the Future*, 54–55.
3. Ellul, *Money and Power*, 10.

people will become better, because their bad behavior now is wholly attrib-
utable to the bad things the bad system does to them.[4]

Of course, he is not saying the opposite of that either, as we can read
from his quote above. People are formed by their built-natural-administered
ecology without a doubt, but this is not the whole story; and this systems
approach, this commitment to social engineering, contains a conclusion
smuggled into its premises that human beings are without anything that
might be called a human nature, that we are, in fact, totally the products of
our *conditions*. Ellul commits to neither biological determinism nor cultural
determinism—and certainly not to some uprooted, post-Nietzschean account of the person as a power-seeking playactor—and nor would I; but he
does point out—as a Christian—that we do have an account, a trans-sys-
temic one, of human nature, individually and collectively, as, among other
things, *fallen*. You can install pretty much any new system you like, and
take ten despotic generations for The New System to overcome the forma-
tive power of preceding social arrangements, and people will still manifest
selfishness, pride, envy, avarice, and all the rest.

Progress, revolution, and even postmodernism[5] are every bit as much
imperial narratives as those they purport to replace. They all aim to encom-

4. Systems-thinking, as we noted in the beginning of the book, has some of the
same tendencies as the post-Enlightenment subject-object/conquest-of-nature thinking, in as much as it attempts to encompass and "control." Once social organization has
been rendered a "system"—which is a helpful way to think of it for certain analytical
purposes—one can begin to think of social organization as something that is manipulable, or reconstructable, in the way a machine or an office is. Systems-thinking can also
lend itself to conspiracy theories; if social organization is like a machine, then a small
group can control the levers and buttons. This is not to say that social organization is
not manipulable, especially by force. It clearly is, though not in any way that is either totally controllable or predictable, because beyond a certain threshold of social complexity, any social organization is subject to disruption by variables that are either beyond
control or unforeseeable. Our global social organization now, which we have unpacked
using the interpretive framework of world-*system* theory, does have many regular features, including the ecosemiotic nature of general-purpose money as we have described
it. These features, through self-organization, have become comparatively stable; and
these same features' stability relies on existing flows and nodes that are identifiable. We
have tried to make the case that what is predictable is that disruption of flows as they
are now; for example, fuel, food, and raw materials (and thereby, disruption of labor
as flow-nodes), will disrupt the self-organization of society and send those who have
accrued the most power through existing regimes looking for fresh strategies to protect
and extend that power (a function of human frailty).

5. Hart, *Beauty of the Infinite*, 5–8. David Bentley Hart criticizes postmodern
orthodoxy in the American academy as "the triumph of rhetoric over dialectics," which
in his view—and the author's—makes postmodernity not "post" anything. By reducing
every question to rationalizations in support of a Nietzschean will-to-power, postmod-
ernists substitute their own encompassing metanarrative (of solipsistic and exhausting

pass, enclose, and universalize, based on the peculiar ideals of a Western "educated" class. Just as the Gospels point us to a refusal to cosign the self-glorification of official authority, I think the same applies to the kinds of encompassing ideologies whose postures of inclusion and tolerance thinly conceal a desire for conquest over the messy and particular.

Dr. Mayra Rivera, professor of religion and Latino/a studies at Harvard University, writes,

> The passion for intellectual questioning that infused early modern discussions of wonder is thus enmeshed in the "rituals of appropriation" of exploration and conquest . . . At stake is more than the recognition of historical complicity; it is more fundamentally a question of the inherent assumptions of modern epistemological and ontological frameworks . . . which begins with the Cartesian ego . . . the connection between Descartes' *ego cogito*[6] and the ideal conquistador, the *ego conquiro*.[7] Dussel argues that the *ego conquiro* precedes and sustains the *ego cogito*, and thus any decolonial project must deconstruct this modern construction of the subject.[8]

If cross and resurrection mean anything at all in the outworking of history—and I believe they do—then they mean that we see the core practice of sin in violence and domination and the core practice of redemption in finding ways to be together without them. What this book has tried to show is that general-purpose money is every bit as much one of the powers as the state, and that in our own epoch these are two faces stamped on either side of the same coin. Mammon is a species of dominion,

---

skepticism) for the modern metanarratives they rightly identify as species of conquest. In large part, this is because they have not transcended the subject-object duality, but reversed the modern search for objectivity (nature) against subjectivity (culture) into "subjectivities" (paradoxically without any coherent "subject" at all) against objectivity. The idea, taken from Nietzsche, is that the way to solve the culture-nature dualism is to disappear them both into "discourse" generated by that vaporous, disembodied "will-to-power." It is just another, slyer Western conquest gambit. Writes Hart: "The truth of no truths becomes, inevitably, truth: a way of naming being, language, and culture that guards the boundaries of thought against claims it has not validated." Christians, while they are forced to engage modernity and postmodernity, are not grounded in either modernity's universalizing pretensions (several of which this book engages) or postmodernity's rhetorical truth-less truth (which the author admittedly finds tedious), but in the story of a crucified Judean rabbi, our Logos, the Word made flesh.

6. "I think."
7. "I conquer."
8. Rivera, "Glory," 171.

intrinsically and inevitably so. Its concealment as such is a function of ideology, another of the powers.

More to the point, however, money is an instrument that creates modern poverty, that sustains it through both enclosure and premeditated scarcity, and that—in large part because we see poverty as an issue of mal-distribution—it facilitates a form of charity that is increasingly impersonal and void of that essential ingredient for Christ's reign: love. Prather says that "creaturely history is the context in and for which Christ's prophetic confrontation of unjust power unfolds, and thus in which all persons are called to have faith and bear witness to God's victory over the powers of evil."[9] What is it over which Christ's power stands? What is the relationship between injustice and the idol of Mammon? How do we bear this witness without withdrawing *and* without taking up the sword? How do we witness to injustice in the face of authorities who cannot witness, and still answer violence with love? Whatever the answer is to those questions, before we can arrive at it we have to disentangle ourselves from the ruling ideology that throws a veil over that answer; and this means a fearless form of discernment. Now, what can we do?

Anti-Christ

When we review the first chapter on climate change, then integrate that reality with the direction we are heading politically and economically, it is with a kind of fascinated terror that we come to grips with the magnitude of these problems. With the magnitude and the *inertia* of that magnitude. Mass-times-velocity equals momentum. When I engage in political discourse or do my little projects to rehabilitate a scrap of soil, I wonder if I am like "The Fishes," the group of armed revolutionaries in the film adaptation of P. D. James's novel *Children of Men*. They continued the armed struggle for the rights of the persecuted refugees, and yet human beings have become unaccountably sterile and had produced no babies for more than eighteen years. Life itself had become, as Sartre so pithily put it, "a blank check written against eternity."[10]

We may wonder if we aren't rearranging the deck chairs on the Titanic. On the other hand, as Merry Brandybuck scolds Treebeard for his neutrality, "But you are a part of this world!" And as Camus shows in his story "The Guest," when Daru attempts to evade the world's conflicts by nestling into

9. Prather, *Christ, Power, and Mammon*, 8.
10. Sartre, "The Wall." In some translations, he says, "counterfeiting eternity."

the Algerian outback, the world is going to enmesh you into its conflicts whether you like it or not.

We have spoken frankly here, more than once, about capitalism; and we are aware that this is a kind of taboo that is further mystified by the popular notion that the only alternative to capitalism is "socialism," and that the only kind of socialism is the repressive state socialism of the former Soviet Union, its imitators, and its client-states. But there were social organizations that predated either capitalism or this form of socialism for much longer than either has existed. The problem for us is that these forms of social organization, like all social arrangements, flourished and finally fell *in the context of their own times.* In our own time, as we have shown, we are likewise caught within the context of our current organizational forms, and within those contexts, there are some alternatives that are possible, some not. Some probable, some not. We can only start here and now, with all that means. We are certainly not advocating a rebirthed Soviet socialism—which is in any case not possible—though we do insist, based on what we can show, that the status quo, which is an *actually presently existing* neoliberal capitalist world system, was birthed out of crisis, has undergone serial crises, and is headed toward crises—economic and ecologic—that will eventually self-destruct. We hope we have shown that general-purpose money and our dependency on it are a key ingredient in that dependency for people, families, communities, nations . . . and churches. No one is advocating the barracks socialism of the twentieth century. But we are faced with a collective choice. We will ride the current structures of power into an abyss of misery and social dislocation; or we will accomplish a survivable crash landing scenario by systematically disentangling ourselves from those structures of power. This will involve the state, whether we like it or not; and it will demand that the state at least facilitate certain forms of redesign that are antithetical to capital accumulation and "growth." Some will cry, "Socialism!" To which I'll say . . . "Whatever!"

Let's drop the scary -ism suffix and speak of practical matters.

Kathryn Tanner notes, "Just as God is love does not mean love is God, God's Kingdom may be the basis for a Christian identification with socialism with it without that implying that socialism on its own merits is to be identified with the Kingdom."[11] I will say this, paraphrasing José Antonio Viera-Gallo, that if a humane and sustainable "socialism" is worked out, it better come riding on a bicycle.[12] The old, authoritarian, industrial model

11. Tanner, "Karl Barth on the Economy," 181.

12. "El socialismo puede llegar sólo en bicicleta." In Andrews, *Columbia Dictionary of Quotations,* 279.

of socialism—captured always within the global power-structures of capitalism and therein bound to general-purpose money—cannot stand. One way or another, the alternatives facing humanity at this juncture require our clear-eyed admission of how far the social injustices and ecological catastrophe have already gone.

> The feeble but honest thing to say is simply that ecosocialism seems possible, as ecocapitalism does not. Socialism may not necessitate, but it at least permits, that collectively assumed and administered usufruct of the earth that the slogan of the Anthropocene urges but can't induce. Any such political approximation to enlightened species-being would likely emerge in a handful of embattled and, with luck, allied countries long before attaining anything like the universality it intended. An international movement to redistribute ecological harm and plenty along lines of equality, within living generations as well as between them and their descendants, would, in other words, face a drawn-out battle against a capitalism dead-set against any such thing. This means, tragically, that by the time the Capitalocene concludes, capitalism will only have a more or less badly despoiled world to bequeath to its successor, whether—updating Rosa Luxemburg—that turns out to be ecosocialism or ethnobarbarism.[13]

There is a pithy quote making the rounds in response to the flurry of dystopian books and films depicting end-of-the-world and zombie-apocalypse scenarios: "It is easier to imagine the end of the world than the end of capitalism." The quote did not, as is frequently claimed, originate with Slavoj Žižek or Fred Jameson; it is a misquotation from literary critic H. Bruce Franklin. In 1979, Franklin wrote an essay called "What Are We to Make of J. G. Ballard's Apocalypse?" It was literary criticism of dystopian science fiction, to be sure. But what Franklin did was accuse Ballard of "mistaking the end of capitalism for the end of the world." Where the misquotation might name a truism, the actual quotation says something more to the point.

> Ballard's imagined world is reduced to the dimensions of that island created by intertwined expressways on which individuals in their cellular commodities hurtle to their destruction or that apartment complex in which the wealthy and professional classes degenerate into anarchic tribal warfare among themselves. And hence Ballard accurately, indeed magnificently, projects the doomed social structure in which he exists. What could Ballard

13. Kunkel, "The Capitalocene."

create if he were able to envision the end of capitalism as not the
end, but the beginning, of a human world?[14]

This speaks to us, I think—to what we find "unthinkable." Because we
are ourselves, the author and most readers, confined within the structures
of patriarchy, industrialism, capitalism, white supremacy, and the realities
of an imperial center that is waning . . . and more dangerously, thrashing
about trying to reestablish its grip. Our enclosure is more than our dependence on money and our captivity within an inherited built environment;
it is also epistemological, reproduced every day by our *way of knowing*.
The *way we know* has been enclosed. We have been epistemologically enclosed, shut out from the commons, employed in the new techno-mills
. . . privatized. So how do we break this intellectual enclosure? How do
we re-form a *way of knowing* that shares an intellectual commons; that
begins breaking down our intellectual models and our over-specialized
intellectual division of labor?

I'm going to suggest it begins with the resurrection of an archaic concept to understand our circumstance: evil. In another film/book allusion,
from *The Thin Red Line*,[15] our narrator, Private Witt, asks, in the face of
the mindless and inevitable cruelty of war, "This great evil, where's it come
from? How'd it steal into the world? What seed, what root *did* it grow from?
Who's doin' this? "

What am I to do? What are we to do? Where do we begin? What is evil?
How do we know its face? Is it just an ultra-rich clown running a nation, a
thuggish racist cop, a serial rapist, a war criminal, a bureaucrat signing an
eviction notice, or a drunken husband beating the hell out of his wife? Is it
money, or some spirit of money, or the lust for money?

What seed? What root?

I have to divert, now, away from the hard diagnostics of science, back
into an unsure anthropology and a story around which the figure of the
Anti-Christ can be rescued from horror-films and jackleg preachers.

Our secular era, this epoch of modernity reaching into the post-
Trumpian Now of crackpot capitalism, with its mad envies and addictions,
its nuclear weapons, and its ceaseless violence, is not an era *against* Christianity, but—as Ivan Illich so provocatively pointed out—the perversely inevitable triumph of evil *from within the church*.[16] The *Anti-Christ*, the seed,
the root from which this evil grew, quickened in the belly of the church,

14. Franklin, "J. G. Ballard's Apocalypse," 104–5.

15. Malick, *Thin Red Line*.

16. No one disputes that Western modernity is historically rooted in European
Christendom.

because the Anti-Christ becomes possible only through the revelation of the Christ. In 1987, Illich stated during an interview,

> My work is an attempt to accept with great sadness the fact of Western culture. [Historian Christopher] Dawson has a passage where he says that the Church is Europe and Europe is the Church, and I say *yes! Corruptio optimi quae est pessima* [the corruption of the best which is the worst]. Through the attempt to insure, to guarantee, to regulate Revelation, the best becomes the worst.[17]

Illich breaks this down into five fundamentals:

The Incarnation happened.

The Incarnation was a surprise.

The Incarnation was a gift.

The Incarnation was not "discoverable," but revealed.

The Incarnation is expressed through love and knowledge.

With this revelation, said Illich, came two sources of risk, one positive risk to the world, and one negative risk to the church: the danger of social disruption to the world and the danger of institutionalization to the church.

The former danger is to families and other bounded groups in society, because the freedom to love across boundaries has great potential to disrupt boundaries. Jesus said this when he described being shunned by one's social family to become part of an ecclesial one. "I have come to set a man against his father, and a daughter against her mother" (Matt 10:35).

The latter danger, that of institutionalization, which is about power and which aligns the church with power, carries with it the potential for the *betrayal* of that new *gifted* freedom. The church becomes its own Judas, rebuking the woman with the jar of nard for deviating from the worldly mission, where Judas may find his own benefit, Judas blithely unaware that she is the first Christian—a story in all four Gospels—who in preparing Jesus's body for burial demonstrates her recognition that salvation will not be through the military Throne of David but by way of the political criminal's cross. The latter danger is to the faith itself, to the unique gift of the Incarnation, should leaders emerge who "try to manage and, eventually, to legislate this new love, to create an institution that will guarantee it, insure it, and protect it by criminalizing its opposite." What has been *divinized* becomes *legalized* and therein degraded. Jesus spoke to this as well, though less directly, when he corrected the Pharisees and Scribes about the rules

17. Cayley, *Ivan Illich in Conversation*, 242–43.

for keeping Sabbath, telling them that the Sabbath was a *gift* to people, not a means for regulating them (Mark 2:27).

This new dimension of love (across boundaries) surprisingly opened by the Incarnation is revealed—neither invent-able nor discoverable—and it is accomplished by *grace*. But just as importantly, it is *embodied*. "*Carne*" means "flesh." In the Parable of the Samaritan, the feeling that preceded this surprising friendship that appears between two ethnically divided men is described in the Gospels by the Greek as "stirred in his guts" (an *enfleshed* reaction) as opposed to the more standoffish "felt compassion."[18]

In the process of *institutionalization*, the personal connection is replaced with ever more impersonal and abstract *systems*, with management schemes performed by detached administrators. "And this is crucial for Illich," says David Cayley. "For him, the answer to the question—who is my neighbor?—is: it could be anybody, so long as it is a *fully embodied relationship* and one that is actually felt as a *personal* call. Remove this embodied quality, turn a personally experienced vocation into an ethical norm, and you have, Illich says, 'a liberal fantasy.'"[19]

Citing the philosopher Husserl, Cayley explains the Parable of the Samaritan another way. Husserl said that people have "home-worlds," places and cultures within one's experience where they feel *at home*.[20] Different peoples have different home-worlds, and between each of the different home-worlds is a kind of no-man's land (forgive this old gendered expression) that doesn't refer to either. We spoke earlier in the book about the *Umwelt*—the world-in-self—that is connected to the *Unwelt* of the other by a *semiosphere* of shared signs and referents. Is that semiosphere particular, intimately enfleshed, and local; or is it generalized, abstract, and impersonally universal?

The Christian notion of a *call* is crucial here. The gift of grace comes as a *calling* that bridges that no-man's land. And Christ's gift "is in [the Parable of the Samaritan] establishing a relationship with the man in the ditch [which] begins a *new world* [with new signs] and thus demonstrates a power that has been super-added to him through the Incarnation, not one that could ever belong to his natural repertoire. He acts, as Illich repeatedly says, on a call."[21]

18. The Greek says the Samaritan was stirred in his σπλάγχνον, *splanchnon*, meaning "innards."

19. Cayley, "Christ and Anti-Christ."

20. And Jesus said unto him, "The foxes have holes, and the birds of the heaven have nests; but the Son of man has nowhere to lay his head" (Luke 9:58).

21. Cayley, "Christ and Anti-Christ."

The church's compromise with worldly power set it on a course where church legalization, institutionalization, and even its governance became inevitable. Illich saw "the mystery of evil," as he called it, that mystery that deposits and conceals the anti-Christ in the belly of Christ's church, as the idea "that man can do what God cannot, namely manipulate others for their own salvation."[22] The criminalization of sin and the legislation of love, said Illich, are the genesis of that "liberal fantasy" that came to pass as Christendom ripened into modernity, where the gift became service industries, systems, or welfare states.[23] Even the great philosophical challenger to liberalism and its business-class apologists, Marx, was initially rooted in Hegel's secularized Christianity, that transfer of power from a perverted Christendom to an armed modern state. Marx, as brilliant an atheist as he was, was haunted by Christ. Marx's own challenge envisioned a kind of secular *eschaton*, or beautiful end time, but this would now be accomplished through revolutionary civil war and technological innovation, not the cross and the call.

Illich's Anti-Christ is not a foulmouthed ogre invading the bodies of innocent girls or a monstrous despot astride a cosmic throne in the Kingdom of Corpses. The anti-Christ wears a suit, pursues a degree in management or law, studies ledgers and scatterplots, administers charity, designs futures, and manages risks. It creeps in through the temptations of the *impersonal* and the *abstract*. And the secret weapon of the Anti-Christ has become general-purpose *money*.

Institutionalization

An old friend will help you move. A good friend will help you move a dead body.

—JIM HAYES

22. Illich, *Rivers North of the Future*, 13.

23. Ravenscroft, "Illich's Critique of Abstract Philanthropy." "It is argued that Illich's thought is animated by a traditional theological understanding of charity as anchored in local, personal bonds and networks of reciprocity, and that his critique of Western economic modernity has much to do with the gradual depersonalization and institutionalization of charity, theoretically and in society, linked to its transmogrification into 'abstract' philanthropy. Drawing on debates around the nature of love and the gift in contemporary theology, philosophy, and social anthropology, the conceptual dynamics of Illich's account of human sociality are made clear. Illich's continual concern throughout his life with defending spaces for meaningful human interaction, and with attacking those institutional and technological forms that threaten the interpersonal dimension of human life, can in this way be read as an outworking of his underlying concern for charity, understood as social bond."

Looked at dispassionately, institutionalization, in addition to its impersonality or because of it, is a function of Dunbar's number.[24] Any group that exceeds a certain threshold in number requires a layer of administration or management above it to organize its activity, suppress potential conflicts, and collect and redistribute goods. This is why anarchism can never "work"[25] except in groups that are fewer than around 150 people.[26]

The problem is, this leadership layer has qualities and characteristics that make it different from those it administers, and it inevitably does three things. The leader group (1) begins making rules not only for the whole, but for the smooth running of the leadership function—best case—and (2) to strengthen the leadership layer—this can be a good or bad thing depending on the specific leaders—and (3) to aggrandize itself at the expense of those led—which requires the leader group to intentionally bewilder those led into believing that what the leader group is doing to aggrandize itself is for the good of the whole.

In the case of rulemaking, especially in complex bureaucratic societies, the rules that apply to the whole (e.g., murder taboos or incest taboos) are expected, understood, and accepted for fairly obvious reasons. But rules that facilitate more "effective" management (e.g., the office is only open from 10 to 4, Monday through Thursday) also have a threshold whereupon they

24. Most of our day-to-day interactions involve either primary or secondary relationships. If you are my spouse or twice-a-week hiking buddy, we have a primary relationship based in mutual care and reciprocal obligation. If you are my insurance agent or my boss, we have a secondary relationship based in formal rules. There is a limited number of primary relationships one person can manage. Anthropologist Robin Dunbar suggests that the average person can only maintain about 150 primary, I-care-you-care relationships. The simple reason for this is that we reach certain cognitive limits, and because there is simply not enough time for more without diffusing the quality of all relationships. Obviously, the number is fuzzy, because with changes in culture come changes in relationships, and because relationships themselves are difficult to define precisely because they are not quantifiable. But if we assume 150 as a hypothetical constant, variable across some range, then the range itself is a valid premise for a few conclusions.

25. Troxell, "Christian Theory." This is not dismissing anarchism as a political *orientation*. Illich was frequently accused of it, and he called Jesus an anarchist. Ted Troxell makes an important distinction between the encompassing anarchism of Kroptokin or Bakunin and what he calls post-anarchism, which, rather than call for the "abolition of the state," and using De Certeau's distinction between "strategy" and "tactics," resists and-or bypasses the state in specific, fluid, and localized ways. Troxell discusses Christian anarchism (e.g., that of Dorothy Day) not so much as an ideology—though it contains ideological critiques—as practices that live out peaceful alternatives as witnesses in a violent world, and rejecting the visions of warlike (and male adventurist) triumphalism that motivate many leftists and anarchists.

26. Krotoski, "Robin Dunbar."

quit being for the good of the whole and begin subordinating the good of the whole to the good of the management layer. The management tail begins to wag the community dog. This dog-waggery is pernicious but not *necessarily* malicious. It is a pain in the collective behind, but through vigilance and good will, this tendency can *theoretically* be checked. In most cases, however, it is not; and this tendency is combined with those that follow. The larger the social organization, the more difficult this dog-waggery is to control, because of what we might call the law of social inertia. Mass times velocity equals momentum; and the granular self-organization of society within these larger administrative, economic, and juridical frameworks tends to minimize the capacity of individual leaders themselves to operate effectively outside these frameworks. And so, in spite of our best intentions, "the beat goes on."

In the case of leadership groups strengthening themselves, motive is crucial, but, then again, good motives do not always produce the intended effects. The management group might want to strengthen its own power to more effectively respond to emergencies. Unity-of-command is a principle wedded to tactical agility, so to speak. On the other hand—motive again—the leader group may take more power out of a desire to impose its will on the group. And, still again, even a power-grab might be motivated by the desire to accomplish something good; but this power might also be sought for something malicious or selfish. Specifics matter, but the problem is, one leader might want more power to do good, then a replacement comes along who uses that established institutional power to do wrong. We can look at our situation between President Obama and President Trump, where the-former strengthened the executive to do many wrongs (carrying water for Wall Street and the military-industrial-media complex, deportations, attacking whistle-blowers, supporting coup-makers and despots, and chronic paranoid bombing abroad), but did so with a certain circumspection and with an eye to stability—making him a kind of known and stable quality—and the latter, at least from what we can glean so far, has the mental and emotional makeup of a tyrannical six-year-old brat, and he has inherited this increased executive power, with even more *unpredictable* consequences.

In the third case, of leader self-aggrandizement, or what we might call *corruption*, the leaders use their positions and power to become rich, mainly, or richer; though we ought not discount the attraction of power itself to feed their feeble egos and give them the capacity to abuse others for their own sadistic pleasure. Ambiguously situated between the latter two cases, human beings who are in positions of power also enjoy mass recognition (fame), and often see the development of *reputation* as a kind of vain hedge against mortality. So you have leaders with an eye to their "legacies," which is still tragi-comically self-aggrandizing.[27] This can serve the good of others in some cases (even though the motive is narcissistic), but it can also be pursued in ways that themselves have unintended and terrible negative consequences.

Add to these the problem of impersonality, and we begin to see how the dangers of institutionalization are also related to *scale*. The larger the enterprise, the more necessary is institutionalization, and the greater the dangers described above. Now apply this insight to the difference between a parish of one hundred souls and a parish of one thousand. More to the point, how is either parish tempted to "organize charity," using the tools of efficiency, in ways that change the beaten Jew along the roadside into a listed client?

This criticism does not easily conform to either Catholic legalisms about "natural law,"[28] or Protestant notions of "orders of creation."[29] Illich's midrash-like take on the Parable of the Samaritan closely resembles "Yoder's critical adoption . . . of the modern concept of a power-structure . . . [and] . . . Yoder's relocation of this conceptuality within a theological cosmology."[30] Neither Yoder nor Illich would suggest that human society is not meant to be ordered; but both want that order to be accountable to "God's own ordering of human life in Christ."[31] No serious thinker in the latter twentieth century could ignore the relationships between German churches and the Third Reich, a state that was simultaneously violent (Yoder's preoccupation) and bureaucratic (Illich's), founded on a project of radical social engineering (the myth of progress).

The impulse to seek an easy answer, a formula we can remember with a rhyme, can mislead us into slotting our options into the Good file and the Bad

27. Stringfellow, *Keeper of the Word*, 247. On *money* to secure legacies: "The idolatry of money has its most grotesque form as a doctrine of immortality. Money is then not only the proof of the present moral worth of a person, but also the means through which his life gains significance after death. If a man leaves a substantial estate, death is cheated, if not defeated, because the money he leaves will sustain the memory of him and his fortune while the poor die and are at once forgotten. It is supposedly important to amass money not for its use in life, but as a monument in death. Money thus becomes the measure of a man's moral excellence while he lives and the means to purchase a certain survival of death; money makes people both moral and immortal; that is the most profound idolatry of money."

28. Aquinas' idea that human beings, through reason and free will, are naturally inclined to conform themselves to Eternal Law with which they are imprinted as creatures of God; and that human beings can therefore naturally discern good from evil.

29. A doctrine that God established various, hierarchical, and interrelated "orders" of creation (i.e., the family, the community, the state, the church, etc.).

30. Prather, *Christ, Power and Mammon*, 95–96.

31. Ibid., 97.

file. If progressive social engineering is Bad, then conservative *laissez faire* must be good. If conservative hard-heartedness and authoritarianism is Bad, then radical abstract compassion wrapped in libertarianism is Good. The way to avoid Constantinianism is withdrawal. The way to avoid withdrawal is a somewhat Constantinian "realism." The problem is that these kinds of categories conform neither to reality nor to the faithfulness of Christ, which each call on us to respond to the particularity of reality, in contexts that cannot be fully foreseen, in ways that manifest the Reign of God in the here and now. This is a reign, a "Kingdom" as Scripture calls it, in which governance is accomplished by courageous prophecy and in a state of *radical vulnerability*. This is the meaning of cross and resurrection.

Yes, we can participate in the overthrow of evils. No, we cannot do it using evil. We are not seeking a triumph for ourselves, but justice and reconciliation. As Prather describes this from Barth:

> Solidarity with specific socio-political movements, not as tangential or secondary to, but as *concretely expressive* of Christian faith and hope in God's reign, rests entirely on the distinction-in-relation between the Spirit of Jesus' humanity and the spirits manifest in the structuring powers . . . the present capitalist order has also faced this decision, and has been found wanting, not merely in the less benign personal decisions of certain owners or bosses, but at the *structural* heart of the system.[32]

Understanding money as an ecological force has only reinforced this conclusion, and it deepens our understanding of *how and why* at the "structural heart" of capitalism there stands a profound rebellion against the Reign of God. That Barth and other Christian socialists—steeped in the conflicts of their own times—may have missed this ecological dimension, and even fallen to one degree or another for the Promethian myth of development with its concealment of the center-margin dynamics—does not mean we declare them totally in error. Their insights into the exploitation of labor still stand, as we can see in any Satanic poor-nation sweat shop, now extended and enhanced by the discovery of how this capital-labor relation is nested in a capitalist ecology that is discernable through the nodes and flows of labor, energy, food, and raw materials worldwide.

32. Ibid., 225.

The Alternatives

Beloved, believe not every spirit, but prove the spirits, whether
they are of God; because many false prophets are gone out into
the world.

—1 JOHN 4:1

The challenge of modernity is to live without illusions without
becoming disillusioned.

—ANTONIO GRAMSCI

We do not possess money. People do not possess idols; they are possessed
by them, especially those who have the least of it. Yet as we have noted again
and again, this is more than a matter of a person possessed by the need for
money or the obsession with its accumulation. We are its structural captives,
which at least means we can face our captivity without worshipping our cap-
tor provided we recognize money-idolatry for what it is. Economics—in the
way that it excludes everything non-monetary, in the way it subordinates all
things to money—is a liturgy for this idol, in the same way that our patriotism is a liturgy for that co-idol, the nation. As Prather describes it, we have
twin idols: Mammon and Leviathan. It is only with this in view that we can
begin to decide what is to be done, based on what can be done.

We can parse words and correct popular misunderstandings as we go
along, but we'll begin with a blunt statement. Wherever capitalism is headed
from here, the continuation of the monetized industrial capitalist epoch
(within which state socialisms were themselves entrapped by industrial
Promethianism, and therefore part of the capitalist order), is suicidal. There
will be no soft landing. Continuing on this same path is already disastrous
for most of the world, and that disaster is creeping back from the margins—
where it had been exported through violence, fraud, plunder, domination,
and unequal exchange—toward the centers. The ecology of general-purpose
money tells us this in the way that its use is contrary to those natural processes that constitute the very biosphere upon which we all depend and of
which we are all a part.

There may be movements for an economic model that is designed
to break us away from economic models and return to uniquely situated,
relocalized, subsistence. Christians may want to critically join such movements. What are needed first are some very radical policy prescriptions; and
whether they are possible is another question.

You can call it whatever you like, but the central state would quickly need to take control over productive processes as a form of triage. New social organizations cannot be created by decree or wholesale abandonment of current systems. If there is a resolution to our crises, then it will take more than a generation, and it will require complex, detailed, and carefully thought-out transitions. When I said triage, I meant exactly that. Such a movement would have to stop the bleeding and restore the airway first. And that would mean a strong (not violent) state that does several specific things as soon as possible.

The most important of those things will be to nationalize the banks, the utilities, and other key industries; to unilaterally and immediately withdraw all US military forces from abroad; to systematically ensure that everyone is housed and fed; to guarantee a universal baseline income to all; to establish civilian control boards over all police agencies and prisons and abolish police tactical units; to make education through graduate school free to all who qualify; to forgive massive amounts of personal debt; and to adopt a single-payer health care system. This is just the lifesaving first step, because people need to be reassured and supported before the real work of *redesign* begins.

Because the complex crisis we face is ecological, any form of governance will have to address these crises head-on; and it will have to aim all its efforts at ultimately restoring a right relation between humankind and non-human nature that liquidates the subject-object dualism. Because general-purpose money is an ecological phenomenon that dissolves traditions, communities, and the biosphere, any transition worth its salt will have to begin the long march to reduce our dependence on general-purpose money, which inevitably means some form of the *radical relocalization* of all basic production, draconian control of "markets," the gradual death by benign neglect of old transportation grids, and the reorganization of political subdivisions around watersheds instead of arbitrary lines drawn on the map.

To this end, the state's role would be crucial. Once key industries and infrastructure are placed under public control and price controls established, nonessential industries would need to be systematically closed down. As they are closed, massive public works training and jobs programs would be established to guarantee uninterrupted full employment at living wages; and those jobs would need to be geared to the transitional projects for repairing environmental damage and setting the stage for thorough-going relocalization. With price controls, the state could print money for this purpose (they've printed about a trillion dollars to bail out bond traders so far). Priority programs would remediate areas and communities where environmental injustices have been the worst. A maximum wage system would need to be established for various professionals—doctors, lawyers, etc. Dramatic conservation measures would need to be taken and enforced, beginning with energy rationing and including any nonessential production that relies on imports that depend upon postcolonial (neoliberal) unequal exchange relations abroad. All subsidies and allowances in agriculture and forestry would be cancelled and/or redirected for both re-localization and sustainability. Any industry that exceeds a certain number of employees and which is not directed wholly by the state would be reorganized as worker-owned. All industry oversight and management would be conducted by subsets of the central authority who are representative of their watersheds. All subsidies to fossil energy extraction and refinement would need to be ended, and a transition program for all workers in those industries into public works.[33]

As to money, and this may be the most radical proposal of all—but it takes into account what we have studied with regard to money as the sign with no referent—one proposal has been a two-money system. Alf Hornborg sums it up:

> Perhaps transforming our money system is the only chance we have. General-purpose money rewards the dissipation of resources with ever more resources to dissipate, until they are gone, or at least inaccessible. The dilemma of sustainability thus seems to be the very juxtaposition of this socio-cultural institution with the . . . facts of entropy, limited land area, and finite stocks of resources. The problem could thus be expressed as the consequences of money in a universe obeying the Second Law of Thermodynamics. If this is indeed recognized as our fundamental problem, it is much less problematic to conclude which of these factors—general-purpose money or the Second Law of Thermodynamics—can be changed through political decisions. Money is a cultural sign system invented by humans and in the long run perhaps the only factor we can hope to transform in the interest of sustainability.[34]

33. Kunkel, "The Capitalocene." This would be critically important. As Kunkel writes: "Fossil fuels now persist, in the face of renewable alternatives, because of massive investments of capital in the fixed infrastructure of their production, refining and transportation. The transition to a post-carbon energy system that every rational person sees must be undertaken with all deliberate speed can't occur without devaluing the assets, natural and built alike, of private and state-owned energy companies. Meanwhile, fossil energy is publicly subsidised at six times the rate of renewables. This subsidy to suicide is reason alone to doubt the possibility of any ecological capitalism."

34. Hornborg, *Global Ecology*, 147–48.

What Hornborg and others have proposed is a dual money system—
which they call a multi-centric economy. The state or other polities issue
two forms of currency. One form would be the existing national currency,
which will be eventually transitioned into a currency for long-distance exchange. The other would be local scripts, exchangeable only within certain
boundaries (watersheds?) and only for subsistence commodities produced
within those boundaries: locally grown food, locally produced tools, re-used
items (thrift shops), organic fuels, materials extracted from local land (wood,
fibers, plants, mulch, compost, et al.), local transport assistance, and local
services. This script would be issued as a substantial portion of the guaranteed minimum income. Local script would be absolutely tax-free and could
be used to hire temporary informal labor. In the short term, this may actually
increase the exchanges using national currency, because it would free more
income for non-local commodities; but over the longer term, the advantages
afforded by local script, in conjunction with policies that promote increased
local production, would strengthen the script as well as stabilize the local
economy. In particular, given that local food production would be exchangeable for local script that is issued as part of a guaranteed minimum income,
this system would promote small-scale, local agriculture, which is an essential—if not *the* essential—component of any larger transition. It would
likewise inoculate local production from the solvent-effect of the national
general-purpose currency, and set the stage for the most important general
change of all: a de-financialized, de-growth economy.[35]

The goal of short and mid-term social control over the economy
through a democratic state is not the stabilization of a social-democratic
state, but the transition to a de-financialized, de-growth economy.

Without this kind of emergency program, what we have now—crisis
wracked and headed for disaster—will stutter along and crash, leaving us
even more vulnerable to authoritarian reactionaries than we already are,
as evidenced by the narrow election of Trump. Long-term and intentional
watershed-based relocalization is far more radical than the nationalistic
and nostalgic Keyenesians of Bernie Sanders' stripe, but a *real* alternative
needs to be articulated, with a vision upon which to build a *real* resistance
to the period of reaction we are now entering. How that looks will depend
on many things that are yet to be discovered in the process of redesigning
the built environment; and if we do not redesign the built environment, that
very environment will return us to our present practical and epistemological default positions on the runaway train.

35. Fournier, "The Politics of Degrowth."

Like it or not, we are already miles along the path of a world emergency. We may fail to take this kind of dramatic action, to mount this kind of resistance, to enter into this kind of mass movement; but if we fail at that, we will categorically leave our grandchildren a desperate, insecure, miserable, and more dangerous world. For far too many around the world and at home, this is already the reality.

> The call is to all Christians, not just a select few, to witness to the way of God, the truth of God, which is different from the powers of the world. But . . . we need to do it in the world in which we live, and to know that world.
>
> —Katharine Temple, Catholic Worker[36]

What are Christians to do? And we are asking in particular what do Western Christians do? What do American Christians do? I would require five earths for everyone on earth to live like the abstractly-average American, and three earths to live like the abstractly-average European. The "standard" of living in the "developed" world exists parasitically upon the poorest. These two irrefutable facts confront us with the momentous moral obligation not merely to redistribute, but to break that parasitic dependency *at our own expense*. And yet we have also demonstrated the difficulty of making this kind of dramatic transition-to-less (far less) is not merely our selfish reluctance to do so, but the many ways in which we ourselves are locked into dependency, locked into this dance of death with those so far *out of sight and out of mind*, locked in by our lack of skills and the determinisms of the built environment, locked in by our current and nested duties and obligations, locked in by our total dependence on general-purpose money, locked into complicity whether we like it or not.

We know the gravitational force of money on the church. Too often in the past, as corporations (churches are corporations now, with IRS charters) and as money-dependent institutions, the church has remained silent in the face of injustices until others have already legitimated resistance. Too often the richest parishioners are the most influential because of the size of their tithes. In this, we need true leaders, just in their treatment of members, vigilant against bureaucratism, resistant to self-aggrandizing power, and inoculated against corruption.

Perhaps before we begin, the church needs to lose its obsession with respectability. Jesus was not respectable. On the contrary, he broke every "respectability" code of his time. The path to the cross is not quiet white Happyville. The middle class church of shined shoes and starched shirts

36. Dietrich and Temple, "Jacques Ellul," 5.

with a weekly dose of organ music and self-righteousness is not equal to the task of witnessing in a world headed toward Syria or Haiti writ large on everyone's horizon.

The church has neither the standing nor the capacity to become Constantinian, and given our history and our calling, it seems we ought to resist the desire to do so. The measures required by any movement of resistance or the articulation of political alternatives are based on the relationship between what we actually have before us and what are *next steps* in that triage. We are not "building the future"[37]—God knows how wrong that notion has gone before; we are calling an ambulance and getting a patient to the hospital. We need to find our footing as resident aliens and enter into practical alliances at each step along the way, as witnesses. Nonviolent, fearless, willing to work and sacrifice and speak truth to power as well as to allies.

But perhaps our most important work is calling to us as parishes/congregations who are uniquely positioned as pre-organized local institutions to begin the practical life-saving work *ahead of and alongside the political work*. While we work for environmental justice, provide sanctuary and succor, and speak truth to power, we need to reclaim and rehabilitate land, water, and housing; begin to create new facts on the ground; and make peace between neighbors.

We cannot overemphasize how important the built environment is for any transition to a de-growth economy; and that begins most fundamentally with water, soil, and food. Dependence on money is in no way clearer than in our food systems. And intensive hand-tended, organic polyculture can produce far more and far more variable food per hectare than extractive industrial agriculture while actually restoring soils to biotic health, capturing carbon, and preventing water pollution.[38] What prevents us now from a transition to ecologically sound agriculture in place of industrial monoculture is the fact that we cannot produce enough food on these smaller scales to match that now produced using industrial methods unless *far more people engage in the practice of growing food*, which requires more people having access to smaller parcels of land and water. Churches should be in the forefront on land reclamation for local, small-scale food production. Churches should be finding ways—especially among the young—to quit sending missions abroad to force subsistence cultures to become more "developed," and start rebuilding their own communities in a direction that points *from* "developed" *to* subsistence. If American churches want a real

37. Such arrogance! One might hope that Christians, at least, would approach these things with an attitude of contrition.

38. Meyer, "Small-Scale Organic Farming."

mission, let us help twenty million more young people to be small-scale farmers, urban agriculturists, permaculture practitioners, truck gardeners, suburban sharecroppers, rooftop growers, food forest designers, hoop-house growers, community gardeners, and gleaners.

The general-purpose money and growth economy is fundamentally based on scarcity. We depend on money, which is deliberately made scarce enough to ensure competition, that is, conflict. We are structured for conflict. Sustainable food production cooperates with nature in a structure based fundamentally on patient abundance. One cilantro plant, grown with little to no maintenance apart from ensuring enough water, produces thousands of seeds. Nature, like grace, is profligate. Food systems that imitate nature are based not on scarcity but abundance, and abundance reduces conflict. This is peacemaking.

Churches can lead efforts toward relocalization, before and apart from its policy complications. The restructuring of the built environment is inevitable, but there are good changes and bad ones. Redesigning the built environment the right way is a duty to us all and a calling for many. It will be difficult at first, then less so, but the direction these things take depend on who will have standing ten years from now to show other people the right way—learned through patient practice—when those others no longer have a choice. This is how we make facts on the ground that will eventually change the people on the ground around them. As the twelve-steppers remind us, "You can't think your way into right acting. You have to act your way into right thinking."

Conspiracy of Friendship

An old civil rights organizer once told a group of us activists who had gathered around one of the many outrages of the day back in the early 1990s, "My first advice to all of you is, don't just do something, sit there." You could hear people scooting their chairs around and see them fidgeting when they heard this. I fidgeted, too.

Most of what we attempted failed. We were pumped up for a fight. We didn't lack resolve or courage or even strategic sense . . . most of the time. We lacked humility and patience. The antidote to that, at least one antidote, is reflection. Nine times out of ten, we need to sit there. Everything we do sets a series of unpredictable ramifications in motion for one thing; but, apart from that, we are as powerless as everyone else. It's only pride that tells us differently.

I had not become Christian back then, and I was a devotee of the myth of progress. Moreover, I was an army vet with some planning skills and some serious think-evil insights about how to get the best of an adversary. This *was* the toughest, *is* the toughest, aspect of my own personality, my own history, to divest of as a Christian who confesses a crucified sovereign who told us to stay awake, to persevere, and to leave the big stuff to God.

When Illich interprets the Parable of the Samaritan to me as a gift of free and *enfleshed* friendship, the old me rankles and bucks, scoots his chair and fidgets. I want to get Davidic on someone's ass, get back out there and correct things, because I've been indoctrinated into believing that this is how we find justice in a world weeping and bleeding with in-justice. Upon reflection, I have to admit, taking on the big stuff is a lot easier than friendship for me. I am far more charitable in the abstract than I am in person. It is easy for me to give and congratulate myself on my generosity; but it is hard for me to be charitable about the brokenness I see across from me, the person breathing the same air as me, the other who reflects my own lonely brokenness back to me. Money given impersonally as charity does that, too.

Illich liked to describe the earliest church, the house churches along the postal routes identified in John's Apocalypse. The liturgy was simple then. It was the conspiracy, *conspiratio*. In Latin, this means breathe to-gether. *Con*, together. *Spiratio*, breath. Spirit in the past was the same word as breath. The living person, the person who still was animated by the soul, or the spirit, was that person who breathes. Sharing breath meant sharing spirit. The *conspiratio*, for early Christians, was a mouth-kiss, and exchange of spirit. Then they ate. The liturgy was kissing then eating together. Then they would talk about their story, the story of the broken people who follow a crucified sovereign. The reason Illich had such an aversion to develop-ment, to bureaucratic society, to over-specialized experts, to contracts, and to impersonal institutions was that these are the antithesis in their imper-sonality to the heterogeneous community of friends who kiss and eat and talk about Jesus.

In our witness, before, during, and after we live and know and act in that world to which we witness as resident aliens, we are united—if we can be faithful—in a conspiracy of friendship. We seek knowledge as best we can. We practice various renunciations to know our freedom as best we can. We seek after the resurrection of the commons and an economics of local conviviality. But our currency is *friendship*, because the Incarnation happened, the Incarnation was a surprise, the Incarnation was a gift, the Incarnation was revealed not discovered, and the Incarnation is expressed through love and knowledge.

Though I speak with the tongues of men and of angels, but have not love, I have become sounding brass or a clanging cymbal. And though I have the gift of prophecy, and understand all mysteries and all knowledge, and though I have all faith, so that I could remove mountains, but have not love, I am nothing.

—1 CORINTHIANS 13:1

Bibliography

Alexis-Baker, Nekeisha. "Market Capitalism: The Religion of the Market and Its Challenge to the Church." *The Ellul Forum* 44 (Fall 2009) 4–10.

Allen, Benjamin S. "Deforestation's Challenge to Green Growth in Brazil." Green Growth Economies Project, Berkeley Roundtable on the International Economy, University of California, Berkeley, September 13, 2011. http://brie.berkeley.edu/publications/WP_202DeforestationGreenGrowthBrazil.pdf.

Alvarez, Robert. "The U.S. Department of Energy's Atomic Defense Budget for FY 2017." Institute for Policy Studies, March 2016. http://www.lasg.org/budget/FY2017/Alvarez_DOE_Budget_2017.pdf.

Amadeo, Kimberly. "What Caused Stagflation, and Can It Happen Again?" *The Balance*, September 24, 2016. https://www.thebalance.com/what-is-stagflation-3305964.

Andrews, Robert. *The Columbia Dictionary of Quotations*. New York: Columbia University Press, 1993.

Araghi, Farshad, and Marina Karides. "Land Dispossession and Global Crisis." *Journal of World-System Research* 18 (2012) 1–5.

Arbesman, Samuel. *The Half-Life of Facts: Why Everything We Know Has an Expiration Date*. New York: Penguin, 2012.

Arnaud, Emilie. "Occupied Palestine: Displacement as of October 2014." Internal Displacement Monitoring Centre, October 27, 2014. http://www.internal-displacement.org/middle-east-and-north-africa/palestine/2014/syria-displacement-in-occupied-palestine-as-of-october-2014.

Beckel, Michael. "Senators Supporting Ethanol Subsidies Reap Riches from Corn Interests." *OpenSecrets*, January 23, 2011. https://www.opensecrets.org/news/2011/01/ethanol-lobby-finds-friends-foes/.

Bennholdt-Thomsen, Veronika, and Maria Mies. *The Subsistence Perspective: Beyond the Globalised Economy*. New York: Zed. 2000.

Bergson, Henri. *Creative Evolution*. Translated by Arthur Mitchell. New York: H. Holt, 1911.

Biddle, Wayne. "Nerve Gases and Pesticides: Links Are Close." *New York Times*, March 30, 1984.

Biello, David. "Electric Cars Are Not Necessarily Clean." *Scientific American*, May 11, 2016. https://www.scientificamerican.com/article/electric-cars-are-not-necessarily-clean/.

Blas, Javier. "Saudi Wells Running Dry—of Water—Spell End of Desert Wheat." *Bloomberg*, November 3, 2015. https://www.bloomberg.com/news/articles/2015 -11-04/saudi-wells-running-dry-of-water-spell-end-of-desert-wheat.

Bohannan, Paul. "The Impact of Money on an African Subsistence Economy." *The Journal of Economic History 19 (1959) 491–503.*

Bollman, Moritz, et al. *World Ocean Review 1.* 2010. http://worldoceanreview.com/wp-content/downloads/wor1/WOR1_english.pdf.

Boone, Peter, and Simon Johnson. "Way Too Big to Fail." *New Republic*, November 7, 2010.

Bovard, James. "Archer Daniels Midland—a Case Study in Corporate Welfare." Cato Institute Policy Analysis No. 241, September 26, 1995. https://object.cato.org/ sites/cato.org/files/pubs/pdf/pa241.pdf.

Bowlby, Chris. "Fritz Haber: Jewish Chemist Whose Work Led to Zyklon B." *BBC*, April 12, 2011. http://www.bbc.com/news/world-13015210.

Brower, Montgomery. "Pulling Strings on Capitol Hill, These Lobbyists Are Trying to Unravel Reagan's Tax Reform." *People*, October 14, 1985.

Bureau of Labor Statistics. "International Comparison of Hourly Compensation." August 9, 2013. https://www.bls.gov/fls/ichcc.pdf.

Burn-Callander, Rebecca. "The History of Money: From Barter to Bitcoin." *The Telegraph*, October 20, 2014.

Campbell, John. "Bayesian Methods and Universal Darwinism." In *Bayesian Inference and Maximum Entropy Methods in Science and Engineering: 29th International Workshop*, edited by Paul M. Goggans and Chung-Yong Chan, 40–47. Melville, NY: American Institute of Physics, 2009.

Carney, Dan. "Dwayne's World." *Mother Jones* (July/August 1995). https://www. motherjones.com/politics/1995/07/dwaynes-world/.

Cayley, David. "Christ and Anti-Christ in the Thought of Ivan Illich." Address to Department of Religious Studies, McMaster University, Hamilton, ON, October 21, 2015.

———. *Ivan Illich in Conversation.* Toronto: House of Anansi, 1992.

Chakrabortty, Aditya. "Mainstream Economics Is in Denial: The World Has Changed." *Guardian*, October 28, 2013. https://www.theguardian.com/commentisfree/2013/ oct/28/mainstream-economics-denial-world-changed.

Conniff, Richard. "What the Luddites Really Fought Against." *Smithsonian*, March 2011. http://www.smithsonianmag.com/history/what-the-luddites-really-fought-against-264412/.

Cooke, Kieran. "Turmoil in Saudi Water Sector as Country Runs Dry." *Middle East Eye*, July 10, 2016. http://www.middleeasteye.net/columns/turmoil-saudi-water-sector-country-runs-dry-465571093.

Corradin, Camilla. "Israel: Water as a Tool to Dominate Palestinians." *Al Jazeera*, June 23, 2016. http://www.aljazeera.com/news/2016/06/israel-water-tool-dominate-palestinians-160619062531348.html.

Cunliffe, Sydney. "British Imperialism and Tea Culture in Asia and North America, 1650–1950." MA thesis, University of Victoria, 2014.

Dale, Edwin L., Jr. "U.S. Trade Deficit Is Cut Markedly as Exports Grow." *New York Times*, April 27, 1973.

Davis, Mike. "Planet of Slums." *New Left Review* 26 (March/April 2004). https:// newleftreview.org/II/26/mike-davis-planet-of-slums.

Day, Keri. "The Myth of Progress." In *Religious Resistance to Neoliberalism: Womanist and Black Feminist Perspectives*, 19–46. New York: Palgrave Macmillan, 2016.

Dietrich, Jeff, and Katharine Temple. "Jacques Ellul: The Word of God in a World of Technique." *Ellul Forum* 31 (Spring 2003). https://journals.wheaton.edu/index.php/ellul/article/view/203.

Donley, Arvin. "The Inside Story of a Groundbreaking Trade Agreement." *World Grain*, July 2, 2013. http://www.world-grain.com/News/News-Home/Features/2013/7/The-inside-story-of-a-groundbreaking-trade-agreement.aspx?cck=1.

Dumaresq, Charles. "Cobalt Mining Legacy." *Carleton University*, 2009. http://www.cobaltmininglegacy.ca/.

Durish, Pat, et al. "Civil Society, Cultural Hegemony, and Citizenship: Implications for Adult Educators." Conference Proceedings, 1999 Adult Education Research Conference, DeKalb, IL. http://newprairiepress.org/cgi/viewcontent.cgi?article=2086&context=aerc.

Ellul, Jacques. *Money and Power*. Translated by LaVonne Neff. Downers Grove, IL: InterVarsity, 1984.

———. *The Technological Society*. Translated by John Wilkinson. New York: Vintage, 1964.

Fairlie, Simon. "A Short History of Enclosure in Britain." *The Land* 7 (Summer 2009). http://www.thelandmagazine.org.uk/articles/short-history-enclosure-britain.

Foster, John Bellamy. *The Vulnerable Planet: A Short Economic History of the Environment*. New York: Monthly Review, 1994.

Fournier, Valérie. "Escaping from the Economy: The Politics of Degrowth." *International Journal of Sociology* 28 (2008) 528–45.

Franklin, H. Bruce. "What Are We to Make of J. G. Ballard's Apocalypse?" In *Voices for the Future: Essays on Major Science Fiction Writers*, Volume 2, edited by Thomas Clareson, 82–105. Bowling Green: Bowling Green University Popular Press, 1979.

Gause, F. Gregory. "Sultans of Swing? The Geopolitics of Falling Oil Prices." Brookings Institution, April 2015. https://www.brookings.edu/wp-content/uploads/2016/06/Falling-Oil-Prices-English.pdf.

Ghizoni, Sandra Kollen. "Creation of the Bretton Woods System." *Federal Reserve History*, November 22, 2013. https://www.federalreservehistory.org/essays/bretton_woods_created.

Ghogomu, Mbiyimoh. "U.S. Factory Workers Make 76 Time More Per Hour than Workers in Indonesia." *The Higher Learning*, April 9, 2015. http://thehigherlearning.com/2015/04/09/u-s-factory-workers-make-76-times-more-per-hour-than-workers-in-indonesia/.

Gilson, Ronald J., and Curtis J. Milhaupt. "Economically Benevolent Dictators: Lessons for Developing Democracies." Columbia Law and Economics Working Paper No. 371, March 6, 2010. http://dx.doi.org/10.2139/ssrn.1564925.

Glick, Reuven, and Kevin J. Lansing. "U.S. Household Deleveraging and Future Consumption Growth." Federal Reserve Bank of San Francisco Economic Letter, May 15, 2009. http://www.frbsf.org/economic-research/publications/economic-letter/2009/may/us-household-deleveraging-consumption-growth/.

Global Policy Forum. "Permanent Bases." 2007. https://www.globalpolicy.org/political-issues-in-iraq/permanent-bases.html.

Goff, Stan. *Borderline: Reflections on War, Sex, and Church*, Eugene, OR: Cascade, 2015.

———. *Full Spectrum Disorder: The Military in the New American Century*. New York: Soft Skull, 2004.

Goldenberg, Susanne. "US Corn-Belt Farmers: 'The Country Has Turned on Us.'" *Guardian*, August 15, 2011. https://www.theguardian.com/environment/2011/aug/15/us-corn-belt-farmers.

Gowan, Peter. "Ways of the World." Interview by Mike Newman and Marko Bojcun. *New Left Review* 59 (September-October 2009). https://newleftreview.org/II/59/peter-gowan-the-ways-of-the-world.

Guccione, Bob, Jr. "Life After Death: SPIN's 1996 Feature on the Unspeakable War in Sarajevo." *Spin*, September 11, 2015. https://www.spin.com/featured/life-after-death-war-in-sarajevo-feature/.

Guimond, Marie-France. "Structural Adjustment and Peacebuilding: Road to Conflict or Peace?" International Development Research Centre Working Paper 8, February 2007. https://www.idrc.ca/sites/default/files/sp/Documents%20EN/Structural-Adjustment-and-Peacebuilding-Road-to-Conflict-or-Peace.pdf.

Hall, Bob. "How Much for a Seat on the Board of Transportation?" *Democracy South*, (April 4, 1997). http://democracyncarchive.org/downloads/archive/priceforBOTseat.html.

Hall, Charles A. S., Jessica G. Lambert, and Stephen B. Balogh. "EROI of Different Fuels and the Implications for Society." *Energy Policy* 64 (2014) 141–52.

Hamburg, Steve. "Methane: The Other Important Greenhouse Gas." Environmental Defense Fund, 2017. https://www.edf.org/methane-other-important-greenhouse-gas.

Hammer, Joshua. "Is a Lack of Water to Blame for the Conflict in Syria?" *Smithsonian*, June, 2013. https://www.smithsonianmag.com/innovation/is-a-lack-of-water-to-blame-for-the-conflict-in-syria-72513729/.

Hart, David Bentley. *The Beauty of the Infinite: The Aesthetics of Christian Truth*. Grand Rapids: Eerdmans, 2004.

Hartsock, Nancy C. M. *Money, Sex, and Power: Toward a Feminist Historical Materialism*. Boston: Northeastern University Press, 1983.

Harvey, Chelsea. "Climate Change: Greenland Loses a Trillion Tonnes of Ice a Year as Melting Rate Triples." *Independent*, July 21, 2016. http://www.independent.co.uk/environment/climate-change-global-warming-greenland-ice-melting-rate-sea-levels-rise-a7147846.html

Harvey, David. *A Brief History of Neoliberalism*. Oxford: Oxford University Press, 2005.

Hazell, Peter B. R. "Green Revolution: Curse or Blessing?" International Food Policy Research Institute, 2002. https://www.ifpri.org/publication/green-revolution.

Hedges, Chris. "Retribution for a World Lost in Screens." *Truthdig*, September 26, 2010. http://www.truthdig.com/report/item/retribution_for_a_world_lost_in_screens_20100927.

Herr, Norman. "Television & Health." *Sourcebook for Teaching Science*, 2017. https://www.csun.edu/science/health/docs/tv&health.html.

Hill, Joshua S. "Solar Panels Soon to Complete Repayment of Energy Debt." *Clean Technica*, December 8, 2016. https://cleantechnica.com/2016/12/08/solar-panels-soon-complete-repayment-energy-debt/.

Hornborg, Alf. *Global Ecology and Unequal Exchange*. New York: Routledge, 2011.

———. *The Power of the Machine: Global Inequalities of Technology, Economy, and the Environment*. Lanham, MD: AltaMira, 2001.

Hornborg, Alf, J. R. McNeill, and Joan Martínez-Alier, eds. *Rethinking Environmental History: World-System History and Global Environmental Change*. Walnut Creek, CA: AltaMira. 2007.

Hudson, Michael. "How the US Has Launched a New Financial World Order—and How the Rest of the World Will Fight Back." *Counterpunch*, October 11, 2010. http://www.counterpunch.org/2010/10/11/why-the-u-s-has-launched-a-new-financial-world-war-and-how-the-the-rest-of-the-world-will-fight-back/.

———. *Super Imperialism: The Economic Strategy of American Empire*. New York: Holt, Rinehart, and Winston, 2003.

Hughes, J. Donald. "Environmental Impacts of the Roman Economy and Social Structure: Augustus to Diocletian." In *Rethinking Environmental History: World-System History and Global Environmental Change*, edited by Alf Hornborg, J. R. McNeill, and Joan Martínez-Alier, 27–39. Lanham, MD: AltaMira. 2007.

Hunt, William, and Scott Stevens. "Permeable Pavement Use and Research at Hannibal Parking Lot in Kinston, NC." NCSU Water Quality Group, May 2001.

Illich, Ivan. *Deschooling Society*. New York: Harper & Row, 1971.

———. "The Educational Enterprise in the Light of the Gospel." Lecture given in Chicago, IL, November 13, 1988. http://www.davidtinapple.com/illich/1988_Educational.html.

———. *Energy and Equity*. Ideas in Progress. New York: Harper & Row, 1974.

———. *Rivers North of the Future: The Testament of Ivan Illich*. As told to David Cayley. Toronto: House of Anansi, 2005.

———. "Vernacular Values." April 12, 1981. http://www.preservenet.com/theory/Illich/Vernacular.html#EMPIRE.

"The IMF and the World Bank: Puppets of the Neoliberal Onslaught." *The Thistle* 13.2 (September/October 2000). http://www.mit.edu/~thistle/v13/2/imf.html.

Inderscience. "How Much Oil Have We Used?" May 8, 2009. https://www.sciencedaily.com/releases/2009/05/090507072830.htm.

International Business Times. "World Energy Day 2014: How Much Oil Is Left and How Long Will It Last?" February 11, 2016. http://www.ibtimes.co.uk/world-energy-day-2014-how-much-oil-left-how-long-will-it-last-1471200.

International Monetary Fund. "Tequila Hangover: The Mexican Peso Crisis and Its Aftermath." In *History of the International Monetary Fund, 1990–1999*, 455–96. https://www.imf.org/external/pubs/ft/history/2012/pdf/c10.pdf.

Islam, Nazrul. "Agro-imperialism: Green Revolution to Biotechnology." *Daily Star*, July 2, 2004. http://archive.thedailystar.net/2004/07/02/d407021501100.htm.

Jacobson, Michael. "To Cut or Not to Cut: Tree Value and Deciding When to Harvest Timber." Penn State Extension, 2008. http://extension.psu.edu/natural-resources/forests/finance/forest-tax-info/publications/forest-finance-8-to-cut-or-not-cut-tree-value-and-deciding-when-to-harvest-timber/extension_publication_file.

Jamail, Dahr. "The Melting Arctic's Dramatic Impact on All Weather Patterns." *Truthout*, January 4, 2016. http://www.truth-out.org/news/item/34276-the-melting-arctic-s-dramatic-impact-on-global-weather-patterns.

Janaro, Jeff. "The Danger of Imperial Overstretch." *Foreign Policy Journal*, July 15, 2014. https://www.foreignpolicyjournal.com/2014/07/15/the-danger-of-imperial-overstretch/.

Jeddah Regional Climate Center. "First National Communication Water Resources." 2017. https://jrcc.sa/First_National_Communication_Water_Resources.php.

Johnston, David, "Have We Passed the Point of No Return on Climate Change?" *Scientific American*, April 13, 2015. https://www.scientificamerican.com/article/have-we-passed-the-point-of-no-return-on-climate-change/.

Kee, Howard Clark. *Community of the New Age: Studies in Mark's Gospel.* Macon, GA: Mercer University Press, 1983.

Kelleher, Dennis M. "The Lessons of Repealing Glass-Steagall." *Huffington Post*, November 11, 2016. http://www.huffingtonpost.com/dennis-m-kelleher/the-lessons-of-repealing-glass-steagall_b_8532666.html.

Kirk, Chris. "American Debt Crisis in 5 Charts." *Business Insider*, May 14, 2016. http://www.businessinsider.com/the-american-debt-crisis-in-5-charts-2016-5.

Krotoski, Aleks. "Robin Dunbar: We Can Only Ever Have 150 Friends at Most." *Guardian*, March 13, 2010. https://www.theguardian.com/technology/2010/mar/14/my-bright-idea-robin-dunbar.

Kunkel, Benjamin. "The Capitalocene." *London Review of Books*, March 2, 2017, 22–28.

Kwa, Aileen. "Agriculture in Developing Countries: Which Way Forward?" Focus on the Global South, Trade-Related Agenda, Development and Equity Occasional Papers 4, June 2001. https://focusweb.org/publications/2001/agriculture_which_way_forward.html.

Kwong, Peter. "The Chinese Face of Neoliberalism." *Counterpunch*, October 7, 2006. https://www.counterpunch.org/2006/10/07/the-chinese-face-of-neoliberalism/.

Lancaster, Don. "Some Energy Fundamentals." *The Blatant Opportunist* 71 (October 2002). http://www.tinaja.com/glib/energfun.pdf.

LeBeau, Phil. "Whoa! 1.7 Billion Cars on the Road by 2035." *CNBC*, November 12, 2012. https://www.cnbc.com/id/49796736.

Leonard, Andrew. "When Guano Imperialists Ruled the Earth." *Salon*, February 29, 2008. http://www.salon.com/2008/02/29/guano_imperialism/.

LeVine, Steve. "Saudi Arabia Has Declared an End to Its Oil War with the US." *Quartz*, June 23, 2016. https://qz.com/714622/saudi-arabia-has-declared-an-end-to-its-oil-war-with-the-us/.

Li Ching, Lim. "Is Ecological Agriculture Productive?" *Third World Network*, November 2008. http://www.twn.my/title2/susagri/susagri64.htm.

Liesman, Steve. "US Household Debt Climbs to $12.26 Trillion in First Quarter." *CNBC*, May 24, 2016. https://www.cnbc.com/2016/05/24/household-debt-climbs-to-1225-trillion-in-first-quarter.html.

Linder, Douglas O. "Oklahoma City Bombing Trial (1997)." *Famous Trials: University of Missouri at Kansas City Law School*, 2006. http://www.famous-trials.com/oklacity.

Liu, Henry C. K. "U.S. Dollar Hegemony Has Got to Go." *Asia Times*, April 11, 2002.

Lohmann, Larry. "'Strange Markets' and the Climate Crisis." In *Crisis financiera o crisis civilizatoria*, 98–122. Quito: Instituto de Estudios Ecologistas del Tercer Mundo, 2010. See http://www.thecornerhouse.org.uk/sites/thecornerhouse.org.uk/files/Crisis%20Financiera%200%20civilizatoria.pdf.

Long, Heather. "Who Owns America's Debt?" *CNN Money*, May 10, 2016. http://money.cnn.com/2016/05/10/news/economy/us-debt-ownership/.

Lowenstein, Roger. "The Nixon Shock." *Bloomberg*, August 4, 2011. https://www.bloomberg.com/news/articles/2011-08-04/the-nixon-shock.

MacIntyre, Alasdair. *After Virtue.* Notre Dame: University of Notre Dame Press, 1984.

———. *God, Philosophy, Universities: A Selective History of the Catholic Philosophical Tradition.* Lanham, MD: Rowman & Littlefield, 2009.

Magill, Bobby. "Fracking Boom Leading to Fracking Bust: Scientists." *Climate Central*, November 1, 2013. http://www.climatecentral.org/news/fracking-boom-leading-to-fracking-bust-scientists-16680.

Malick, Terrence. *The Thin Red Line*. Screenplay. 20th Century Fox. 1998.

Maryknoll Office of Global Concerns. "Peak Oil, Low Prices." *NewsNotes*, January-February 2015, 16–17. http://maryknollogc.org/sites/default/files/newsnotes/attachments/NewsNotesweb_0.pdf.

McDonald, Charlotte. "How Many Earths Do We Need?" *BBC News*, June 16, 2015. http://www.bbc.com/news/magazine-33133712.

Meikle, Scott. "Aristotle on Money." *Phronesis* 39 (1994) 26–44.

Melendez, Eleazar David. "Financial Crisis Costs Tops $22 Trillion, GAO Says." *Huffington Post*, February 14, 2013. http://www.huffingtonpost.com/2013/02/14/financial-crisis-cost-gao_n_2687553.html.

Merchant, Carolyn. *The Death of Nature: Women, Ecology, and the Scientific Revolution*. New York: Harper & Row, 1980.

———. "Women and Nature: Responding to the Call." University of California, Berkeley, 1997. http://nature.berkeley.edu/departments/espm/env-hist/articles/97.pdf.

Meyer, Nick. "UN Report Says Small-Scale Organic Farming Only Way to Feed the World." *Technologywater*, December 14, 2014. http://www.technologywater.com/post/69995394390/un-report-says-small-scale-organic-farming-only.

Mies, Maria. *Patriarchy and Accumulation on a World Scale: Women in the International Division of Labour*. New ed. London: Zed, 1999.

Mitchell, Lawrence. "Financial Speculation—the Good, the Bad, and the Parasitic." *The Conversation*, November 11, 2014. http://theconversation.com/financial-speculation-the-good-the-bad-and-the-parasitic-33613.

Moore, Jason W. "Anthropocene or Capitalocene?" *VersoBooks Review* (blog), December 1, 2015. http://www.versobooks.com/blogs/2360-jason-w-moore-anthropocene-or-capitalocene.

———. *Capitalism in the Web of Life: Ecology and the Accumulation of Capital*. Brooklyn: Verso, 2017.

———. "The Capitalocene, Part I: On the Nature and Origins of Our Ecological Crisis." March 2014. http://www.jasonwmoore.com/uploads/The_Capitalocene__Part_I__June_2014.pdf.

———. "The Capitalocene, Part II: Abstract Social Nature and the Limits to Capital." June 2014. http://www.jasonwmoore.com/uploads/The_Capitalocene___Part_II__June_2014.pdf.

———. "Cheap Food and Bad Money: Food, Frontiers, and Financialization in the Rise and Demise of Neoliberalism." *Review: A Journal of the Fernand Braudel Center* 33.2–3 (2012) 225–61.

———. "The End of Cheap Nature or: How I Learned to Stop Worrying about 'the' Environment and Love the Crisis of Capitalism." In *Structures of the World Political Economy and the Future Global Conflict and Cooperation*, edited by Christian Suter and Christopher Chase-Dunn, 285–314. Berlin: LIT, 2014.

———. "The Rise and Fall of Cheap Nature: A Short History." University of Washington, January 12, 2016. https://geography.washington.edu/news/2016/01/12/jason-w-moore-rise-and-fall-cheap-nature-short-history.

———. "Silver, Ecology, and the Origins of the Modern World, 1450–1640." In *Rethinking Environmental History: World-System History and Global Environmental*

Change, edited by Alf Hornborg, J. R. McNeill, and Joan Martínez-Alier, 123–42. Lanham, MD: AltaMira. 2007.

———. "Transcending the Metabolic Rift: A Theory of Crises in the Capitalist World-Ecology." *Journal of Peasant Studies* 38 (2011) 1–46.

———. "Wall Street Is a Way of Organizing Nature: Interview." *Upping the Anti: A Journal of Theory and Action* 12 (May 2011). http://www.jasonwmoore.com/uploads/Moore__Wall_Street_is_a_Way_of_Organizing_Nature__2011.pdf.

Moore, Jason W., and Kamil Ahsan. "Capitalism in the Web of Life: An Interview with Jason Moore." *Viewpoint*, September 28, 2015. https://www.viewpointmag.com/2015/09/28/capitalism-in-the-web-of-life-an-interview-with-jason-moore/.

Murphy, David J., C. A. S. Hall, and Bobby Powers. "New Perspectives on the Energy Return on (Energy) Investment (EROI) of Corn Ethanol." *Environment, Development and Sustainability* 13 (2011) 179–202.

Muzeum, Deri. "How the Romans Used Crucifixion—Including Jesus'—as a Political Weapon." *Newsweek*, April 4, 2015. http://www.newsweek.com/how-romans-used-crucifixion-including-jesus-political-weapon-318934.

Myers, Ched. *Binding the Strong Man: A Political Reading of Mark's Story of Jesus*. Maryknoll, NY: Orbis, 1988.

———. "God Speed the Year of Jubilee." *Sojourners*, May-June 1998.

NACLA. "The Food Weapon: Mightier than Missiles." Chap. 2 in "U.S. Grain Arsenal." *Latin America and Empire Report*, October 1975. http://la.utexas.edu/users/hcleaver/357L/357Lsum_s4_NACLA_Ch2.html.

Nader, Ralph. "Imperial Failure: Lessons from Afghanistan and Iraq." *Counterpunch*, October 12, 2015. http://www.counterpunch.org/2015/10/12/imperial-failure-lessons-from-afghanistan-and-iraq/.

Ovetz, Robert. "Privatization Is the Real Tragedy of the Commons." *Environmental News Network*, July 28, 2005. http://www.enn.com/top_stories/article/2169.

Oweiss, Ibrahim M. "Petrodollars: Problems and Prospects." Address to the Conference on the World Monetary Crisis, Columbia University, March 1–3, 1974. http://faculty.georgetown.edu/imo3/petrod/petro2.htm.

Paarlberg, Don. "Tarnished Gold: Fifty Years of New Deal Farm Programs." *Imprimis* 16.11 (November 1987). https://imprimis.hillsdale.edu/tarnished-gold-fifty-years-of-new-deal-farm-programs/.

Parry, Robert. "The Victory of 'Perception Management.'" *Consortiumnews*, December 28, 2014. https://consortiumnews.com/2014/12/28/the-victory-of-perception-management/.

Peck, Emily. "Women Work More Hours than Men, Get Paid Less." *Huffington Post*, October 27, 2016. http://www.huffingtonpost.com/entry/gender-wage-gap_us_58123342e4b0390e69ceaa8e.

Petras, James. "The Great Land Giveaway: Neo-Colonialism by Invitation." Centre for Research on Globalization, December 1, 2008. http://www.globalresearch.ca/the-great-land-giveaway-neo-colonialism-by-invitation/11231.

Peter G. Peterson Foundation. "U.S. Defense Spending Compared to Other Countries." June 1, 2017. http://www.pgpf.org/chart-archive/0053_defense-comparison.

Pettinger, Tejvan. "Hot Money Flows." *Economics Help*, November 28, 2012. http://www.economicshelp.org/blog/glossary/hot-money-flows/.

Phelps, Glenn, and Steve Crabtree. "Worldwide, Median Household Income about $10,000." *Gallup*, December 16, 2013. http://news.gallup.com/poll/166211/worldwide-median-household-income-000.aspx.

Polanyi, Karl. *The Great Transformation: The Political and Economic Origins of Our Time*. Boston: Beacon, 1944.

Ponting, Clive. *A New Green History of the World*. Rev. ed. New York: Penguin, 2007.

Prather, Scott Thomas. *Christ, Power and Mammon: Karl Barth and John Howard Yoder in Dialogue*. London: Bloomsbury, 2013.

Price, David. "Energy and Evolution." *Population and Environment: A Journal of Interdisciplinary Studies* 16 (1995) 301–19.

Rademacher, Lexi. "The Three Agricultural Revolutions." https://spark.adobe.com/page/OTqy7WtKSU5tM/.

Ravenscroft, Simon. "Modernity and the Economics of Gift and Charity: On Ivan Illich's Critique of Abstract Philanthropy." *Telos* 174 (Spring 2016) 149–70.

Reich, Robert. "America's Biggest Jobs Program: The US Military." *Christian Science Monitor*, August 13, 2010. http://robertreich.org/post/938938180.

Reid, Carlton. "The Real Speed of Cars Is just 3.7mph." *Roads Were Not Built for Cars* (blog), April 9, 2012. http://www.roadswerenotbuiltforcars.com/ivanillich/.

Rivera, Mayra. "Glory: The First Passion of Theology?" In *Polydoxy: Theology of Multiplicity and Relation*, edited by Catherine Keller and Laurel C. Schneider, 167–81. New York: Routledge, 2010.

Robinson, Jerry. "The Rise of the Petrodollar System: 'Dollars for Oil.'" *Financial Sense*, February 23, 2012. http://www.financialsense.com/contributors/jerry-robinson/the-rise-of-the-petrodollar-system-dollars-for-oil.

Rosenthal, Elizabeth, and Andrew W. Lehren. "Relief in Every Window, but Global Worry, Too." *New York Times*, June 20, 2012. http://www.nytimes.com/2012/06/21/world/asia/global-demand-for-air-conditioning-forces-tough-environmental-choices.html.

Ruggiero, Gregory. "Latin American Debt Crisis: What Were Its Causes and Is It Over?" *Independent Study*, March 15, 1999. http://www.angelfire.com/nj/GregoryRuggiero/latinamericancrisis.html.

Sachs, Jeffrey D. "From His First Day in Office, Bush Was Ousting Aristide." *Los Angeles Times*, March 4, 2004. http://articles.latimes.com/2004/mar/04/opinion/oe-sachs4.

Santa-Cruz, Arturo. *Mexico-United State Relations: The Semantics of Sovereignty*. New York: Routledge, 2012.

Sartre, Jean-Paul. "The Wall." 1939. http://chabrieres.pagesperso-orange.fr/texts/sartre_thewall.html.

Schaefer, Kevin. "The Tipping Point." *The Circle*, October 2015, 22–23.

Schneider, Keith. "Dwayne O. Andreas, Who Turned Archer Daniels Midland into Food Giant, Dies at 98." *New York Times*, November 16, 2016. https://www.nytimes.com/2016/11/17/business/dwayne-o-andreas-former-archer-daniels-midland-chief-dies-at-98.html.

Selg, Peter. *Rudolf Steiner, Life and Work*. Vol. 1, *1861–1890: Childhood, Youth, and Study Years*. Great Barrington, MA: SteinerBooks, 2014.

Semuels, Alana. "White Flight Never Ended." *The Atlantic*, July 30, 2015. https://www.theatlantic.com/business/archive/2015/07/white-flight-alive-and-well/399980/.

Shah, Anup. "Structural Adjustment—a Major Cause of Poverty." *Global Issues*, March 24, 2013. http://www.globalissues.org/article/3/structural-adjustment-a-major-cause-of-poverty.

Shaughnessy, Larry. "One Soldier, One Year: $850,000 and Rising." *CNN: Security Clearance*, February 28, 2012. http://security.blogs.cnn.com/2012/02/28/one-soldier-one-year-850000-and-rising/.

Shiva, Vandana. "Sacred Cow or Sacred Car?" *Zed: Environment*, September 23, 2016. https://www.zedbooks.net/blog/posts/sacred-cow-sacred-car/.

Silber, William L. "How Volker Launched His Attack on Inflation." *Bloomberg*, August 20, 2012. https://www.bloomberg.com/view/articles/2012-08-20/how-volcker-launched-his-attack-on-inflation.

Silberglitt, Richard, et al. "Critical Materials: Present Danger to US Manufacturing." RAND Corporation, 2013. http://www.rand.org/content/dam/rand/pubs/research_reports/RR100/RR133/RAND_RR133.pdf.

Simpson, Sarah. "The Arctic Thaw Could Make Global Warming Worse." *Scientific American*, June 1, 2009. https://www.scientificamerican.com/article/the-peril-below-the-ice/.

Sovacool, Benjamin K. "Valuing the Greenhouse Gas Emissions from Nuclear Power: A Critical Survey." *Energy Policy* 36.8 (2008) 2950–63.

Strange, Susan. "What Theory? The Theory in Mad Money." Centre for the Study of Globalisation and Regionalisation Working Paper No. 18/98, December 1998. http://www2.warwick.ac.uk/fac/soc/pais/research/researchcentres/csgr/research/abstracts/18/.

Strauss, Benjamin, and Scott Kulp. "20 Countries Most at Risk from Sea Level Rise." *Weather Channel*, September 25, 2014. https://weather.com/science/environment/news/20-countries-most-risk-sea-level-rise-20140924.

Stringfellow, William. *A Keeper of the Word: Selected Writings of William Stringfellow*. Edited by Bill Wiley-Kellerman. Grand Rapids: Eerdmans, 1994.

Strother, Emma. "On Water Scarcity and the Right to Life: Bolivia." Council on Hemispheric Affairs, June 27, 2013. http://www.coha.org/on-water-scarcity-and-the-right-to-life-bolivia/.

Sutter, Robert G., et al. "Balancing Acts: The U.S. Rebalance and Asia-Pacific Stability." Sigur Center for Asian Studies at George Washington University, August, 2013. https://www2.gwu.edu/~sigur/assets/docs/BalancingActs_Compiled1.pdf.

Swift, Jaimee A. "It's Not just Flint: Environmental Racism Is Slowly Killing Blacks across America." *The Grio*, January 24, 2016. http://thegrio.com/2016/01/24/flint-water-environmental-racism-blacks/.

Sydow, Momme von. "Sociobiology, Universal Darwinism, and Their Transcendence." PhD diss., Durham University, 2001.

Taibbi, Matt. "A Rare Look at Why the Government Won't Fight Wall Street." *Rolling Stone*, September 18, 2012. https://www.rollingstone.com/politics/news/a-rare-look-at-why-the-government-wont-fight-wall-street-20120918.

Tainter, Joseph. "Complexity, Problem-Solving, and Sustainable Societies." In *Getting Down to Earth: Practical Applications of Ecological Economics*, edited by Robert Costanza, Olman Segura, and Joan Martínez-Alier, 61–76. Washington, DC: Island, 1996.

Tanner, Kathryn. "Karl Barth on the Economy." In *Commanding Grace: Studies in Karl Barth's Ethics*, edited by Daniel L. Migliore, 176–97. Grand Rapids: Eerdmans, 2010.

Taussig, Michael T. *The Devil and Commodity Fetishism in South America*. Chapel Hill: University of North Carolina Press, 1980.

Temple, Katharine. "The Myth of Progress." *Sojourners*, March 1977. https://sojo.net/magazine/march-2016/archives-march-1977.

Tencer, Daniel. "Number of Cars Worldwide Surpasses 1 Billion; Can the World Handle This Many Wheels?" *Huffington Post*, February 19, 2013. http://www.huffingtonpost.ca/2011/08/23/car-population_n_934291.html.

Time. "The Top 10 Things You Didn't Know About Money." April 2016. http://content.time.com/time/specials/packages/article/0,28804,1914560_1914558,00.html.

Tolkien, J. R. R. *The Lord of the Rings*. Part 1, *Fellowship of the Ring*. London: Allen & Unwin, 1954.

Tracy, Jared M. "Perception Management in the United States from the Great War to the Great Crash." PhD diss., Kansas State University, 2012.

Troxell, Ted. "Christian Theory." *Journal for the Study of Radicalism* 7.1 (2013) 37–60.

Turgeon, Andrew. "The Great Pacific Garbage Patch." *National Geographic Encyclopedia*, September 19, 2014. https://www.nationalgeographic.org/encyclopedia/great-pacific-garbage-patch/.

United Nations Development Programme. *Human Development Report 2007/2008*. http://hdr.undp.org/sites/default/files/reports/268/hdr_20072008_en_complete.pdf.

University of Virginia, Miller Center of Public Affairs. "The President and the National Security State during the Cold War." 2017. http://archive.millercenter.org/cpc/education/president-and-national-security-state-during-cold-war.

U.S. Department of Energy, Office of Scientific and Technical Information. "Ilya Prigogine, Chaos, and Dissipative Structures." December 19, 2016. https://www.osti.gov/accomplishments/prigogine.html.

U.S. Department of Treasury. "Major Foreign Holders of Treasury Securities—2016." http://ticdata.treasury.gov/Publish/mfh.txt.

Vidal, John. "The 7000km Journey That Links Amazon Destruction to Fast Food." *Guardian*, April 6, 2006. https://www.theguardian.com/business/2006/apr/06/brazil.food.

Vulliamy, Ed. "Venezuelan Coup Linked to Bush Team." *Guardian*, April 21, 2002. https://www.theguardian.com/world/2002/apr/21/usa.venezuela.

Wagner, Stephen C. "Biological Nitrogen Fixation." *Nature Education Knowledge* 3.10 (2012). https://archive.is/3Rumq.

Waldman, Scott. "Antarctica Ice Shelf Is Breaking from the Inside Out." *Scientific American*, November 29, 2016. https://www.scientificamerican.com/article/antarctica-ice-shelf-is-breaking-from-the-inside-out/.

Washington Post. "Special Report: The Black Budget." 2014. http://www.washingtonpost.com/wp-srv/special/national/black-budget/.

Weisz, Helga. "Combining Social Metabolism and Input-Output Analyses to Account for Ecologically Unequal Trade." In *Rethinking Environmental History: World-System History and Global Environmental Change*, edited by Alf Hornborg, J. R. McNeill, and Joan Martinez-Alier, 289–304. Lanham, MD: Rowman & Littlefield, 2007.

Weisbrot, Mark. "Hard Choices: Clinton Admits Role in Honduran Coup Aftermath." *Al Jazeera*, September 29, 2014. http://america.aljazeera.com/opinions/2014/9/hillary-clinton-honduraslatinamericaforeignpolicy.html.

———. "Obama's Latin America Policy: Continuity Without Change." Center for Economic and Policy Research, September 2013. http://cepr.net/documents/publications/obamas-latin-america-policy-2011-05.pdf.

Wehrey, Frederic. "The Authoritarian Resurgence: Saudi Arabia's Anxious Autocrats." Carnegie Endowment for International Peace, April 15, 2015. http://carnegieendowment.org/2015/04/15/authoritarian-resurgence-saudi-arabia-s-anxious-autocrats-pub-59790.

Williams, Michael. "The Role of Deforestation in Earth and World-System Integration." In *Rethinking Environmental History: World-System History and Global Environmental Change*, edited by Alf Hornborg, J. R. McNeill, and Joan Martinez-Alier, 101–19. Lanham, MD: AltaMira, 2007.

Wise, Jeff. "The Truth about Hydrogen." *Popular Mechanics*, November 31, 2006. http://www.popularmechanics.com/science/energy/a926/4199381/.

Wise, Timothy A. "Agricultural Dumping under NAFTA: Estimating the Costs of U.S. Agricultural Policies to Mexican Producers." Global Development and Environment Institute, Tufts University, Working Paper No. 09-08, December 2009. http://www.ase.tufts.edu/gdae/Pubs/wp/09-08AgricDumping.pdf.

———. "Mexico: The Cost of US Dumping." *NACLA Report on the Americas*, January/February 2011. http://www.ase.tufts.edu/gdae/Pubs/rp/WiseNACLADumpingFeb2011.pdf.

———. "Who Pays for Agricultural Dumping? Farmers in Developing Countries." Global Development and Environment Institute, Tufts University, July 29, 2010. http://www.ase.tufts.edu/gdae/Pubs/rp/GC29July10Wise.pdf.

Wittgenstein, Ludwig. *Philosophical Investigations*. Translated by G. E. M. Anscombe. 2nd ed. Oxford: Blackwell, 1958.

Woolley, Suzanne. "Do You Have More Debt Than the Average American?" *Bloomberg*, December 15, 2016. https://www.bloomberg.com/news/articles/2016-12-15/average-credit-card-debt-16k-total-debt-133k-where-do-you-fit-in.

Xanthos, Nicolas. "Wittgenstein's Language Games." *Signo* (2006). http://www.signosemio.com/wittgenstein/language-games.asp.

Youngquist, Walter. "Alternative Energy Sources—Myths and Realities." *Electronic Green Journal* 1.9 (December 1998). http://escholarship.org/uc/item/3df8697r.

Zhou, Moming. "U.S. Oil Production to Peak at 43-Year High Before Trailing Off." *Bloomberg*, June 9, 2015. https://www.bloomberg.com/news/articles/2015-06-09/u-s-boosts-oil-output-estimate-to-43-year-high-on-well-backlog.

Zickel, Raymond E., ed. *Soviet Union: A Country Study*. Washington, DC: Federal Research Division, Library of Congress, 1991.

Index

Biblical citations